# COOKING OVER COALS

by Mel Marshall

ILLUSTRATIONS BY JOE BOREN

**WINCHESTER PRESS**

# THIS BOOK IS
# FOR MOTHER

A PORTION OF THE MATERIAL IN THIS BOOK HAS
APPEARED IN SLIGHTLY DIFFERENT FORM IN *Argosy,*
*Camping Journal,* AND *Gourmet;* PERMISSION OF
THE EDITORS OF THESE MAGAZINES TO REPRINT
IS GRATEFULLY ACKNOWLEDGED.

LIBRARY OF CONGRESS CATALOG CARD NUMBER: 76-150383

ISBN: 0-87691-003-9

BOOK DESIGN BY IRVING PERKINS

PUBLISHED BY WINCHESTER PRESS
460 PARK AVENUE, NEW YORK 10022

PRINTED IN THE UNITED STATES OF AMERICA

# Contents

**Introduction**   **1**

I **What, How and Why**   **9**

II **Meat and the Outdoor Chef**   **27**
MARINADES AND SAUCES / ANTELOPE / BEAR / BOAR /
BUFFALO / CARIBOU / DEER / ELK / MOOSE / MOUN-
TAIN SHEEP

III **Pots and Pans on a Bed of Coals**   **68**
POT ROAST / MEAT LOAVES AND PATTIES / STEWS /
VARIETY MEATS

IV **Small Game—An Infinite Variety**   **85**
BEAVER / MUSKRAT / OPOSSUM / PORCUPINE / RAB-
BIT / RACCOON / RATTLESNAKE / SQUIRREL / WOOD-
CHUCK / SMALL GAME STEWS

V **Waterfowl and Reed Birds**   **107**
DUCK / GOOSE / MUDHENS OR COOTS / JACKSNIPE /
WOODCOCK

VI **Upland Game Birds**   **128**
DOVES / GROUSE / PHEASANT / PIGEONS / QUAIL /
TURKEY

# Contents

**VII    Fresh-Water Fish**                                                        **158**

SAUCES / BLACK BASS / CARP / CATFISH / EEL / LAKE
TROUT / MUSKELLUNGE / PANFISH / PIKE / PICK-
EREL / SHAD / STURGEON / SUCKERS / WHITEFISH /
TROUT

**VIII    Salt-Water Fish**                                                        **188**

ALBACORE / BARRACUDA / BLUEFISH / CODFISH /
FLOUNDER / HADDOCK / HALIBUT / OCTOPUS / SAL-
MON / SNAPPER / SQUID / STRIPED BASS / SWORD-
FISH / WHITING / WHITEBAIT / GRUNNION

**IX    Shellfish**                                                                **208**

MOLLUSCS: ABALONE / CONCH / CLAMS / MUSSELS /
OYSTERS / SCALLOPS    CRUSTACEANS: CRAB / CRAW-
FISH / LOBSTER / SHRIMP / FROGS' LEGS / TURTLE

**X    Soups, Stews, & Vegetables**                                                **241**

SOUPS / BEANS / CABBAGE / CORN / EGGPLANT /
MUSHROOMS / ONIONS / POTATOES / TURNIPS / CAR-
ROTS / RICE / SQUASH

**XI    Bread, Cakes, & Eggs**                                                     **263**

LOAF BREADS / BISCUITS / PAN BREADS / CORN MEAL
BREADS / PANCAKES / EGGS

**XII    "A Little Something Sweet"**                                               **286**

DESSERTS / CANDIES / CAMP COFFEE

**Appendix**                                                                       **300**

COMMERCIAL SUPPLIERS OF GAME MEATS                                                  300
SHEEPHERDER STOVE & SELF-POWERED SPIT                                               303
SMOKE-COOKING, DRYING, AND SALTING                                                  306
OUTDOOR GRUB-BOXES                                                                  308

**Index**                                                                          **311**

# Foreword

*Hot dogs do not a cookout make,*
*Nor plain grilled steaks a chef.*

MANY OUTDOOR COOKS never progress beyond these two staples of the backyard grill, but the aspiring patio chef is not altogether to blame for this lack of versatility. Most of today's literature on outdoor cooking swings between two extremes. Either it consists of a multiplicity of unlikely ways to disguise frankfurters and hamburgers, or it features complicated dishes that would challenge a *cordon bleu* operating in a well-equipped kitchen. Faced with a choice between these two extremes, the backyard cook throws up his hands and settles for the monotony of the familiar old standbys.

This book tries to explore the vast middle ground between the oversimple and the too-complex. It is a rewarding area, well scouted by pioneers and frontiersmen who of necessity cooked outdoors every day, month after month. They learned to get the most out of a bed of coals, to do things the easy way, and they created dishes which most of today's outdoor cooks have never met.

Hunters and fishermen, campers and hikers, few in number until recent years, kept alive the lore of outdoor cooking during a time when any man who cooked at all was considered, at the least, eccentric, and the man who cooked outdoors was looked on as some sort of nut.

## Foreword

Things have changed. Today, smoke from millions of backyard grills threads into suburban skies. Those who respond to the pleasant challenges of outdoor cooking often extend their interest to camping, boating, fishing, hunting. These new devotees of the open cooking fire discover that fish fresh from the water, wild game, and wild birds make mass-produced foods taste pallid. As a result, there is more interest now in the cooking of game than at any time in this century. In recognition of this interest, and because all outdoor cooking originated in game cookery, many of the recipes in this book are based on game. This does not mean that you must be a fisherman or hunter to use and enjoy them. In all but two or three recipes, commercial meats will give very good results, and all but a few of the dishes given can be cooked indoors, if you wish.

Whatever and wherever you cook, this book tries to include that priceless special ingredient—pleasure. Cooking should do more than merely produce edible food. It should provide as much pleasure for the cook as it does for those who eat the dishes he has prepared. Nervous, reluctant, keyed-up cooks seldom turn out good meals. The best cooks have learned to take the sage advice given in quite a different context: Relax and enjoy it. So stir some pleasure into the pot at your next cookout. You will find it increases your own fun just as it increases the enjoyment of those who share the food you serve.

M.M.

# Introduction

## Beyond the Frank
## and the Burger

AT ONE TIME OR ANOTHER, most outdoor cooks swear fervently that never again will they tie themselves down with culinary chores while the rest of the bunch is having fun. Usually the swearing results from an experience something like this:

You're cooking for a party of friends, at your own backyard grill, or on a cookout, or in camp. You see the hues of perfection appear on the food on the grill—steaks a rich mahogany, lamb cubes delicately golden, chicken a crackling crusty tan. It's the moment to eat, but the crowd is elsewhere. You're all by yourself at the cooking fire.

If you're at home, your friends are probably petting Junior's aardvark or admiring your wife's new night-blooming osmosis. If the site is more remote, your cookout or camping buddies are chasing the chipmunks or bird-watching, or gazing at the trout jumping. You're not sure where they are, and don't really care; all you know is that you're calling for them to come and get it, and the food is overcooking.

By the time they finally straggle up, you're peering through an

1

## Introduction

eye-stinging haze of smoke at overdone steaks curling up like black potato chips, bone-hard lamb cubes, shriveled sooty chicken. Or, if you stubbornly dished up the food when it was ready, it's now congealing in its fat on cold plates. Either way, the meal and your temper are both ruined.

Take courage. You don't have to chain yourself to the grill when you cook outdoors, or watch the food like a private eye watching an errant spouse. It's possible to prepare an outdoor meal, whether for two or for twenty, and still enjoy freedom from pot-watching. It is also possible to cook foods outdoors that can be served when it's convenient, not for some split-second deadline when they must either be eaten or thrown away. You can serve a wonderful dinner to a dozen guests without having to float a bank loan to finance a stack of steaks. Most important, it is possible to cook foods other than frankfurters, hamburgers, and chicken on an outdoor grill; not just possible, but easier and more enjoyable.

You can do all these things if you really want to, if you're willing to spend a little time acquiring an understanding of basic outdoor cooking procedures and the reasons why they are basic. No matter how good a cook's intentions, he cannot operate intelligently without this understanding. Human nature being what it is, a lot of cooks don't follow what they consider to be arbitrary and unnecessary instructions given in recipes because they don't understand clearly why those instructions are important.

When pioneers erected their first crude shelters, women cooked over campfires, but once land was cleared and a cabin built, the woman moved to her indoor kitchen. It might have been only a crane and spit over a hearth, with a shelf or two and a table close by, but it was her kitchen. After she got that indoor kitchen, any cooking done outdoors promptly became the man's responsibility.

Outside meant more then than a backyard or patio, and most men's jobs took them outdoors. Not all settlers who broke frontiers stayed close to home and farmed. Great numbers of men worked away from the home place; they were trappers, miners, lumber-jacks, cowhands, railroad builders. They traveled far, and there were no drive-in restaurants to accommodate them while on the road; usually there weren't even any roads. These men cooked for themselves, and many of them came to cook very well indeed, if only in self-defense.

Generally they cooked game of one sort or another, so that over the years outdoor cookery and game cookery became virtually synonymous. That is why so many of the recipes in this book begin with wild game, but don't let that bother you. Commercial meats can be substituted in all but a few specialty recipes, and if you want to give butcher's cuts a suggestion of wild game flavor, there is a marinade recipe on page 31 especially for that purpose. There is also, in an appendix beginning on page 300, a list of sources that will supply you with almost every kind of wild meat from antelope to zebra. And, if you prefer to do your cooking indoors, or like to enjoy outdoor-style cooking during periods of bad weather, most recipes give directions for times and temperatures for a gas or electric range.

But please don't be misled into thinking that you can substitute commercial meats for game and still enjoy the unique flavors game affords. The flavor of any meat involves its tone and texture as well as its taste; the total flavor of the flesh of wild animals is built during their entire life spans and is the result of a diet of wild foods and wilderness living. It is not to be duplicated by the flesh of animals bred under controlled conditions, fed scientifically balanced rations, and raised under a caretaker's eye. But the substitutes suggested have been tested and will produce satisfactory results.

Nor can all outdoor cooking processes be precisely duplicated indoors. The quick dry heat from live coals differs from that of a gas or electric broiler or grill—no oven can cook as gently as a Dutch oven buried in coals. This quick dry heat encountered in outdoor cooking makes marinating an important step in cooking meats on a grill or spit. If you would like to find out how important this step is, take identical pieces of meat from the same cut, marinate one, and cook both for the same length of time over the same fire. Then let your taste be the judge.

**3**

## Introduction

If there is one basic commandment to observe in outdoor cooking, it is that the meat be cooked to perfection, whether it be steak, roast, or stew, wild game or commercial cut, red meat, fish, or fowl. Through the years, I have talked about outdoor and camp cooking with men who presided over the lumber-camp cook shanties, the chuck wagons of trail drive and roundup, the dining cars of rail-laying crews. The men they fed worked hard and got hungry, and demanded good meals. So did the solitary workers who fended for themselves—the range-riding cowhand, the lone prospector, the fur trapper, the sheepherder. Even when eating alone, they took pains to feed themselves well.

Until "air-tights," as canned foods were called during their early years, became common, the outdoor cook had plenty of meat, but very little to cook with it. Generally, he had no eggs, only the simplest seasonings, and his vegetables were confined to the root types that do not spoil quickly. These can be counted on the fingers of one hand—potatoes, turnips, carrots, onions, cabbage. This is why the recipes you will encounter here draw largely on these vegetables. Not only are they traditional, but somehow dishes served outdoors taste better when ingredients are kept simple and hearty.

The early-day cooks were not only sharply limited as to choice of ingredients and seasonings, they had no corner supermarket handy where they could replenish depleted supplies. If the camp ran out of salt, they learned to season the roast or stew with a few drops of gall or a sprinkling of gunpowder. If they ran out of flour, they made do with corn meal. They learned to bake bread—and even cakes and pies—in a Dutch oven buried in the coals. They knew how to tenderize a freshly killed deer with a marinade and then how to hold the juices in its fat-free flesh by dousing the meat with bourbon and touching a match to it before cooking it. And they knew which cuts of a range-run steer were tender enough to be cooked at once and which cuts had to be aged a few days.

Indeed, the skill of the early-day outdoor cook was partly an intimate understanding of the anatomy of the animals he butchered

4

for the pot. The rest of it was knowledge and use of cooking processes that made often leathery-tough meat not only chewable, but actually tasty. A lot of his discoveries were accidental, but then, so was the discovery of champagne. And we can profit by his discoveries, since they enable today's outdoor chef to use less expensive cuts of meat in cooking with surprisingly good results.

Meat from any freshly killed animal, whether wild game or range-run cattle, has a common characteristic. It has very little fat in its tissues, and is quite tough until aged. When tossed on the grill over that quick dry heat from open coals that we noted earlier, all meat dries out quickly, loses juices and flavor, and toughens before it cooks. Only a few choice tidbits from any large animal are suitable for cooking by broiling or grilling immediately after the beast has been killed. This is true even of the pen-finished cattle whose meat is sold by today's butchers. Even though these steers are fed rations designed to produce a softer-fibered flesh with higher in-tissue fat content, aging is still required to make them table-tender. And at the risk of being unduly repetitive, marinating is important when cooking any cut of meat over coals.

Breaking down the tough tissues by grinding is the easiest and quickest way to tenderize meat. It is also the cheapest, which accounts for the popularity of hamburgers with today's outdoor cooks. In the early days there were few meat grinders around, so hamburgers didn't appear on camp menus. No self-respecting camp cook would have served a hamburger patty anyhow. These men understood quite well that meat cooked on a grill, over the direct heat of open coals, must be seared completely and quickly to hold in the juices that give it flavor. By its very nature, a hamburger patty cannot be seared over an open fire. If you've wondered why the hamburgers you cook on your patio grill are dry and tasteless, juicy only if you cook them very, very rare, this is the answer.

Of all meats selected for grill-cooking, ground meat is the worst possible choice. If you simply must cook hamburgers outdoors, there is a way to do it. On page 73 you will find a method by which you can cook a tasty, juicy hamburger outdoors.

## Introduction

This brings us to consideration of the frankfurter as a candidate for outdoor cooking. It outranks the hamburger in popularity. Fortunately, the great frankfurter controversy that erupted about the middle of 1969 served to place this item in its proper perspective. Many people learned for the first time that hot dogs are not necessarily economical or even desirable as food. With a fat content of 30 per cent, frankfurters cost more than steak. The nitrates and nitrites added to them as preservatives are suspect as damaging essential body chemistry, while the dye used in coloring them is officially classed as a carcinogen, or cancer-causing substance. These revelations dimmed the frankfurter's appeal considerably, and when the controversy was ended by permitting hot dog manufacturers to include a substantial portion of chicken meat in what had formerly been an all-beef food, the appeal paled still more.

Without getting any further involved in the question of the frankfurter as a healthful or economical food, it does have one characteristic that rules out its use as a recipe ingredient. Unlike other sausages, it is completely precooked by processes that lock the flavor of its dominant spices into the meat it contains. There is no way to alter the flavor of a frankfurter, nor does it have the ability to impart any flavor to foods with which it is cooked. For all practical purposes, the frankfurter is an inert cooking ingredient.

The frankfurter is complete and unalterable and it can only be heated, placed in a bun, and smeared with strong sauces such as mustard and ketchup. This book contains no "recipes" for "cooking" frankfurters.

Why, then, are burgers and franks so popular with today's outdoor chefs? The answer is very simple—their use is a perpetuation of the lack of understanding of outdoor cooking processes and suitability of ingredients. It is this same lack of understanding that confuses outdoor cookery with smoke cookery.

Novices writing and talking about outdoor cooking spread a lot of nonsense about the desirability of foods cooked on grill or spit having a "smoky taste." Perhaps the gist of a statement by one of the greatest master chefs of all time, Auguste Escoffier, will help to refute this misconception. Escoffier wrote—and the quotation is a synthesis, not a word-for-word translation: "Whatever fuel is used in grills, it is essential that it produce no smoke, for if smoke either from fuels used or from the falling of fat from cooking is allowed to bathe the food, it will surely acquire a most disagreeable taste."

If flavorful outdoor cooking is your objective, then pay no attention to those dramatic full-color pictures that adorn magazine articles on the subject, showing flames from a blazing bonfire rising to engulf a spitted roast, or bathing a row of hamburger patties or frankfurters resting on a grill. Such productions are the work of a school of cooking more concerned about how food looks than how it tastes; adherents of this school aim to please the eye rather than the palate.

There is an authentic and legitimate cuisine of smoke cookery. It dates from prehistoric times, was common to the aborigines of all continents, was first recorded in recipes by the Chinese, and is still in use today. Smoke cookery is confused with smoking meats to preserve them. Smoking is a method of food preservation used with hams, bacon, some sausages, and kippered fish. Barbecuing stems from smoke cookery, but belongs to a separate branch of the family. Smoking is a process of preserving food; any resulting flavor imparted as a by-product should not be mistaken as the primary objective. Amateur chefs burn up a lot of money, throwing costly hickory chips on coals to produce the "smoky flavor" they have been told is desirable. Poppycock. If a smoky flavor is all you want, why bother with cooking food? Just stand downwind from the fire and inhale.

Smoked foods are discussed in some detail on page 306, if you want to pursue the subject further. If your interest is in smoke cooking, there are several good books dealing exclusively with that specialized subject.

Neither smoke cookery nor general outdoor cooking should be mistaken for barbecuing. And whatever you call your patio grill or outdoor cooking area, please don't call it a "barbecue." A barbecue is not a thing, but an event. A barbecue is neither a grill nor an

## Introduction

outdoor fireplace, nor is it just any meat cooked outdoors. Properly speaking, the only meat entitled to be called barbecue is that which has been inundated in a spicy sauce and then cooked lingeringly in a sealed pit in the ground over a bed of dying coals. So call your outdoor culinary activities almost anything you please—grilling, charcoal broiling, spit roasting. Call your outdoor cooking area whatever you like; just don't call it or your indiscriminate outdoor cooking a "barbecue."

Those who use such loose, inaccurate terminology are the type who put tomatoes into chili con carne. The result may be edible, but it's not the real thing. No one who has stood by while a barbecue pit is opened, and then eaten real barbecued meat, would ever make such an error. Every Rolls-Royce is an automobile, but not every automobile is a Rolls; all barbecued meat is cooked outdoors, but not all meat cooked outdoors is barbecue. For authentic barbecue cooking, consult page 39. For genuine, tomatoless chili con carne, turn to page 55.

Barbecuing, like most outdoor cooking, recalls the days before all landscapes were manicured, when there was open country and the rivers ran clear as does the resurgence of interest in camping, fishing, and hunting. The interest in these latter two is not, as a vocal minority bitterly proclaims, an inheritance of some ancient and evil lust for blood. The interest is a nostalgic acknowledgment that our ancestors enjoyed something we have almost lost—the flavor of foods received direct from nature, the savoring of simple ingredients.

# I

---

# What, How, and Why

LET'S LOOK OVER the hardware involved in cooking over coals, to judge the advantages and disadvantages of different types of facilities, utensils, tools, and fuels.

Since home is where the heart is, home is the obvious place to start. In your patio or backyard you can cook as well, though perhaps not as stylishly or conveniently, over the same primitive type of arrangement you would use at a temporary camp or cookout site as you can with the most elaborate equipment. Generally, this means a simple firepit with stones or bricks along two sides to support and level a mesh or rod grill, perhaps with a pair of forked sticks driven into the ground so that a spit or rod to support hanging pots can be placed over the cooking fire.

Certainly, if you do a fair amount of outdoor cooking at home, a more elaborate arrangement is better. Next in order of simplicity, then, is the portable pressed metal grill correctly called a brazier. The better grades usually have a crank-and-chain device enabling you to adjust the distance between grill-rods and coals; the more elaborate versions will probably have a power-driven spit. These small braziers are handily portable, easy to store, relatively efficient, if you are willing to accept their limitations that curtail the scope of your cooking. Most of these portable braziers are far too shallow; they will not accommodate a bed of coals deep enough for a long period of cooking. Some are so small that the coals they hold will not provide enough heat to cook a whole fowl or a large cut of meat. And those braziers that do provide spits generally lack the reflector-flue so vital to successful spit-cooking of roasts, hams, or whole birds.

Recently, several types of braziers fueled by natural or butane gas have appeared; these use chunks of a ceramic material in their beds to simulate the heat of natural coals. These braziers are usually permanent installations, though one type is attached to its fuel source by a long flexible hose that gives it some mobility. Those I have tested work very well indeed, but they share the limitations of the natural fuel braziers—small grilling surfaces and no reflector.

Go back to kitchens of two or three centuries ago, in which meats were cooked every day on spits. You have probably looked at several pictures of such kitchens, without realizing the significance of the spit arrangements they show. In such kitchens, spits were not set back deep into the fireplace, directly over the coals. They were at the front of the hearth, where the chef could attend his meats without being broiled himself.

What cooks food on a spit is not direct heat rising from a bed of coals directly beneath it, but the flow of superheated air from those coals, directed across the food by a properly shaped hood or back-chimney. Bathed in this constant stream of very, very hot air —up to 1200 degrees in pyrometer tests—food cooked on a spit has different characteristics of flavor and texture than food cooked in a convection oven or Dutch oven. Spit-cooking is the only true roasting process; oven-cooking should correctly be called baking, and Dutch-oven-cooking, braising.

Juices from food being spit-roasted should not be allowed to fall on the coals, but should be caught in a drip pan placed under the spit. When you try to cook on a spit directly over coals, you are troubled by constant flare-ups from dripping juices, a smoking fire that imparts foul flavors to the food, your face and hands burned from spatters as you try to baste, and food burned outside and raw inside. Some type of hooded reflector is a must on any brazier or firepit to be used for spit-cooking. Few manufacturers of free-standing braziers include this necessity.

If you own a brazier without a hood or reflector-flue, a tinsmith can snip one out in a few minutes, to fit either circular or rectangular models. One third of a circular brazier should be enclosed with a reflector that curves inward toward the brazier's center. The back and one fourth of the sides of square or rectangular braziers should be enclosed. In spit-cooking, your coals should bₑ pushed to the back of the firepit to allow a drip pan to be placed under the cooking meat.

Obviously, something besides a hand-crank is needed to turn the spit. Old hearths had some very ingenious mechanisms, including geared weights, clockworks with wound-up springs, and dogs running on an endless belt. Today electricity replaces these devices, but is available only in backyards, not at remote cookout or camping sites. However, in an appendix, page 300, you will find a spinning cage that is powered by a twisted rope, a device that can be quickly improvised and used anywhere to rotate a cut of meat over a circular bed of coals, thus providing the equivalent of spit-roasting.

Most outdoor chefs who use backyard facilities often will want some kind of permanent firepit-grill of mortared stone or brick. No two chefs have the same idea of exactly what they want, so here are a few suggestions to help you plan your new one or modify your present one.

Most people find a hip-high grill surface most convenient; this height allows them to look after both food and fire without too much bending and stooping. Crank-and-chain pulleys to raise and lower the grill are nice but not essential; it will be shown later in this chapter how you can tailor your bed of coals to your cooking needs. Plan a grill surface at least four feet long by two feet wide. You can use just part of it when you cook small quantities, but you cannot stretch a too-small grill area.

**What, How, and Why**

Perhaps the most practical and satisfactory permanent arrangement you could plan would have a two-section grill, allowing you to use half the firepit for grilling or spit-roasting, the other half for Dutch oven cooking. Or a separate firepit could be built to accommodate your Dutch oven, with space as well for a sheepherder stove —a Sibley stove, to use its correct name—which is another convenient adjunct to outdoor cooking.

A Sibley stove is a sheet-metal box with an open bottom. It is 12 to 16 inches deep, 24 to 36 inches long, 18 to 24 inches wide, and has rods much like a grill running across the short dimension, a few inches from its rim. These rods hold pans when the stove is in use. One end of the box is hinged to form a flap door. On top, at the end opposite the door, a hole is cut and provided with a flange or collar large enough to accept a short length of stovepipe. In use, the sheepherder stove is placed over an open firepit dug in the ground, a fire built in the pit and allowed to die to coals. The interior is then used for roasting or baking and the top as a big griddle, or as a convenient warming plate.

There are several versions of the sheepherder stove. Some have solid bottoms and the fire is built in the stove itself. My own favorite is a portable folding version designed for me by a hunter friend who operates a metal fabricating shop. It is described in an appendix on page 303.

No matter how you plan your outdoor cooking area, its heart remains the open firepit with grill and/or spit. How many layers of gilt you put on the lily is up to you. If you want to go all out, do as a number of others have. Buy a used wood- or coal-burning range and brick it into a portion of your grill, to provide you with oven, griddle, and top-of-range cooking area for skillets or saucepans.

More on the practical side is your selection of grill rods and their spacing. Heavy stamped mesh with wide openings makes a very satisfactory grill, as do rods spaced up to two inches apart. An auxiliary grill is very handy; this is of the type commonly called an oyster grill, and is made of thin, closely spaced rods. The wide mesh or wide-spaced heavy rods are fine for steaks, half-fowl, and large meat cuts; the oyster grill makes it easier to cook fish and other fragile foods, or foods cut into small pieces. It is used by laying it atop the wider-spaced grill. A wide variety of basket grills will be found on the market today, in several shapes, suitable for fish, thin-sliced meats, and foods that are difficult to handle or turn on a flat grill surface.

These basket grills are also used in conjunction with the "roti," or vertical grill, a commonplace in Europe, which is late in arriving on the U.S. scene. The roti is a three-sided, deep box, looking like a U laid on its side. It has double walls—an outer wall of perforated metal, an inner wall of grill rods. The space between the two walls is filled with live coals, and food clamped in a basket grill lowered into the open space, so that a steak, for instance, cooks on both sides at the same time, in the manner that bread is toasted in an electric toaster. The roti takes up only a square foot of space, and is very handy when only two or three are being served.

Your cooking tools for grilling and spit-roasting are few and simple. Long tongs are essential. Food cooking on a grill is difficult to turn with a fork, and the tines thrust into the meat release its juices and rob it of flavor. Tongs do the job with greater efficiency and fewer scorched fingertips. There are small mops with long handles made expressly to be used in basting; a brush with soft, thick bristles does an equally good job. Actually, some strips of clean rags tied to a stick will work as well as mop or brush, and can then be disposed of by burning.

In preparing meats for grill or spit, a larding needle or larding knife is handy; most spit-roasted meats (especially game) should be larded before cooking. A curved upholsterer's needle makes easy work of closing the cavities of fowl and fish after stuffing them for the spit or grill. Your work area will profit if you provide a large flat hardwood block on which cutting and chopping can be done.

To tend your fire, you need a metal poker or stirring-rod of some sort. A rake or hoe from a set of child-sized garden tools is ideal for smoothing a bed of coals. For a dollar or less military surplus stores sell a small folding trenching shovel that is just the right size for handling charcoal lumps, or for moving live coals in quantities. A toy water pistol, with a pinch of baking soda added to its water, is better than anything else for dousing a sudden flare-up in a bed of coals, or for spot-cooling hot spots.

Now we have arrived at a moment of truth. Many calm, sedate individuals, who can discuss such divisive subjects as politics, taxes, and national fiscal policies without ruffling their tranquillity, grow choleric when pots and pans are mentioned in connection with outdoor cooking. They are firmly committed to the belief that only foods cooked over the direct heat of coals on grill or spit qualify for this category.

Both tradition and practical considerations are against them. The several utensils discussed in the following paragraphs have a long and honorable association with outdoor cooking. Their use extends the scope of the outdoor chef to a tremendous degree by allowing him to utilize ingredients and combinations that would be impossible if he confined himself to the grill or spit.

*Dutch Oven*

First on the list is the heavy cast-iron Dutch oven, followed closely by the equally heavy cast-iron skillet—or, if you can find one, the double skillet. And notice that cast iron is specified. Shun utensils of thin pressed metal as you would shun the virus of the common cold.

Buy the biggest Dutch oven you can find. When you shop for one, be sure you know what you're looking for, as most stores today call any deep roasting pan with a tight-fitting lid a Dutch oven. Not so. The Dutch oven you want is made of cast iron, is either round or oval in shape, and has a flat dished top of cast iron that will hold a layer of live coals. It will have no wood or plastic anywhere about it. Some Dutch ovens are made with plain flat bottoms, others have short, stubby legs; legs or lack of legs is unimportant, it's that flat dished top you're after.

A Dutch oven is the best helper an outdoor cook can own. Its uses are many. It is, of course, designed to be buried in the coals

*Skillet-type
Dutch Oven*

with a layer of live coals heaped on its top, to cook roasts that will emerge tender and juicy from long exposure to slow, gentle heat. But in a Dutch oven you can also bake bread, cakes, biscuits, and puddings. You can use it as a stewpan, soup pot, skillet, and even a dishpan. In it you can not only bake, you can braise, boil, sauté, or deep-fry.

*Double Skillet*

As versatile as the Dutch oven, lacking only its ability to cook in large quantities, is the double skillet, also of heavy cast iron. This utensil is a matched pair of skillets, one shallow, one deep, with an interlocking tongue-and-slot hinge opposite the handle, and a

**15**

grooved rim which seals the two pans together. This feature enables the double skillet to be used in the same manner as a Dutch oven, buried in the coals as a small roaster or baking pan. And, as in the case of the Dutch oven, when you buy one, get the biggest size available.

If these sound like old-fashioned utensils, that's exactly what they are. They are manufactured today from old patterns, thanks to the

*Spider*

demand created by the greatly increased interest in outdoor cooking. Also being manufactured once more are cast-iron spiders, footed griddles, cast-iron teakettles and skillets, stewing pots, and muffin pans. Most of these are exact replicas of utensils once considered outmoded, but invaluable to anyone cooking over coals.

*Bean Pot*

Spiders, familiar to antique buyers, are frying pans or skillets with long legs. They may have dished covers designed to hold live coals, or plain flat or domed tops. The purpose of the legs is to allow them to be used over a thin layer of coals for slow sautéing, or the coals

**16**

may be heaped high, until they contact the bottom of the spider, for quick frying.

Footed griddles have legs shorter than those commonly found on spiders, and the legs serve the same purpose as those on the smaller pan. The cast-iron teakettle will keep water really hot with a minimum of heat on its bottom, very handy on a cold windy day.

Cast-iron utensils will never win any prizes for beauty of design, but they sweep the field in the utility competition. Thick cast-iron pans are heavy, of course, but to most camp cooks today weight is no problem. There are back-packers who will justifiably want utensils of light pressed steel or pressed aluminum, but for those who cook in backyard or patio, or confine themselves to auto-accessible campgrounds for cookouts, a few extra pounds mean nothing compared to the added utility of cast iron.

All cast-iron utensils must be seasoned. This is a simple process. Put a pound or so of unsalted pork fat into the utensil, put the pan on hot coals and let the fat get smoking hot. Remove the pan and let the fat cool slowly and naturally. Discard the fat, wipe the pan clean, and heat slowly until it is smoking hot once more. Let cool, wipe, and the seasoning job is done. Once seasoned, cast-iron utensils are as free of sticking problems as are those lined with Teflon, and a great deal more rugged. Spoons, metal pancake turners, even knives, do not mar their inner surfaces.

Used regularly and cleaned properly, cast-iron utensils need little care. Detergents should never be used in washing them; they should be scoured with very hot water and a rough cloth or plastic scouring-pad. If very dirty, they can be scoured with hot water and sand. Once every year or so, the crust that forms on their outer surfaces can be knocked off with a small piece of wood. If foods being cooked in any cast-iron utensil begin to stick to sides or bottom, the utensil should be reseasoned.

Used in outdoor cooking, the chief virtue of cast-iron utensils is that they hold and distribute heat evenly, important since a bed of coals may have hot and cold spots. Cast-iron pans can be used on the griddle, high enough above the coals for the gentle heat needed

**17**

to scramble eggs. Or they can be put directly on live coals to get them to the intense heat required for searing meats. Unlike pots and pans of pressed steel or aluminum, cast-iron utensils do not melt, warp, or become pitted. And they are very, very rugged.

My own double skillet—ownership of which is contested by my wife—has been used regularly for over thirty years, and is better than it was when new. It has been scoured with sand from the beaches of both the Atlantic and the Pacific, the Sea of Cortez, and the Gulf of Mexico. It's been washed in mountain streams and lakes at altitudes above 10,000 feet, and in the mouths of rivers where they rumble into the sea. It's been used as skillet, roaster, baking-oven, dishpan, chopping block, and pillow. Once it was used as a weapon, to kill a rattlesnake that invaded our camping area. Its two halves have seen service on kitchen ranges as often as on outdoor fires, and it is still used indoors in preference to copper-bottomed, ceramic, glass, or enameled steel pans. It has cooked meals for me alone, in solitary camp, and for crowds of twenty or more. It seems indestructible, and with luck I will still be using it thirty years from now.

It is the heavy Dutch oven and iron skillet that give the outdoor chef freedom from pot-watching and from a split-second mealtime scheduling. Foods cooked too long on grill or spit become dried out, tasteless, tough. Using the Dutch oven and double skillet to pot-roast, braise, stew, and sauté at low temperatures, foods can be cooked slowly and served when it is convenient for everyone to eat. In the Dutch oven, there is almost no point at which food must be served or be ruined, for the final stage of cooking in a Dutch oven is done at such a low temperature that the foods are really only being kept hot.

About the only non-cast-iron utensil you need to consider for outdoor use is your coffeepot. This should be of enameled steel, the old-style conical pot that turns out boiled coffee. (A recipe for camp coffee appears on page 298.)

Other necessary tools are few and simple. A pancake turner; a pair of long-handled spoons, one plain, one with a slotted bowl;

**18**

some kind of mixing bowl, or perhaps two. These, like the coffee-pot, should be of enameled steel, so you can heat water in them, or cook in them, if you wish.

*Coffee Pot*

Then there are your camp knives. Indoors or out, no cook is better than his knives. Many cooks are drawn to knives with shiny blades, and shiny blades almost invariably mean stainless steel, and stainless steel knives will not hold an edge. Stainless steel knives can be used in the kitchen—and ruined in the electric knife sharpener, which is the best friend of the man who sells knives and the worst enemy of the man who uses them. All the electric knife-sharpeners I have tried run at such high speed that they draw the temper from any knife blade exposed to them. Certainly an electric sharpener should never be used on a good and valued knife.

Invest in three knives with blades of drop-forged high carbon steel. Be sure they have man-sized handles. Get a butcher knife with an eight- or ten-inch blade; a utility knife, often called a "bull cook" knife, with a tapering seven-inch blade; and a four-inch paring knife. Before you ever use them, put an edge on them with a carborundum stone followed by a whetting on a hard Arkansas stone. Keep a steel handy and whisk the blades along it regularly. If this sounds too invloved, go to your butcher and ask him to translate, or to show you how to sharpen and maintain a knife. Indoors or out, a dull knife is a cook's curse.

Don't worry about your carbon steel knives rusting. After a little use, the action of food acids on the blades will make them virtually rustproof. Don't wash them with detergents, which breaks down this protective coating. Wash them in hot, hot water and wipe them clean while the blades are still hot. With the three knives described above, you can handle any outdoor cooking chore from skinning out an elk to mincing parsley for garnish.

As for dishes, the cheap, heavy ware used in short-order restaurants is best for outdoor use. Metal, plastic, and paper plates let food cool too quickly. Metal cups are an abomination; if you try to drink from them before coffee is stone cold, your reward is a blistered lip. Enameled metalware is not much better. Paper plates, even in holders, grow soggy under the influence of gravies and sauces and hot food juices. Their only virtue is that they save a lot of dishwashing.

Whatever its uses, aluminum foil is not a cooking utensil, and after disposing of a personal prejudice, I'll go into details. The prejudice is not against foil as such, but against those who leave wads and bits of it cluttering up the landscape. Like no-deposit bottles and aluminum cans, foil is one of man's most indestructible creations. Tin and steel rust, paper dissolves under rain and snow; but foil shines forever, a permanent reminder of man's sloppiness.

My prejudice is not caused just by the unsightliness of the litter. Many wild animals, including deer, woodchucks, squirrels, and rabbits, eat aluminum foil. In time it kills them, not the quick, clean death of a hunter's bullet, but a slow and agonizing one, as the foil irritates their stomach membranes until they swell and close the animal's digestive tract. The animal then starves with its stomach full. If you must use foil, bury discarded pieces very, very deeply, or take it home to dispose of.

Now for foil as a cooking utensil. Wrapping and sealing foods in foil, then burying them in coals or oven-baking them, is mistakenly thought by many to produce baked food. It does not. Technically, food is roasted only when cooked on the spit; food cooked in an oven is baked, though the usage of years has conditioned us to accepting oven-baked meats as being roasts. But foods sealed in foil are neither baked nor roasted, they are steamed, as in a pressure cooker.

Foods cooked in this fashion produce moisture from their own juices, and this moisture is reabsorbed as steam by the food cooking. In some instances this is a desired result. In others, it damages flavor and destroys texture. The potato is a good example. A baked potato, whether cooked in the oven or buried in coals, is fluffy, dry, flaky. A potato baked in a sealed foil wrapping boils in its juices and comes out hard and soggy. If you want a boiled potato, boil it to begin with, and save the cost and trouble involved in wrapping foil around it.

Most foil-wrapped food, cooked by whatever methods, closely resembles that produced in the huge pressure cookers used by institutions such as jails and hospitals. It is soggy, tasteless, and impersonal. Foil is handy for wrapping leftovers, making dripping pans, folding into a drinking cup, and other uses as well. It is of little use in cooking.

Foods buried in coals for cooking should go in wearing only their own skins. If you make pockets of ashes to bury them in, then cover them with live coals; they will not burn or char. If you object to the idea of brushing ashes off the food you eat, wrap it in wet newspapers, using several layers. As the food cooks, the newspaper layers will dry out, allowing trapped steam to escape, and you'll enjoy real coal-roasted instead of pressure-cooked foods.

What about seasonings? Well, that depends a great deal on where you're doing your outdoor cooking. If you're in your own backyard, a few steps from the kitchen, the sky's the limit. If you're back-packing and restricted as to weight, that's another story. This is a cookbook, not a camper's manual, but you will find a few suggestions for both auto campers and back-packers in an appendix on page 308.

We are now at the point where we can consider the cooking coals themselves—and the word "coals" cannot be stressed too hard. Just as the glamorous illustrations of spit-cooked roasts bathed in flames are misleading, so are the romantic scenes in Westerns that show the camp cook ladling beans or stew out of a huge pot suspended over a blazing inferno of a campfire. Such a cook would not last long in a real roundup or trail drive. His beans would be thrown in his face by the first cowhand tasting them. Good camp cooks, like all good outdoor cooks, used the Dutch oven in which to cook beans or stews.

Whether cooking over coals or in utensils, the outdoor chef must learn to judge the quirks of his coals and must know his utensils before he can function with smooth assurance. There are no heat regulators or timers on outdoor cooking-fires. Luckily, acquiring this judgment and knowledge isn't a hard job.

There is no short cut to the preparation of your cooking fire. Here, patience is the watchword, patience and an understanding of the various fuels you might be called on to use. Let's look at fuels before taking up the matter of timing.

Plain unadorned charcoal is about the most satisfactory of all fuels for outdoor cooking, though it makes very little sense to carry bags of charcoal into camp or cookout sites where wood is abundant. Given a supply of almost any wood, you can make your own charcoal simply by building a fire and letting it burn down. And while hardwood cooking coals are very nice indeed, they certainly are not essential. At one time or another, I've cooked over coals left from burning pine in the Rockies and Sierras, driftwood with its chemical impregnations from the ocean's waters, mesquite wood on the plains of Texas (and cow chips when there was no mesquite), half-dried corncobs in the Midwest, dead saguaro cactus on the desert, pin oak in the Gulf South, ash, beech, and hickory in the Smokies, and elsewhere have used coals from such diverse woods as madrone, larch, apple, maple, fig, cedar and cypress.

Point—you do not cook over a blazing, smoking fire, but over a bed of coals. By the time the coals are ready to be used for cooking, all sap, bark, and moisture should have been burned from the wood.

Some woods are more desirable than others for outdoor cooking, of course. The U.S. Department of Agriculture has made pyrometer and performance tests of the most common American woods and has graded them according to the amount of heat their coals give, evenness in burning, quantity of smoke emitted, and the tendency of each wood to crackle and throw sparks. Woods with the best ratings from these tests, are, in the order of grading, hard maple, hickory, red oak, white oak, pecan, dogwood, beech, birch, and ash. The smoky woods that come off best are, in order, southern pine and Douglas fir, though the latter throws sparks badly. In the medium-rated group of woods are soft maple, walnut, cherry, gum, sycamore, elm, white pine, cypress, redwood, and cedar; the last three are the spark-tossers. Receiving the lowest ratings are chestnut, basswood, aspen, cottonwood, yellow poplar, spruce, larch, and tamarack; again, the last three throw sparks while burning, and will on occasion throw them even after being reduced to coals.

Don't let these ratings confuse you. The woods rated best and those rated medium, with the spark-throwers excepted, will all produce coals of approximately the same intensity. The poor-rated woods tend to leave light, feathery coals. You can use them for cooking if you begin your fire with enough wood to create a size-able bed of coals, a very deep bed. The harder woods burn to longer-lasting coals, so that when they are used your cooking-bed needs to be only three or four inches deep, instead of the eight to ten inches required for a softwood coal-bed. But almost any wood will leave cooking coals if you build your fire early and burn enough to create a sufficiently deep bed.

Charcoal is easier to use in backyard and patio because it has already undergone its preliminary burning. Whether you use charcoal, or create your own by starting from scratch with sticks of wood, your objective is to create an even bed of coals. Its entire area should be a bright red, with no white hot spots, if you are grilling meats. The temperature or evenness of your bed of cooking coals can be maintained by blowing across it, or fanning it gently —but so gently that you do not stir up ashes and tiny cinders to rise and come to rest on the food. If you are grill-cooking or spit-roasting a large cut of meat or an entire fowl, your coals should be a dull red, with a distinct cast of purple. And the coals heaped around your Dutch oven should be dull red, too, with fresh live coals heaped on top of and around them.

### What, How, and Why

Replenishing a bed of cooking coals that will be used over a long period of time can be done by gently raking away the top layer of ashes and then pushing the entire bed higher by gently prodding its perimeter. If you are using charcoal, fresh lumps or briquettes should be placed around the outside edges of the cooking-bed, in contact with it, until the fresh charcoal is glowing red. As you push your coals up, the fresh ones stay at the bottom, to keep the intensity of the entire bed even.

Some outdoor chefs find it difficult to start charcoal, and resort to kerosene, gasoline, or patent liquid "fire-starters." Try this method instead: Cut both ends from a tall coffee can or juice can and use a big nail to punch a double row of holes an inch or so apart and an inch up from its bottom edge. On the firebed of your grill, crisscross strips of kindling wood or corrugated cardboard. Set the can on this kindling and fill it with charcoal chunks or briquettes. Light the kindling, then blow gently along the bottom of the can. Within minutes, all the charcoal in the can will be ablaze. Using pliers or a heavy potholder, lift the can off, leaving a heap of burning coals. Put fresh charcoal lumps all around the heap, being sure they make contact with those that are burning. When the fresh charcoal is burning well, and you have added all you will need for your cooking-bed, rake the heaped coals smooth. When the last flickers of flame die away, you are ready to cook.

Now to find out how effective your fire is, and to determine the timing for grilling or spit-roasting. Check the effective heat of a bed of coals by holding your hand, palm down, six inches above the grill on which the food will be placed. If you can bear the heat for only two seconds, you have bright coals and high heat. Five seconds, and your coals are medium dark giving medium heat. Seven to ten seconds, and you have dark coals giving low heat. Only don't burn your hand while testing. The instant your palm gets uncomfortably warm, jerk it away. You're testing coals, not trying to prove how tough you are.

To check out a cooking utensil, you need two or three sheets of good rag bond paper. Don't use "erasable" papers or newsprint or

**24**

the thin slick sheets used in duplicating machines. The erasables have a coat or impregnation of silicones or resins; the others contain unassimilated chemicals used in processing the paper.

Cut your good rag bond paper into squares, three or four inches in size. Take an ungreased pan, lay a piece of paper on its bottom, and put the pan on the coals. If the paper turns dark brown in four to five minutes, you are cooking over high heat. If the paper is golden in five minutes, the heat is medium; if it is only a light tan, the heat is low. By remembering the type of coals on which your tests are made, you can judge how your pans will react to each kind of heat, and time your cooking accordingly.

Baking times for breads and cakes in a Dutch oven can be found by the same kind of paper test. Biscuits will be delightfully fluffy and completely cooked in a Dutch oven in the same amount of time required to turn a square of paper a very dark brown, usually 15 to 18 minutes. Breads and cakes in Dutch ovens generally need to be cooked the same amount of time needed to reduce a square of paper to a black, brittle char, usually 35 to 40 minutes. Precise timing of meats cooked in a Dutch oven is not of great importance; a quarter- or even half-hour of extra time will not harm the dish a bit.

Certainly you will not need to make these timing tests every time you cook. Their chief value is to the novice, or to the cook who has acquired a new pan. The longer you cook over coals the easier it is to compensate for the inevitable variables encountered in outdoor cooking—differences in air temperature, wind velocity, altitude, and so forth, all of which play a part in timing when cooking outdoors. Generally these variables are minor, though occasionally you will find a vagrant wind whipping your coals to an intensity rivaling those in a blacksmith's forge, making it necessary to reduce cooking time 50 per cent or more.

Winds, location of firepit, and other variables are very important when you try to use a reflector oven. For that reason, this book will not try to cover the reflector-type oven, for it never performs the same way twice. As for gasoline and butane-fueled camp stoves, they are of limited utility in serious cooking. They are handy for heating coffee, or warming up a dish already cooked, or frying an egg. They are accessories to outdoor cooking, and are chiefly valuable in tents, bus or pickup campers, trailers, and cabins. They are useful when cooking must be done indoors during periods of bad weather, or in woodless areas.

In planning outdoor meals, keep things simple. Too much gear, too many dishes, too many pans, are like seven cooks seasoning the same pot of soup—the result is apt to be confusion. If you're going to have a *fête champêtre* in the grand style, call in a caterer to provide *paté de fois gras,* truffled duckling, and champagne. The most rewarding outdoor meals are those in which the food is plain and robust. It is not an occasion for precious vintage wines; serve young, hearty wines, or beer or ale. If you insist on serving hors d'oeuvres, they should be compatible with the rest of the meal. There are several suggestions among the recipes in the following pages for this type of appetizer.

And when you begin searching among the recipes to find something to fix for your next cookout, don't be surprised or disappointed if you don't find dishes that involve elaborate sauces and fancy fixings. Good outdoor cookery is basically a one-pot proposition. Dishes requiring a string of saucepans, sauces calling for clarification, reduction, straining, and stirring belong in the kitchen, not outdoors.

In the recipes that follow, you should find enough new ideas to make you the neighborhood's king of outdoor chefs. But wear the honor gracefully. Be generous. Tell your friends where you got your recipes and ideas—then they might match your skill, but they won't always be running to you for help.

# II

---

# Meat and the Outdoor Chef

OUTDOOR COOKING and game cooking meant the same thing for a long span of years, and most of the best recipes for cooking meat over coals originated with the hunter. So most of the recipes in this chapter follow tradition by beginning with wild meats, but instructions for substitution are given in all but one or two cases.

Most people who do not enjoy wild game have never tasted it under the proper conditions. The greatest number of the antigame group have had bad experiences with soured meat, meat that has been carelessly or improperly handled. Others have had meat that was rushed from field to table without being aged, then cooked without being marinated. Some hunters today look on refrigeration and freezing as a substitute for natural aging, and bypass the hanging period of ten to twenty days required to allow the natural enzymes present in the meat to break down tough connective tissue. Others try to substitute commercial tenderizers.

In cold weather, game can be hung outdoors in a shady place, and the normal changes in temperature from night to day will make it possible to age an antelope or deer in five to six days, an elk or moose—these bigger animals quartered—in ten days. Aging in

## Meat and the Outdoor Chef

the constant temperature of a meat storage room in a locker plant or butcher shop will take ten to twenty days.

Neither freezing nor tenderizers is a substitute for aging any meat, wild or commercial, by hanging. Commercial tenderizers are based on a synthesized enzyme that is found in its natural state in the papaya. This synthetic enzyme attacks the protein chain of the meat, and causes the flesh to become mushy and flabby in texture. The natural enzymes in the meat itself, and the tannins present in a wine-based marinade, work to soften the connective tissues which are the real culprits that make meat tough.

Before wild game can be aged or brought to the table, it must be cleaned and skinned. Any wild game, furred or feathered, must be cleaned and cooled quickly to prevent it from souring. While this is important with all animals harvested by the hunter's bullet, it is of the greatest importance in large game animals, which will continue to give off body heat for a long time after they die.

Field-dressing should be done at the spot where the animal fell. This includes pulling its carcass to let the head and neck slope down-hill, or propping the carcass up with a branch or two so that blood can drain from an opening made in the jugular vein. After bleeding, the belly should be split with a shallow cut from rib cage to crotch, all intestines removed, genital areas cut away, and usable portions such as the liver and heart removed from the entrails. At the same time, any parts of the flesh that have been tainted by a bullet passing through entrails and gall bladder and then penetrating edible meat should be trimmed out. Unless the lungs have been badly shot-torn and retain a large quantity of blood, they can be removed at camp after the carcass has been skinned and the breast cavity opened. Following field-dressing, the body cavity should be propped open with pieces of branches so cooling will begin at once.

This generalization applies to any antlered game such as deer, elk, antelope, and so on, as well as to bear, boar, and other large animals. When any animal, large or small, has physical features requiring special attention in cleaning for the pot, these will be given in connection with recipes for cooking that particular animal.

## Marinades and Sauces

Use of a marinade in preparing the meat of wild game for cooking can be classed as a necessity; marinating commercial meats that are to be cooked on grill or spit is a wise precaution. The process of cooking over coals is inherently a dry one; that is, the heat from coals is brisker and drier than that of the oven or broiler of a kitchen range. Marinating adds moisture deep inside the meat fibers as basting does not. It also has a gently tenderizing effect.

Marinades are not part of the seasoning, but of the cooking process—a marinade should enhance the flavor of meat without adding a pronounced flavor itself. There are exceptions. In the following marinade recipes you will find one designed to add a "gamy" flavor to commercial cuts of meat. And in dishes such as Hassenpfeffer and Sauerbraten the marinade becomes the basis for the sauce in which the meat is served.

Thin cuts of meat such as chops and thin steaks will need an hour or so in the marinade. Roasts require a longer exposure to allow the liquid to penetrate the meat completely. Overnight is not too long a time to marinate some large cuts, especially when the meat is from an old, tough animal. The meat should be turned in the liqiud several times during the marinating period, and if the meat is not covered completely, some of the marinade should occasionally be spooned over the top. Before going to the grill, spit, or roaster, meats that have been marinated should be wiped dry, for wet meat will not sear properly or brown satisfactorily. All the marinade recipes that follow make approximately 1 quart. They can be doubled when more marinade is needed to cover a large cut of meat being marinated in a big container.

### MARINADE #1

For relatively tender meats such as young venison, small game.

| | |
|---|---|
| 2 cups dry red wine | ½ dozen cracked peppercorns |
| 2 cups cool water | ¼ teaspoon salt |
| ¼ teaspoon powdered basil | |

For a lighter flavor, use rosemary instead of basil; for a heavier overtone, substitute sage or oregano. Combine all ingredients; marinate thin cuts 1 to 2 hours, thick steaks or roasts, 4 to 6 hours or more.

## MARINADE #2

For very dry game meats such as mature deer or antelope; for commercial meats such as lamb. Also for small game, upland birds.

| | |
|---|---|
| ½ cup peanut oil | 1 crushed and crumbled bay leaf |
| 1 cup dry vermouth | 2 cups cool water |
| ½ cup brandy | |
| 1 lemon, or 3 tablespoons fresh lemon juice | |

Blend the liquids thoroughly; if a whole lemon is used, roll it under your hand on a firm flat surface, then slice very thin and add with bay leaf. Stir this marinade often as it is being used, as it tends to separate. Marinate thin cuts at least 2 hours, turning occasionally. Thick cuts such as roasts require at least 6 hours, or overnight. When marinating overnight, be sure there is enough marinade to cover the meat completely.

## MARINADE #3

For very old, tough animals such as mature elk, moose, bear, boar; for mature beef graded Good.

| | |
|---|---|
| ½ cup red wine vinegar | ¼ teaspoon cracked whole cloves |
| 2 cups cool water | |
| 1 cup dry red wine | pinch mustard seed, crushed |
| juice of 1 lemon (3 tablespoons) | 1 teaspoon salt |
| 2 teaspoons cracked peppercorns | |

Mix the liquids in the order given, add the spices and salt. Let the marinade stand 20 to 30 minutes before using.

Steaks and chops ½ inch to ¾ inch thick should be marinated from 2 to 3 hours and turned occasionally. Thick cuts such as roasts should be marinated overnight.

## MARINADE #4

To give commercial meats a gamy flavor. Not recommended for use with wild game.

| | |
|---|---|
| 1 cup port wine | 2 cups cool water |
| ½ cup dry gin | |

If you want a very pronounced flavor added to the meat, crush two juniper berries in the liquid. Vodka can be substituted for gin by crushing one juniper berry in the vodka before adding it to the mixture.

Marinate thin cuts 2 to 3 hours, turning occasionally; thick cuts such as roasts should be marinated a minimum of 6 hours.

## BARBECUE MARINADE OR SAUCE

Let it be clearly understood that this is not a substitute for real barbecued meat, which is pit-cooked after being swathed with a different kind of sauce (see page 39 for this grand old recipe). At best, this adds a barbecue-type of flavor to grilled or roasted meats. It is used after the meat has been cooked.

| | |
|---|---|
| 1 cup peanut oil | pinch of garlic powder or |
| ½ cup strong black coffee | onion powder (not both!) |
| ½ cup tomato juice | ¼ teaspoon Nepal pepper or ½ |
| 2 tablespoons red wine vinegar | teaspoon cayenne |
| ¼ cup dry red wine | ¼ teaspoon dry mustard |
| 2 tablespoons brown sugar | ½ teaspoon salt |

Warm the oil in a saucepan and beat in the coffee, tomato juice, and vinegar. Do not allow to boil. Remove from heat, add the wine and dry ingredients, and stir until they are dissolved.

**Meat and the Outdoor Chef**

Marinate sliced precooked roast meat in the warm liquid for 30 minutes to 1 hour before serving. Serve additional warm sauce with the meat.

### GREEN SAUCE

This is a potent mixture. Like the classic Aioli Sauce it resembles, Green Sauce should be eaten only when you plan no close face-to-face contact with others for 24 hours. It should be used in very, very small quantities. A little bit goes a long way.

| | |
|---|---|
| 4 large cloves garlic | 2 undrained anchovy fillets |
| 2 cups fresh parsley | 1 cup olive oil or peanut oil |

Chop the garlic coarsely. Strip the leaves of parsley from their stems before measuring, then chop parsley and garlic together until very, very fine. Add the anchovy fillets and chop until they are blended with the garlic-parsley mixture. Transfer to bowl or other container, add the oil, and stir thoroughly. Let stand at room temperature 30 minutes before using, stir occasionally. This sauce keeps well, growing more potent as it ages. It should be stored in a tightly closed container in the refrigerator, but always served at room temperature.

### HOT ONION SAUCE

Less powerful than Green Sauce, this Hot Onion Sauce is not intended to be used in cooking, but as a table condiment. It goes well with sturdy meats, and does wonderful things when stirred in small quantities into a bowl of beans, or used to season cooked rice.

| | |
|---|---|
| 1 medium-sized white onion | ½ cup grain vinegar |
| 2 small chili Tepines, Petines, or Japonais peppers | ¼ teaspoon salt |
| | pinch of sugar |

Grate the onion, chop the peppers very fine, mix with vinegar, salt, sugar. Let stand in a covered container 1 hour before using.

As we move into the actual cooking jobs, it might be well to mention once again that while recipes are categorized by types of wild game because of tradition or personal association, commercial meats can be used in preparing all but one or two. And in recipes involving roasting, timing is given for the spit or Dutch oven, the sheepherder stove, and the kitchen range.

## Antelope

There are two great antelope ranges in North America. The southern range begins in western Oklahoma and extends across the Texas Panhandle and central New Mexico into eastern Arizona; the northern range begins in the high country of northern Colorado and goes through Wyoming, Montana, and Idaho.

Antelope are small, their meat dry and virtually fat-free; it tends to be stringy if cooked too rapidly. It should be marinated if you want to enjoy it at its best in chops, steaks, and roasts.

### ANTELOPE CHOPS PIEDMONTESE

This method of cooking antelope was given me by Eugene Gonella, of Merced, California. Gene is a native of Italy's Piedmont section, where the process is used in cooking the native chamois as well as lamb and goat.

| | |
|---|---|
| 3 antelope chops or 2 steaks per serving, cut about ½ inch thick; substitute venison, lamb, veal, baby beef | Marinade #2, page 30 several large sprigs of fresh basil salt |

After at least 2 hours in the marinade, drain the steaks or chops, catching the liquid in the marinade bowl. Tie the basil sprigs into little whisks or brushes and soak them in the marinade a few minutes. Wipe the chops dry, sear them, then arrange them on the grill to leave as little open space as possible between each piece of meat. Cook 4 to 6 minutes on each side over medium coals, beating the meat briskly with the sprigs of basil, dipping the sprigs into the marinade from time to time. Do not salt until the meat is cooked. This method is suitable only for use outdoors, as spatters from the beating makes it rather messy. But the delicate flavor that results is worth a few spatters.

### ANTELOPE ROAST

whole rack or saddle of antelope; substitute venison, lamb
Marinade #2, page 30
thin slices of pork fat or salt

pork, enough to cover the roast
salt, pepper, flour

Marinate a rack of meat 4 to 6 hours, a saddle 6 hours or longer. Wipe the meat dry, reserve the marinade liquid. Mix salt, pepper, and flour together in a ratio of ¼ teaspoon salt and ⅛ teaspoon pepper to each tablespoon of flour, prepare enough to rub into the roast; the quantity needed will vary with the size of the cut. Rub the seasoned flour mixture into the meat. If salt pork is to be used, trim off rind and blanch by dipping into boiling water for about 2 minutes to reduce its saltiness. Cover the entire surface of the roast with the slices of fat; they can be secured by tacking them to the roast with stitches of heavy cord or small skewers.

Spit-roast the meat 25 minutes per pound; during the final 10 minutes of cooking remove the pork fat to allow the meat to brown. Baste during this final cooking with the reserved marinade.

In a sheepherder stove, cook 12 minutes per pound in an open roasting pan. In a kitchen range, cook 15 minutes per pound at 350 degrees. When oven-cooked, the covering of pork fat should be removed and the meat basted two or three times during the final 15 to 20 minutes of cooking.

Serves 8 to 10.

34

## BRAISED ANTELOPE WITH DUMPLINGS

2 pounds antelope meat cut in
   1-inch chunks; substitute
   venison, lamb, veal, baby beef
Marinade #2, page 30 (with
   commercial meats use
   Marinade #4, page 31
salt, pepper

butter or cooking oil
water or game stock
2 cups milk
2 eggs
2 cups flour
¼ teaspoon salt
¼ teaspoon baking powder

Marinate 1 to 2 hours, then wipe the meat dry and dust it very lightly with salt and pepper. Reserve the marinade liquid. Heat just enough butter or oil to grease the inside of the Dutch oven or the deep half of the double skillet. Over bright coals, bring the pan to smoking heat and sear the meat cubes well, stirring so that all sides are browned. Remove pan from heat, pour in the reserved marinade, and add enough water or game stock to bring the level of liquid to 1 inch. Cover and let simmer 20 minutes, stirring occasionally.

Beat the eggs and milk together. Sift flour, salt, and baking powder together, add to the egg-milk mixture, and beat until smooth. Pour this batter over the meat and liquid in the pan in a smooth layer. Close pan, bury in coals, cook 45 minutes to 1 hour.

To cook in a sheepherder stove, use a closed pan and put in the oven after adding the dumpling batter, then cook 20 to 25 minutes. In the kitchen oven, follow the same procedure, but cook 30 minutes at 325 degrees.

Serves 6 to 8.


## SFERIA: ARABIAN ANTELOPE MEATBALLS

A longtime colleague in the broadcasting industry, Bill Musladin of Oakland, California, brought me this recipe from North Africa, where he was stationed during World War II. It is also used to cook mutton and the meat from young camels.

3 pounds antelope meat, bits and trimmings left from butchering; substitute lamb, mutton, veal, baby beef—or young camel

3 cups minced onion

4 tablespoons minced green pepper

2 tablespoons minced cardamom seeds

1 egg

½ teaspoon salt

flour for dredging

clarified butter or cooking oil

Mince meat and onion, pepper, and cardamom seeds very fine, by chopping or putting through a meat grinder using the coarsest blade. Beat the egg lightly, and add it and salt to the meat mixture. Roll into oblong cylinders about the size and shape of a man's thumb. Dredge these in flour, and fry in deep fat until brown and crisp on the outside.

Traditionally, the cooking fat is either sesame seed oil or clarified butter; the butter can be prepared by heating butter until liquified, allowing it to settle, and pouring off the liquid, leaving solids in the pan. Peanut oil or any neutral vegetable oil serves as well, as do bacon drippings (unless you adhere to Moslem dietary laws).

Serves 6 to 8.

## Bear

Bear meat is best in early autumn, when the animal has put on about half the fat it will carry into winter hibernation. Even then, bear meat tends to be very rich. Due to the bear's omnivorous eating habits, flavor of the flesh will vary widely. If weather conditions are right, with the cold days and below-freezing nights that are often encountered even in autumn in high country, the carcass of a freshly killed bear benefits by being hung outdoors and doused with water each night so that an ice-glaze forms on it. A bear carcass should be hung at least four weeks. All excess fat should be trimmed away before the carcass is hung, and when butchering the meat, all visible fat should be removed.

Forequarters of a bear furnish the most desirable meat, as the hindquarters are more heavily muscled and thus tougher. Greatest delicacies are the tenderloin and paws. Several of the specialty houses and game farms in the appendix on page 300 sell bear meat; your butcher may be able to get it for you from one of his suppliers. Recipes which follow are for the smaller bears, black or brown, not the big grizzly and Kodiak types. A little incidental information—the liver of the polar bear should never be eaten; it contains Vitamin A in quantities toxic to the human system. The commercial meat closest to bear meat is pork.

### GRILLED BEAR TENDERLOIN

Greatest of all delicacies from the bear is this strip of meat that hugs the backbone. A suitable substitute is the boned eye-meat from a section of ribs; neither need be marinated when cooked as follows:

| | |
|---|---|
| whole bear tenderloin or the eye of a section of 5 to 6 ribs butchered out in one strip; substitute pork tenderloin, filet of beef | ¼  teaspoon salt |
| | ¼  teaspoon Nepal pepper or ½ teaspoon cayenne |
| | ½  teaspoon fresh grated nutmeg |
| | ½  cup honey |
| ¾  cup flour | 2  tablespoons cider vinegar |

Sift together the flour, salt, pepper, and nutmeg. Warm the honey and blend with the vinegar, then stir in the seasoned flour to make a smooth paste. The paste should be about the consistency of whipped cream; the quantity of flour may need to be adjusted.

Wipe the meat well and sear it on the grill over bright coals, turning frequently so that it browns evenly. When it has been seared, begin brushing on the honey paste, turning to allow the paste to form a thin crust. Cook 40 to 45 minutes, serve by slicing across the grain of the meat.

Serves 8 to 10 generously.

## GRILLED BAKED BEAR PAWS

There is no substitute for bear paws, nor can they be successfully cooked indoors. This meat is slightly gelatinous and tastes like a light marrow with overtones of ham and chicken, but it is a unique flavor that is hard to describe precisely.

4 bear paws, unskinned, and a supply of clean clay
½ cup red wine vinegar
½ cup warm water
2 tablespoons melted bacon drippings
½ teaspoon salt
⅛ teaspoon fresh-ground black pepper

Encase the claws in clay, bury in coals, and cook 6 hours. When the clay is cracked away, skin and fur come with it. Trim the front of the paws to remove the claws. Wrap the paws individually with several turns of light wire to keep the paws from falling apart when they are grilled. Mix vinegar, water, bacon drippings, salt, pepper. Put the paws on the grill over bright coals, cook 10 to 15 minutes, basting very frequently. Turn midway during the cooking period.
Serves 6 to 8.

## Boar

Three separate animals are included in this category. The wild boars of the Ozark-Smoky Mountains are domestic swine run wild, but through more than a century of freedom these boars have acquired all the wild characteristics of their remote ancestors. The boar of California's Monterey Peninsula area is a true European wild boar, descended from escapees imported to stock a private game reservation. The javelina or peccary of the Southwest, found in Texas, Arizona, and northern Mexico, is a wild pig rather than a boar, but should not be downgraded because of its size, for javelinas travel in herds and will tackle anything they encounter. Wild boar meat is sold by several of the game suppliers listed in the appendix on page 300.

Boars are cleaned and the carcasses dipped in boiling water and scraped like any hog, but the javelina has a pair of musk glands on either side of its backbone between rib cage and hips which must be removed at once after the animal has been killed. Both wild boar species and the javelina are classed as pork, though their meat is much leaner and firmer than domesticated pork. None of the three species offers meat that lends itself to grilling or spit-roasting; cuts from all three should be braised, pan-roasted, or barbecued.

### BARBECUED FRESH BOAR HAM OR SIDE

Unless you have an unusually big backyard or the unrestricted use of a nearby vacant lot or a farm with a back 40 where you can dig a barbecue pit, better save this until you get into a wilderness camp where you can dig all you want to.

Your pit should be dug in solid, not sandy soil. For a single ham, it should be 3 feet deep, 2 feet wide, 3 to 4 feet long. To barbecue a pair of hams, increase the length rather than the width. To handle a side of boar weighing 100 to 125 pounds, the pit will need to be 4 feet deep, 6 feet long, 4 feet wide.

When the pit is completed, build a fire in the bottom three to four hours before you plan to put in the meat. Use oak or hickory or some other hardwood; barbecuing is one type of outdoor cooking that does require smokeless, longlasting coals. Keep the fire going until you have a bed of coals 8 to 10 inches deep.

While the wood is burning down, you can be preparing the barbecue sauce, unless you take care of this the day before the barbecue. The following sauce was originated by one of the South's great barbecue chefs, the late George Washington Jones.

| | |
|---|---|
| 5 pounds red ripe tomatoes | 1 large sweet onion |
| 1 quart cold water | 1 large lemon |
| ½ cup brown sugar | 1 tablespoon chili molido |
| 1 tablespoon salt | 1 teaspoon powdered oregano |
| 2 cups cider vinegar | ½ teaspoon freshly ground |
| 2 cloves garlic, peeled | pepper |
| 2 bay leaves | 1 teaspoon dry mustard |

Scald tomatoes and dip them in cold water, peel. Chop coarsely, holding them over the cooking pot to conserve their juice. Add water and put the pot to simmer over low heat. Add sugar, salt, vinegar. Thread the garlic and bay leaves on a string and add them to the pot. Stir the sauce frequently, crushing the tomato pulp as you stir. Grate in the onion. Core but do not skin the lemon, and add it whole. As you stir, press the lemon occasionally to liberate its oils and juices. Add the remainder of the seasonings. Stir, being sure to scrape the bottom well, as the sauce will tend to stick and form a crust on the bottom of the pot; this crust will burn quickly. Simmer 30 to 40 minutes, until the tomato solids dissolve. Remove garlic and bay leaves; remove the lemon, but squeeze it thoroughly over the pot to extract all its juice. Keep the sauce warm until ready to use.

Meanwhile, back at the barbecue pit, the fire should have burned down to a bed of glowing coals. Skewer the ham or hams on a rod 3 to 4 feet longer than the pit; a piece of concrete reinforcing rod is ideal. Brush the meat generously with the sauce, then wrap several turns of wire around it in a wide-spaced spiral to keep it from falling off the skewer as it becomes meltingly tender. Suspend the meat over the center of the bed of coals; it will probably be necessary to make small slits at each end of the pit in which to drop the skewering rod, to bring the meat below the level of the pit's rim. Cover the pit with a sheet of metal big enough to extend beyond its edges a foot on all sides. Using dirt left when the pit was dug, cover the metal plate with a 6- to 8-inch layer, tamping around the edges to seal well.

Go away and forget the barbecue for 12 to 14 hours.

Open the pit, take out the meat, and swab it at once with a good coat of warm sauce. Carve and serve, keeping extra sauce handy to spoon over the sliced meat after it is on the plates. Traditional accompaniments for a barbecue are boiled pinto or red beans, sour pickles, and coleslaw in the Southwest; in the South, fried potatoes, pickles, and a tossed lettuce and tomato salad.

Any meat can be barbecued by the method given above, and the sauce serves equally well with beef as with pork. The time in the pit for a side of beef would be about 16 to 18 hours, less for smaller cuts.

This is not the only way to barbecue meat, of course. In Hawaii, the pit is lined with stones and the fire built on them, then the coals removed, meats placed on the stones on layers of leaves, covered with more leaves, and the pit filled. In China, a sealed container is used instead of a pit. There are other U.S. methods, too. One is to cut the meat into 15- or 20-pound chunks, lather it well with sauce, wrap it in butcher's paper, then in wet burlap bags secured with twists of wire, and place the bundles on the coals; the dirt is then shoveled into the pit. Another method is to have a grid of metal rods ready to lower into the pit on top of the coals, and place the sauced meat on the grid. A metal plate is used to cover the pit in this method. Timing for either of these methods is 10 to 12 hours.

Always remember, though: If meat hasn't been cooked over dying coals in a sealed pit, don't call it barbecue.

### GRILLED SPARERIBS WITH BARBECUE SAUCE

This is what far too many people fondly believe is real barbecue. It is grilled meat served with a barbecue sauce.

| | |
|---|---|
| rack of spareribs; allow about 4 ribs per serving | Barbecue Sauce from page 31 1  teaspoon salt |

Bring a large pot of water to a rolling boil, add salt, drop in the sections of ribs, let cook 3 to 5 minutes. Remove, drain well, blot dry. Marinate the ribs in the barbecue sauce 1 to 2 hours. Cook on the grill for 40 minutes over medium-bright coals, turning frequently and basting often with the sauce. The ribs can be spit-roasted 35 to 40 minutes, basting frequently. In a sheepherder oven, cook the ribs in an open pan 40–45 minutes, turn at midpoint, baste several times as the ribs cook. In the kitchen oven, cook 1 hour at 350 degrees, basting frequently; turn at midpoint of the cooking time. Serve additional sauce in a separate dish. Be sure to skim excess fat from the sauce.

### SMOTHERED JAVELINA CHOPS

Originated by my ingenious wife, this proved the ideal way to cook the small, lean chops from javelina as well as the bigger, tougher chops from wild boar.

| | |
|---|---|
| 8 javelina chops or 4 boar chops; substitute pork chops, allowing 1 per serving unless very small | 1 cup boiling water |
| | 2 to 3 cups vegetable soup |
| | 1 lemon sliced very thin, seeds removed |
| 1 tablespoon peanut oil | 1 teaspoon salt |

Heat the oil sizzling hot in a deep skillet. Sear the chops quickly on both sides. Pour in boiling water, cover pan, cook 10 minutes at low heat. Spread lemon slices over the meat, pour in the soup, add salt. Cover pan, cook 35 to 40 minutes. If fat rises to the surface, skim it off. If the soup thickens too much, add a spoonful or two of warm water and stir. The liquid should cover the meat during the entire cooking period. Pour a portion of the sauce over the chops after they are placed on their warmed serving plates.
Serves 4.

### JAVELINA SCRAPPLE

Any kind of pork can be used to make scrapple, but wild boar or javelina is especially good, since it is so fat-free.

head (skinned, eyes, brain,
and tongue removed) of
javelina or boar, neck, shanks,
and trimmings; substitute
neck, head, and trimmings of
pork
2 teaspoons salt

2 bay leaves
2 cups white corn meal
1 teaspoon oregano
1 hot chili pepper
¼ teaspoon freshly ground
pepper

Put the meat into a large pot and cover completely with cold water. Add salt, pepper, and bay leaves and bring to a rolling boil, then allow to simmer 1½ to 2 hours, until the meat separates from the bones. Skim froth and scum from the surface occasionally; add more water if needed.

Strain broth into a clean pot. Pick meat free of bones and chop in very small pieces. Skim off any fat that has risen to top of broth as it cools. If ice is available, drop some pieces into the broth; the fat will collect on the ice and may be lifted out with it.

Bring 2 quarts of the broth to a rolling boil. Add the corn meal a tablespoon at a time, stirring vigorously as each spoonful is added. Powder the oregano and chili pepper and add them to the mixture. When the broth begins to thicken, add the chopped meat. Cook 20 minutes, stirring briskly. The mixture will plop and spatter and pop blobs out at you as it grows thicker, so be prepared to dodge. When the scrapple is thick enough so that it resists the stirring spoon, it is done.

Pour it into a lightly greased square or rectangular pan, and set in a cool place. In about 3 hours it will be firm enough to be turned out by inverting the pan over waxed paper, foil, or a platter. To serve, slice in ½-inch slices and sauté gently until both sides are crusty and crisp. Serve with fried eggs, or top slices with poached eggs. Scrapple will keep 3 to 4 days in a cool place, or up to 2 weeks in the refrigerator.

Serves 8 to 10.

## Buffalo

After the great slaughter of buffalo reduced their numbers to a piti-ful tag end of about 600 animals in 1880, the native bison has come back. Not in the wild state, however. Today's buffalo are in three major herds and a scattered number of smaller herds. Two of the big herds are on federal reservations, but both the government and private herd owners sell animals. Some require that you order a minimum of a half carcass, others will provide you with cuts such as roasts, chops, hump, and so on. A few private owners will let you shoot your own.

Buffalo meat is somewhat coarser in texture than beef, but has a sweeter flavor. It tends to be fat, and excess fat should be trimmed away before the meat is cooked. Most of the buffalo sold today is aged in the same fashion as commercial meats and is comparable in tenderness to U.S. Grade Good beef. For cooking over coals, it should still be marinated.

### BUFFALO STEAKS WITH MARROW

This is the buffalo hunter's own way of preparing steaks; if you want to try it, include a request for a marrowbone when ordering buffalo meat.

3- to 4-pound buffalo, 1½-
    to 2 inches thick; substitute
    beef chuck or forearm
Marinade #1

½ cup marrow
⅛ teaspoon Nepal pepper or ¼
    teaspoon cayenne

Buffalo marrow is buttery-soft and can be worked at room tem-perature; if beef marrow is used the bone should be warmed before the marrow is removed.

Blend the salt and pepper with the marrow. Remove steak from marinade after 1½ to 2 hours, wipe dry. Place steak on grill over bright coals for 2 minutes, turn and spread marrow over the hot side. After 3 minutes, turn and spread the other side with marrow. Cook 5 minutes, turn and spread more marrow on the hot meat. Turn once more and spread again. Cook 5 more minutes and remove from grill. Let the meat rest 5 to 10 minutes on a warm platter before slicing to serve.

Cooking time as given above results in a rare to medium-rare steak. If you want the meat cooked more thoroughly, extend the final period of cooking time. But please don't overcook. Whether as steak or roast, good meat deserves a better fate than carbonizing.

Serves 6.

### SON-OF-A-BITCH STEW, PLAINS STYLE

Two stews have a right to this name. One originated in the buffalo hunters' camps around 1850 and was based on an Indian dish made from buffalo; it is this one that is the Plains Style stew. The Border Style, which is based on venison or goat meat, is a quarter of a century older; it was born on the Texas-Mexican border, and its chief descendant is chili con carne.

There are several versions of the naming of the dish. Take your choice of the two most likely. One: A tenderfoot buffalo hunter, having eaten the stew for the first time, asked its ingredients, and on being told what it contained, said to the cook, "Sir, only a son-of-a-bitch would cook up a dish like that!" Two: After eating the stew for the first time, one cowhand asked another what was in it, and the second replied, "I'll be a son-of-a-bitch if I know, but it sure was tasty!"

Into the original buffalo version of the stew went the lining of the animal's second stomach, the liver, heart, brains, kidneys with a chunk of kidney suet, a few pounds of flank meat and some marrow; it was seasoned with salt, pepper, and gall from the bladder. The chuck wagon or beef version required parts from two animals. A mature steer furnished red meat, heart, kidneys, tripe, liver, marrow, and suet; an unweaned calf provided sweetbreads, brains, and the marrowgut, which is the closed and unused lower intestine of a nursing calf. Chili peppers replaced gall in the chuck wagon version's seasoning.

Today, the traditional ingredients of either version are hard to find. What follows is the modernized stew that chuck wagon cooks began preparing in later days. It was given me by Charlie Bell, of Skellytown, Texas; Charlie by his own admission was "born in a corner of the Goodnight JA Ranch calf pasture on a windy day" and for more than fifty years worked for the JA as a cowhand.

| | |
|---|---|
| 2 pounds beef flank or brisket | 4 or 5 hot red chili peppers |
| 1 beef or calf heart, cleaned | 1 teaspoon oregano |
| 1 pound tripe | ½ teaspoon coarse-ground black |
| 1½ pounds calf's liver | pepper |
| 2 quarts water | 4 beef kidneys |
| ¼ pound beef marrow or beef | 4 pair sweetbreads |
| suet | 2 pounds calf's brains |
| 2 tablespoons salt | |

Dice the flank meat, heart, tripe, liver, and suet coarsely, into ½-inch cubes. Cover with 2 quarts water in a big pot, bring to a boil, then reduce to a simmer. Skim off any froth or scum rising to the top as it cooks. As soon as the liquid is simmering clear with no more froth appearing, add salt, chili peppers, oregano, and pepper. Simmer 30 to 40 minutes, fish out the chili peppers, mash them to a pulp, and return the pulp to the pot. The meat of the heart will be the last to get tender—when it can be pierced easily by a fork, dice the kidneys and sweetbreads and add them to the pot. Cook 10 minutes, then add the brains. When the brains are dissolved, the liquid will be thick, like a cream soup. At this point, the stew is ready to serve, in big, deep bowls with hot sourdough biscuits.

Serves 12 to 15.

### BOILED BUFFALO TONGUE

Buffalo tongues were usually the only meat taken by hide hunters from the animals they killed. When buffalo hides were bringing

$1.50 to $2.00 at the Kansas hide depots, and buffalo hams had no buyers at 3¢ a pound, the tongues were worth 30¢ apiece. Eastern restaurants scrambled for the tongues, which were among their most expensive menu items.

Buffalo tongue much resembles beef tongue, except that its flesh is very dark, almost black, and is softer in texture.

| | |
|---|---|
| whole uncooked buffalo tongue; substitute beef tongue | 3 bay leaves |
| | ½ clove garlic |
| 1 medium-sized onion, quartered | 1 teaspoon salt |
| | 6 cracked peppercorns |

Cut away the clump of gristle and hard veins at the base of the tongue and wash well. Put in a large pot with water to cover, add the onion, bay leaves, garlic, and salt, bring to a boil, then reduce to a simmer and cook 1½ to 2 hours. During the first 20 or 30 minutes, skim the froth and scum that will rise to the top of the water. Test for tenderness by piercing the base with a fork or skewer; when the tines enter easily, add the peppercorns and cook 10 minutes more. (Peppercorns impart a bitter flavor to liquids in which they are boiled for prolonged periods.)

Drain the tongue well, allow to cool. Skin, beginning at the base. The tongue may be sliced and eaten with a sauce, such as Green Sauce on page 32. Or the slices can be dredged in flour and sautéed lightly in butter. If the tongue is ground with a dash of lemon juice, cayenne or Nepal pepper, and a touch of onion, it makes a patélike spread to serve as an hors d'oeuvre.

## Caribou

Probably the most numerous of all antlered animals on the North American continent today, the caribou's range is the frozen tundra of the Arctic Circle, in Canada and Alaska. The meat is lean, like most venison, and is available commercially.

### CARIBOU RIBS WITH THICK VEGETABLE SAUCE

Perhaps the closest approach to frontier living in modern times was the life of about three hundred colonists persuaded by the federal government to settle in the Matanuska Valley of Alaska in the 1930s. The settlers were promised aid in taming this twentieth-century frontier, but it never quite reached them. Like pioneers of all eras, they soon found themselves living off the land. One of the original colonists, Albert Snell of Oakland, California, passed on to me a pair of recipes that became very popular in preparation of the caribou which became the colonists' principal meat.

| | |
|---|---|
| 3 pounds of caribou ribs, cut like short ribs into chunks of about 1 pound each; substitute beef short ribs | 2 tablespoons brown sugar |
| | 4 medium-sized potatoes |
| | 6 carrots |
| | 2 large sweet onions |
| Marinade #1 | ½ cup white beans |
| beef use Marinade #4 | 1 teaspoon salt |
| 4 thick slices bacon or salt pork | ½ teaspoon pepper |
| | 2 tablespoons vinegar |

Fry bacon or salt pork in Dutch oven until it is very crisp; the salt pork should be blanched in hot water for 2 or 3 minutes if it is used. Remove bacon from pan, drain off excess fat; there should be ¼ inch of fat left. Bring fat to smoking heat and stir in the sugar to caramelize it, scrape the pan well, and add the ribs. Peel and dice coarsely the potatoes, carrots, and onions, crumble the bacon or salt pork, and mix with the diced vegetables. Put vegetables, including beans, in pan between and over the ribs, sprinkle the salt, pepper, and vinegar over the tops of the vegetables.

Close the Dutch oven and bury in coals, cook 2 to 2½ hours. Remove meat to a warm platter, slip out the bones, cut into serving-sized pieces. The vegetables in the pot will have disintegrated; mash them and stir them well. If too thick, add warm water or meat stock to bring the mixture to the consistency of a thick purée; if too thin, cook 10 to 15 minutes over bright coals, stirring frequently. Cover the meat with the sauce, serve.

Serves 6 to 8.

### SPICED CARIBOU SHANKS

| | |
|---|---|
| 5 to 6 pounds of shanks cut into 3-inch lengths, skinned and wiped dry; substitute venison, veal, or lamb shanks | 2 tablespoons cider vinegar |
| | ½ cup cold water |
| | 1½ cups pitted prunes |
| | 1 cup dried apricots |
| 3 tablespoons flour | 1 teaspoon powdered allspice |
| 1 teaspoon salt | 1 teaspoon powdered cloves |
| 2 tablespoons peanut oil or butter | |

Put flour and salt in paper sack and shake the pieces of shank in the sack to coat them. Heat oil or butter very hot, brown shanks well. Mix vinegar with water, pour into pan, close pan tightly, and cook over slow coals 1 hour. Add water occasionally if needed; the pan should never be dry.

Chop prunes and apricots coarsely and soak in cold water. At end of the indicated cooking time, add the chopped fruit and spices. Close pan and cook 25 to 30 minutes over very low coals. This dish can be cooked in a sheepherder stove over dying coals or in the kitchen oven at very low heat. Use a pan with a tight-fitting cover.

Serves 4.

# Deer

There are said to be more deer in North America today than ever before. Because most states, from New England to Hawaii, have open deer seasons, it is the hunter's favorite big game animal. The deer's size is as widely varied as its distribution, ranging from desert deer little bigger than billygoats to mule deer almost as large as elk. Venison is a very dry, very lean meat, requiring marinating if it is to be cooked by a dry-heat process such as grilling; roasts should be larded for spit-roasting, or cooked with moisture in the roasting pan if the oven is used.

## VENISON LIVER, CAMP STYLE

The liver of a deer is justifiably considered the hunter's prize and his own private reward. It spoils quickly and must be cooked almost at once after being removed from the carcass. Its flavor is so delicate that only the simplest seasonings should be used in preparing it.

deer liver, cleaned, cut into
  ½-inch slices; substitute
  finest calf's liver
flour

salt
peanut oil, butter, or bacon
  drippings

Put flour and salt in a paper bag, shake the slices of liver in the bag until each slice is lightly coated. Sauté very gently over low heat in peanut oil, butter, or bacon drippings, using just enough to cover the bottom of the pan, about 2 minutes per side. The liver is done when no pink liquid flows after it is stuck with a fork or knife tip.
  Serves 4 to 6.

## VENISON CHOPS OR STEAKS, SWISS STYLE

12 chops or 4 steaks cut ½ inch
  thick; substitute similar cuts
  from any antlered game, or
  veal or baby beef
1 cup flour
cooking oil or fat

1½ cups cold water
½ teaspoon salt
1 small sweet onion
½ clove garlic
large dash black pepper

Since the recipe uses a moist cooking process, no marinating is necessary. However, if commercial meats are used you might want to marinate for 1 to 2 hours in Marinade #4

**50**

Wipe the meat dry and dredge very lightly in flour. In a dry skillet, brown the remaining flour over very low heat until it is a dark tan. Scrape from skillet onto a piece of clean paper or into a dish.

Put enough cooking oil or fat into the skillet to form a very thin film on its bottom. Bring to smoking heat and sear the chops or steaks on both sides, not more than 1 to 2 minutes per side. Remove meat.

Put water into a small, clean jar; add the browned flour and salt and shake briskly until a smooth mixture forms. Pour this into the skillet in which the meat was seared and stir well, scraping the pan to loosen the browned bits that will be clinging to its bottom. Grate the onion or mince it very fine. Crush the garlic with a knife blade on a firm, flat surface. Add onion and garlic to the flour mixture, add pepper, stir well; put in the browned pieces of meat. The liquid in the skillet should cover the meat; if it does not, add additional warm water. Cover the skillet and cook over slow coals 20 to 30 minutes, until the meat is tender to a fork. Stir occasionally, scraping the pan, to keep the sauce from burning. Adjust seasoning.

Serves 4.

## VENISON STEAKS OR CHOPS IN SOUR CREAM

4 venison round steaks cut ¾ to 1 inch thick, or 12 chops cut the full thickness of the ribs; substitute similar cuts from any antlered game, or veal or beef

Marinade #1
    beef use Marinade #4

¾ cup butter or peanut oil (do not use margarine, as some margarines now contain chemicals that keep them from blending with acid ingredients such as sour cream)

1¼ pints sour cream
    salt
    pepper

Marinate venison 2 to 3 hours; beef in Marinade #4, 3 to 4 hours. (If beef is used in this dish, you will need one-half recipe of Marinade #1 for the sauce.)

In the skillet, heat 1 tablespoon butter or oil to smoking, wipe meat dry and sear on both sides. Add 1 tablespoon butter or oil after the meat is seared and sauté gently over medium coals 8 to 10 minutes per side. Remove meat to a hot platter.

Add the remaining butter or oil to the skillet, scrape the pan well to loosen any bits clinging to its bottom. Strain 1 cup of Marinade #1 and stir into the pan juices, then stir in the sour cream a spoonful at a time, stirring well as each is added. Do not allow to boil or bubble up while the sour cream is being blended. Taste sauce and adjust seasoning with salt and pepper, pour over meat and serve.

Serves 4.

### ROAST VENISON

Simple seasonings in cooking meat—especially game—outdoors reward you by revealing the meat's own delicious flavor. When the meat has been tenderized and its moisture content increased by marinating, you can cook it by any method you choose—grill, spit, Dutch oven, sheepherder stove—and know the results will be pleasing.

If there is any secret to roasting over coals, it is in the preparation of the meat to be cooked. A large roast should be marinated at least 6 to 8 hours; overnight is not too long a time. Turn occasionally, and spoon some of the marinade over the top of the meat. Then wipe the meat dry. If you have a larding needle, cut the pork fat or salt pork (which should have its rinds trimmed off and be blanched in hot water 2 to 3 minutes) or bacon fat into strips that will fit the needle. If you have no larding needle, cut the fat into strips just a trifle narrower than the blade of your thinnest knife; bury the knife blade in the meat, twist the blade, and with a spoon handle slide a strip of fat into the opening along the blade. Space your larding strips 3 to 4 inches apart. Any tag ends of fat protruding from the surface of the roast after larding should be trimmed away. If you have larded with a needle, use the knife tip to insert thin slivers of onion and garlic into the meat; if you lard with a knife, slide the slivers in with the fat.

whole haunch, saddle, or
rack of venison, or a roast
cut from either; substitute
similar cuts of veal, lamb, or
beef
Marinade #1, or #2

for commercial meats,
Marinade #4
5 or 6 thin slices of pork fat,
salt pork, or bacon fat
salt, pepper
½ cup thin slivers of onion
1 clove garlic cut in thin slivers

Dust the marinated and larded roast lightly with salt and pepper. Allow 18 to 20 minutes per pound on the spit, 12 to 18 minutes per pound on the grill over medium coals. When roasting on either of these, baste the meat with the marinade mixture, and when using the grill, turn the roast every 10 to 15 minutes. When roasting in the Dutch oven, put a layer of thin slices of fat on its bottom and place the roast on them, bury in coals, and cook 30 to 40 minutes per pound, or longer. In a sheepherder oven, cook 10 to 12 minutes per pound in a tightly closed pan, again with a layer of pork fat on the bottom. In the kitchen range, allow 15 minutes per pound in a tightly closed pan. The pan can be uncovered during the final 15 to 20 minutes of cooking to brown the roast. Roasts cooked in a Dutch oven can be browned on the spit or grill, if you wish.

Traditionally, red currant jelly is the accompaniment for roast venison. Some cooks use the jelly as is, others modify it by thinning it with a dash of hot water, others thin with a little warmed port wine or cassis.

Allow about ½ pound of meat per serving.

### SON-OF-A-BITCH STEW, BORDER STYLE

On page 45 you met the buffalo and chuck-wagon version of this famous stew; now get acquainted with the border version, which is based on venison or goat meat. It, too, has a history. When the volunteer militia of the young Texas Republic repelled one of several Mexican invasions in the 1830–1840 period, the ragged troops had no trappings of modern armies, such as commissaries and PXs. Standing guard along the Rio Grande, the Texans inherited from the departed Mexican troops a band of camp followers; the Mexican term for these ladies is *lavanderas,* since among other functions they did the washing for the soldiers. They also cooked whatever the men could scrounge from the deserted countryside.

Now, the deer native to that region at that time was small, weighing only 60 to 70 pounds field-dressed. There were also a few stray goats wandering along the riverbanks, and both deer and goats provided the army's meat. Every bit of meat had to go into the pot, and the *lavanderas* had little to use for seasoning except the native wild marjoram, called oregano, and the hot red peppers from deserted gardens. From these scant ingredients the *lavanderas* created the Son-of-a-Bitch Stew, which was called by its equivalent name in border Spanish profanity, *Chingao Cabron.* The dish known today as chili con carne is a lineal descendant of the *lavenderas'* stews, and the stew itself was commonly cooked in border deer camps when I hunted that area during the 1920s.

| | |
|---|---|
| 4 to 5 pounds of trimmings from a deer: flank and neck meat, plus the heart, tongue, brain, kidneys, and testicles; the only substitute meat matching in flavor is goat meat or the flesh of a scrub calf slaughtered because it is too scrawny to raise | ½ pound salt pork or fat bacon<br>1 tablespoon salt<br>3 red Bell peppers<br>1 hot chili pepper, Tepine or Japonais, or 1 teaspoon chili molido<br>6 onions, quartered<br>1 clove garlic<br>¼ teaspoon oregano |

Reserving the kidneys and brains, cut all the meat, including the salt pork, into chunks ½ to ¾ inch in size. Put in a pot and cover with cold water, bring to a boil, then reduce to simmer slowly. Skim off the froth and scum that will rise during the first minutes of simmering; when no more froth appears, add the salt, chopped peppers, onions, and chopped garlic, and the oregano. Cook 30 to 40 minutes, until the pieces of the heart are tender. Chop the kidneys and add, then the brains. When the brains dissolve, the stew is ready.

Some cooks like to thicken the stew with a tablespoon or two of *masa,* which is the fine-grained corn meal used in making tortillas and tamales. This meal is available in most stores in packages labeled *Masa de Harina.*

Serves 8 to 10.

## VENISON CHILI CON CARNE

Of all meats, venison makes the best chili, and of all the meats entitled to be called venison, that from the deer produces the superior chili con carne. If you buy beef from which to make chili, get the lowest grade you can find; it contains the least amount of natural fat, and greasy chili is an abomination. By the time cheap beef has undergone long cooking, and has come under the intoxicating influence of the peppers in the pot, it will be as tender as prime grade. Chili con carne can be made from ground meat, and often is, but the best is prepared from meat chopped into fingertip-sized bits.

No matter what you've read or heard, genuine chili con carne does not contain tomatoes. Putting tomatoes in chili is the equivalent of dousing raw oysters with chocolate sauce. Recipes calling for tomatoes in chili are concocted by those who confuse chili with Italian spaghetti sauce or who think that because chili con carne is red, it must therefore contain tomatoes. Nor should kidney beans ever be associated with chili con carne, in spite of the recommendations of a few misled recipe-writers; the traditional beans accompanying chili are either pintos or plain red beans.

What follows is the traditional recipe for *chili con carne de venado,* as it has been prepared for more than a century by cooks in the area where the dish originated. And while chili may be made with almost any meat, *chili de venado* is the chili of Olympus.

| | |
|---|---|
| 3 pounds of venison: flank, neck, any trimmings left from butchering; substitute very lean beef | 1 teaspoon powdered oregano |
| | ¼ teaspoon *cominos* (cumin) |
| | 2 cloves garlic or ¼ teaspoon garlic powder |
| ¼ cup beef suet or lard | 1 teaspoon salt |
| 2 to 3 teaspoons chili molido | 2 medium-sized hot onions |
| 3 or 4 small hot chili peppers (optional) | |

Chop the meat into fingertip-sized bits. Render the suet, removing the solid residues before they become black and burned. With the liquid fat at smoking heat, brown the meat a small quantity at a time. (Ground meat can be used in making chili, at the sacrifice of a certain amount of flavor. When using ground meat, brown in a very small amount of very hot fat, breaking the meat up into grain-sized bits.)

When all the meat has been browned, drain any excess fat from the pan, sprinkle the meat with the chili molido, cover the pan tightly, and let cook 15 minutes over very low heat; stir once or twice. (A word here about chili molido. This is powdered dried chili pepper pods, and varies considerably in potency between the several brands marketed on a national scale. Some brands are so mild as to be almost sweet, others pack a great deal of authority. You will have to experiment to find the one that best suits your taste.)

Pour enough water into the pan to cover the meat completely. Stir in the oregano, *cominos*, garlic, and salt. If you like a very, very hot chili, put in several pods of the fiery Tepine or Japonais peppers. Cover pan and cook over very low heat, stirring occasionally, for 1 hour. Grate the onions, or chop them very fine, and add them, together with more water if needed to cover the meat. Cook 1 hour, or until the onion bits dissolve.

Before serving, let the pan stand 10 to 15 minutes and skim off any grease that rises to the top. If you can wait, refrigerate the chili in the cooking pot overnight, or set it in a cool place; this will allow the fat to form a cake or crust on top of the sauce, and this crust can then be lifted off in large pieces and discarded. Chili con carne will keep in a covered pan or dish in the refrigerator for a week to ten days.

Makes approximately 12 generous bowls.


**VENISON MINCEMEAT**

The originator of this toothsome venison mincemeat is Jim Armstrong of Arcata, California, who is also a pretty good hand at turning out chili con carne.

| | |
|---|---|
| 1 pound venison; substitute very lean beef | 1 orange, peeled and seeded, all pith and membrane removed |
| 1 pound beef suet | ¾ pound brown sugar |
| 1 pound seedless dark raisins | ½ teaspoon each: allspice, nutmeg, cinnamon |
| ½ pound seedless white raisins | |
| ⅔ pound currants | 2 teaspoons salt |
| 1 pound apples, peeled and cored | 1 pint brandy |
| | ½ pint Jamaican dark rum |
| ½ pound pecans | ¼ pint white port |

Chop the venison into fairly uniform pieces about fingertip size or smaller. Over the lowest possible heat, in an ungreased, uncovered pan, cook until it is very, very dry. The cooking may be done over surface heat or in a low oven. The meat should not be seasoned.

Mince the suet as fine as possible, or pass it through a grinder, using the finest blade. Chop all remaining ingredients into a fine mince. Blend the seasonings and liquors and combine them with the solid ingredients, stirring well with a wooden spoon. Put the mincemeat into a wide-mouth crock or jar; if a jar is used, wrap brown paper around the outside and secure with gummed tape. Cover the container with several folds of cheesecloth, tied loosely around the mouth. Put in a cool, dark place for one month. Once a week, uncover and stir thoroughly with a wooden spoon. If too much of the liquid is absorbed, add a little more brandy.

Makes 2 quarts.

# Elk

Standing second to the deer in popularity as a big game animal is the elk. The flesh of elk is moister and less firm than that of deer, but has the rich flavor characteristic of all venison. Since elk meat has a higher fat content than deer venison, it sours even more readily. Because of the size of an elk carcass, it is usually impractical to hang it whole, but the animal should be quartered for hanging. Elk meat is available from several of the commercial game suppliers listed in the appendix on page 300. Any of the recipes previously given for deer meat are equally suitable for elk; conversely, all of the following recipes can be prepared with deer meat.

### ROAST STUFFED ELK HEART

whole elk heart; substitute deer or beef heart
4 or 5 slices of very dry bread
1 large sweet onion
1 teaspoon celery salt
½ teaspoon salt
¼ teaspoon cayenne

½ cup dry red wine
½ cup peanut oil or other light cooking oil
1 egg
2 tablespoons flour
2 cups cold water

Clean the heart by cutting small slits into each cavity and removing all veins and membranes; wash well, dry with a cloth or paper towels. Break the bread into coarse pieces or chop into ½-inch cubes. Chop the onion coarsely. Combine bread, onion, and all seasonings; blend 1 tablespoon of the oil with the wine, stir into the bread mixture, then break the egg into the mixture and stir well to coat the individual pieces. Stuff the heart with the bread mixture, close the slits with a stitch or two of coarse thread. Rub the outside of the heart with oil, using about 1 tablespoon, then roll in flour until it is well coated.

Heat the remaining oil in a Dutch oven, and brown the heart in the hot oil. Add 2 cups cold water to the oven, close it, and bury in coals for 2 to 2½ hours. In a sheepherder oven, cook in a tightly closed pan for 1½ to 1¾ hours; in the kitchen oven, about 3 hours at 325 degrees. Slice across the grain of the meat to serve.

Serves 6.

### ELK LIVER DUMPLINGS

Elk liver is to deer liver as beef liver is to calf liver, and is better in a mixed dish than broiled or sautéed. In a hunting camp in Oregon, Elmer Meyers of Klamath, California, showed me how to make these dumplings.

| | |
|---|---|
| 1½ to 2 pounds elk liver cut in ½-inch slices; substitute beef liver | 1 teaspoon salt |
| | 1 cup tomato ketchup mixed with 2 cups water, or 3 cups tomato juice |
| 10 slices dry bread | |
| ½ cup milk | 2 or 3 drops Tabasco Sauce or |
| 2 tablespoons bacon drippings | ⅛ teaspon cayenne |

Plunge the slices of liver into briskly boiling water and cook 3 to 4 minutes; remove, drain, and mince very fine or grind. Heat the milk and soften the bread in it; blend with the liver, bacon drippings, and salt. Bring the ketchup-water mixture, or the tomato juice to a slow simmer, and add to it the Tabasco or cayenne. Form the liver mixture into golf-ball-sized dumplings and drop them in the simmering juice. Cook 15 to 20 minutes, stirring so the dumplings will cook evenly.

Serves 6 to 8.


## SALT-COOKED ELK STEAK

| | |
|---|---|
| large steak of about 4 pounds, in one piece, cut 2 to 2½ inches thick; substitute beef | 4 to 5 pounds table salt |
| | 2 large brown paper bags |
| | freshly ground black pepper |
| Marinade #1 | |

Marinate the steak 2 to 3 hours, turning occasionally. Remove from marinade, drain, wipe dry. Wet the paper bags and nest one inside the other to form a double bag. Moisten the salt to form a thick paste. With the bags on a flat surface, spread a layer of the wet salt 1 to 1½ inch thick on the bottom, and place the steak on this. Cover with another layer of salt, being sure to pack salt around the edges of the meat. Press the bags flat, fold edges and close mouth to form a compact package.

Lay the bagged steak on a good layer of bright coals and cover with coals 4 to 5 inches deep. Go away for a half-hour if you like your steak rare; 35 to 40 minutes if you want it medium-rare or medium. Do not overcook, though; 45 minutes should be maximum cooking time. Scrape away the top layer of coals, lift out the packaged steak with a shovel or flat board, crack away the salt crust, and lift the steak out onto a warm platter for slicing. It will not taste too salty, but you should avoid any further seasoning than a light dusting of freshly ground pepper.

## Moose

Biggest of North American antlered game, the moose is growing scarce in his former haunts, though he can still be hunted in some areas of the U.S. Northeast, as well as in Canada and Alaska. Mrs. Sylvia Fox, who with her husband, Jack, operates the Villa San Jose in Morelia, Michoacan, Mexico, was given a handful of moose-meat recipes by her grandfather, who was a bullcook in the North Woods when moose was a lumber-camp staple. The following are from her files.

### MOOSE MEAT WITH APRICOTS

4 pounds moose flank meat; substitute flank from any antlered game, or beef
Marinade #3
    beef substitute Marinade #4

1½ cups dried apricots
½ cup minced raw carrots

3 cups dry bread crumbs
1½ teaspoons salt
2 teaspoons powdered thyme
dash cayenne
½ cup meat stock or broth
1 tablespoon bacon drippings
½ cup cold water

Remove the tough outer membrane from the piece of flank and pound the meat well with a mallet or back of a cleaver, then trim into a rectangle. Marinate 2 to 3 hours, drain well.

Chop the apricots coarsely and combine them with the carrots, bread crumbs, and seasonings. Moisten with the stock and work into a smooth mixture. Spread this evenly over the piece of flank meat. Roll the meat jelly-roll style and tie with heavy cord.

Heat bacon drippings in a Dutch oven and brown the roll of meat evenly. Add ½ cup cold water to the pan, close the Dutch oven, and bury in coals; cook 2 to 2½ hours. In a sheepherder stove, in a closed pan, cook 1¼ to 1½ hours; in the kitchen oven, cook 2 hours at 350 degrees.

Serves 6 to 8.


### ROAST MOOSE LIVER

8-pound piece of moose liver
  ½ to ¾ cup flour
    1 cup bacon drippings or cooking oil
    3 or 4 medium-sized sweet onions

1½ teaspoon salt
½ teaspoon paprika
  dash nutmeg
¾ cup buttermilk or ½ cup sour cream thinned with ¼ cup warm water

Rub the cleaned liver with flour and brown in hot fat in the bottom of a Dutch oven, turning the meat to brown all areas evenly. Slice the onions, sprinkle lightly with flour, and brown quickly in very hot fat in a separate pan. Combine the seasonings and sprinkle them over the onions, then pour the buttermilk or thinned sour cream over the onions and liver.

Cover the oven, bury in coals, and cook 1½ to 2 hours; overcook rather than removing too soon. When cooking this in a sheepherder stove, use a closed pan and cook 1 hour; in the kitchen range, 1¼ hours at 325 degrees. You can test for doneness in a sheepherder or kitchen oven by piercing the liver with a slender knife or long skewer—if no pink liquid flows when the instrument is withdrawn, the liver is done.

Thin slices on toast make an unusual appetizer.

Serves 10 to 12.

### MOOSE MEATBALLS WITH PRUNES AND APPLES

| | |
|---|---|
| 2 pounds of trimmings such as flank, neck; substitute elk or beef | ½ cup milk |
| | ½ teaspoon salt |
| | ⅛ teaspoon pepper |
| ½ pound bacon or sausage meat | 1 egg |
| 2 apples, cored and peeled | 1 cup tomato ketchup |
| 12 to 14 pitted prunes | 2 tablespoons cider vinegar |
| 1½ cups bread crumbs | 1 cup warm water |

Put the meat through a grinder twice, putting the bacon, apples, and prunes, through with it the second time. (If sausage meat is used, it can be added after the second grinding.) Combine the bread crumbs, milk, and seasonings with the ground meat. Break the egg over the mixture and blend it in well. With a very gentle touch, press into golf-ball-sized meatballs.

Mix the ketchup and vinegar with 1 cup warm water. Grease a Dutch oven lightly and dot the meatballs on its bottom. Pour in the ketchup-vinegar-water mixture. Close the Dutch oven, place it on a bed of coals, and cook 40 to 45 minutes, opening occasionally to turn the meatballs so they will cook evenly in their liquid bath. The meatballs should be almost completely covered as they cook; more liquid may be needed.

Serves 8 to 10.

## Mountain Sheep

Not to be confused with its shy cousin, the stub-horned mountain goat, which is considered inedible, the Rocky Mountain sheep or bighorn may be hunted in several areas. Colorado, Wyoming, Arizona, New Mexico, Nevada, as well as Alaska and Canada, all have open seasons on the bighorn. The desert bighorn can be taken in several states of northern Mexico. The aoudad, an imported bighorn, can be hunted with special permit in the Palo Duro Canyon of

Texas; there are also several private fee-hunting preserves in Texas and Arizona where these sheep will be found.

Closer kin to the antelope than to antlered game, the flesh of the bighorn is lighter in texture than venison, and very, very dry. It can be cooked using any of the recipes for antelope beginning on page 33.

## MOUNTAIN SHEEP ALBONDIGAS

In the late 1920s, Owen "Pat" Kilday, for many years Sheriff of Bexar County, Texas, took a group of friends into northern Mexico on a mountain sheep hunt. He generously included a teen-age boy —myself—in the party. The hunting was rough and the game scarce, but from the one sheep brought in the Mexican camp cooks prepared a meal of the meatballs called *Albondigas*.

| | |
|---|---|
| 2 to 3 pounds of meat, trimmings, neck, flank; substitute lamb, veal, baby beef | 1 teaspoon mild chili molido |
| | 1 egg |
| | lard or bacon drippings |
| | 4 very ripe tomatoes |
| 1 pound bacon | salt |
| 2 cloves garlic | |

Chop the meat and bacon very fine, adding the garlic and chili powder while chopping. Beat the egg lightly and mix it with the meat, shape into small thick cakes about 1½ inch in diameter and more rounded than flat. Heat ½ inch of fat and cook the meatballs on one side until brown. Turn, and chop the tomatoes on top of the meat so their juice will run into the cooking pan. Sprinkle lightly with salt. Cover the skillet and cook gently 20 to 25 minutes. Stir once or twice.

This becomes a one-dish meal if ½ to ⅔ cup of rice is added when the tomatoes begin to simmer, and several thick slices of onion laid on top of the ingredients cooking in the pan. If rice is added, more salt will be needed; taste to adjust seasoning before serving.

Serves 8 to 10 without rice; 10 to 12 with rice.

## AOUDAD SHEEP STEAKS

Introduced experimentally in 1948, the maned aoudad sheep from Africa have thrived in the Palo Duro Canyon, in the Texas Panhandle. Breeding stock has already been provided from this herd to other states having comparable terrain, and chances seem good that the aoudad will become a reasonably common big game animal of the future in the West and Southwest.

In 1965 a limited number of permits were issued for the first aoudad sheep hunt in North America. Verl Hawbaker of Amarillo, who divides his time between hunting antiques for business and wild game for pleasure, was one of the half-dozen successful hunters. Mrs. Hawbaker cooked steaks from the aoudad by the method she has found successful in handling elk, antelope, and deer, but found that marinating improved the meat, which resembles that of antelope rather than the firmer-textured venisons.

| | |
|---|---|
| 4 steaks ¾ to 1 inch thick; substitute antelope, elk, or beef | flour bacon drippings salt, pepper |
| Marinade #2 beef use Marinade #4 | 2 large sweet onions, sliced |

Marinate the steaks 2 to 4 hours. Before wiping dry, pound them with a tenderizing mallet or the back edge of a heavy cleaver. Wipe dry, press firmly into flour, wipe off excess. Sauté gently in bacon drippings over low heat 4 to 5 minutes per side, turn only once. Season by sprinkling with salt and pepper after the meat has been turned. Lay the onion slices on the meat and cover the pan. After removing from heat, let the pan remain covered 10 minutes. When the steaks and onions have been removed to a warm platter, return the pan to the heat, sprinkle with a thin layer of flour, scrape and stir until the flour is lightly browned, then add warm water or meat stock to make a thin gravy.

Serves 4.

# Kabobs

This style of cooking is also called skewer cookery, cooking *en brochette,* hibachi cooking, and shashlik. While the terms are loosely interchangeable, hibachi cooking is practiced indoors, over small individual grills, and shashlik is applied correctly only to lamb that is skewer-cooked. Those now engaged in hibachi-cooking, or those contemplating embracing it, should take a sober second look at the dangers involved in the indoor use of charcoal fires. Hibachis originated in Japan, where traditional methods of home construction result in very well-ventilated structures, and the exhaustion of oxygen from burning charcoal in a room is not as apt to occur as in the tightly sealed homes of the U.S. It is even dangerous to use a charcoal grill in a garage with opened doors.

Kabobbing, or skewer-cooking, is better suited to soft-fleshed commercial meats than to game, though young and tender wild animals do provide some meats that are suitable. Any game intended for skewer-cooking should be marinated after being cut into 1- to 1½-inch cubes, and use of a marinade improves commercial meats cooked in this style. Skewers should be square or rectangular rather than round, as foods impaled on round skewers tend to slip when being turned.

Special marinades, such as lime juice for fish, will firm up soft-fleshed foods so they will stay on the skewers better. Such items as sweetbreads need parboiling to firm them; onions and green peppers also need parboiling, but the purpose in this case is to tenderize them so they will be done at the same time as the meat with which they are cooked.

Endless combinations of foods can be cooked on skewers. Here are a few compatible combinations:

lamb cubes with cherry tomatoes, small onions, eggplant cubes

veal or beef cubes with the above, or with potato and pepper chunks

pork cubes with chunks of apple and yam or sweet potato
kidneys with bacon and mushrooms
scallops lightly parboiled, wrapped in bacon, and tiny onions
oysters—see Angels on Horseback, page 218
shrimp with cherry tomatoes, chunks of sweet red pepper

Skewer-cooked foods need frequent basting, either with a light neutral oil, such as peanut oil, or an oil-wine mixture seasoned with herbs of your choice, or one of the herbed butters from page 164. The use of manufactured bottled salad dressings is not recommended; most of these products contain no natural ingredients except water, and are merely combinations of chemicals which may react unpredictably to heat. If you require proof, look at their labels.

## PEMMICAN

By a process of trial and error, most aboriginal peoples came up with some kind of iron rations that they could carry with them on their nomadic journeys from campsite to campsite. That evolved by the American Indians came to be called pemmican by the white man, though each tribe had its own pemmican made from herbs, meats, and berries found in its own territory. The pemmican given here was worked out with the help and advice of a Comanche Indian friend, Sammy Eagle Tail Feather, who remembered from his early childhood how the pemmican of his tribe was made and how it tasted. Unfortunately, by the time our collaboration began, many of the wild plants used originally had vanished under the plow, the hooves of cattle, and the city pavements. But Sammy said it was "almost as good" as the buffalo-gut-cased pemmican that he once enjoyed.

Ideally, a pemmican will satisfy hunger without creating thirst. It will sustain energy when taken in very small bites and chewed for a long time; this, too, helps to alleviate thirst. It will not spoil, nor will its taste pall when it is the only food available day after day. Comanche pemmican was made from sun-dried buffalo and deer jerky, several kinds of tart wild berries including the chokecherry, and the sweet mesquite beans, all pounded into a fine paste with pecans and honey.

| | |
|---|---|
| 3 ounces dried beef jerky | 1 tablespoon honey |
| 5 ounces raisins | 2 tablespoons peanut butter |
| 4 ounces unroasted peanuts or pecans | ¼ teaspoon Nepal pepper or ½ teaspoon cayenne |

Put meat and raisins through a meat grinder twice, using the finest blade. Pound or chop the nuts, or reduce them to powder by using an electric blender, since their oil will cause them to darken if they are passed through a metal-bladed meat grinder. Warm the honey slightly and combine it with the peanut butter, then mix it with the other ingredients, including the pepper. Blend very thoroughly. It will form a thick paste, and will keep for several months without refrigeration in a closed jar or lidded plastic container. It should be eaten in very small bites, by itself, a half-teaspoon or so at a time. Sources where good jerky can be purchased will be found in the appendix on page 300.

### UNHAPPY HUNTER'S DINNER

When game has been nonexistent or fish uncooperative, the cook is forced to fall back on this universal camp joke.

| | |
|---|---|
| 4 large boiled potatoes | 2 small onions |
| 4 thick slices bacon or salt pork (blanched) | 2 tablespoons flour |
| | 1½ cups milk |
| 2 tablespoons corn meal | large pinch of pepper |

Peel and slice the potatoes. Roll the bacon or salt pork in the corn meal and fry it crisp, put it on plates where the potato slices have been divided. In the fat left in the frying pan, sauté the onions lightly. Shake the flour and milk (which must be cold) together in a jar or bottle, pour over the hot fat in the skillet and stir over medium-high coals into a smooth tan gravy; add pepper as you stir. Pour the gravy over the potatoes and bacon, and eat while contemplating the general cussedness of Nature. Serves 4.

# III

---

# Pots and Pans on
# a Bed of Coals

Too MANY outdoor chefs look down their noses at any recipe calling
for utensils, though as we have seen in preceding chapters, the use of
such utensils as the Dutch oven relieves the cook from worries about
pot-watching, critical timing, or even about the type and quality of
the coals over which he is cooking.

There is much more to the art of outdoor cooking than the preparation of primary cuts of meat. Some of the dishes utilizing trimmings, lights, and even leftovers offer the chef a real opportunity to
shine. Such dishes also make outdoor cooking more economical, and
in days when food budgets are stretched to the point of strain, this
virtue certainly cannot be ignored.

Those outdoor chefs who scorn the use of utensils overlook an obvious fact—utensils were invented or evolved by people who had
tired of the sameness of grill-cooked and spit-cooked meats, Pot
roasts, stews, meat loaves, pot puddings, and all the dishes utilizing
pieces that do not adapt themselves well to grilling and spit-roasting
as well as those that convert leftovers to fresh offerings are reason
enough for the outdoor cook to welcome utensils to his bed of cooking coals.

## POT ROAST

Most meats, whether game or commercial, respond joyfully to the moist heat of slow pot-roasting. Some, the less expensive grades of commercial beef and the tougher cuts of game, come very close to demanding it. And there has never been a better utensil than the Dutch oven for cooking pot roasts. When used to cook commercial meats, no marinating is really necessary, though use of a marinade with these cuts will help their flavor. Game should be marinated in one of the mixtures given beginning on page 29. You make the choice.

| | |
|---|---|
| 4- to 6-pound roast | 4 or 5 medium-sized onions |
| slices of lean bacon or salt pork | salt, pepper |
| 4 or 5 medium-sized potatoes | marinade or cold water |
| 4 or 5 carrots | |

If a marinade is used, reserve the liquid after draining the meat.

Line the bottom of the Dutch oven with thin slices of bacon or salt pork; if salt pork is used it should be trimmed and blanched 2 or 3 minutes in boiling water. Put the meat on the bacon slices. Peel and halve the vegetables and arrange them around the meat. Dust with salt and pepper. Strain the reserved marinade mixture into the pot, or add cold water to a level of 1 to 1½ inches.

Close the oven, bury it in coals, cook 2½ to 3 hours. Overcooking will do no harm. In a sheepherder or kitchen oven, use a heavy roasting pan with a tight-fitting cover. Cook 1½ to 2 hours in a sheepherder oven, 2 hours at 350 degrees in the kitchen range.

Serves 8 to 10.

## BRAISED MEATROLL

| | |
|---|---|
| 3- to 4-pound piece of flank meat | salt, pepper |
| ½ pound salt pork or fat bacon | 2 tablespoons butter or cooking oil |
| 2 medium-sized potatoes | 1 tablespoon butter |
| 1 cup dry white wine | |

Flank meat being tough and stringy, use of Marinade #1 or #2, page 29 is advised.

Remove the white outer membrane from the meat. Pound on a firm flat surface with a tenderizing mallet or the back of a heavy cleaver. Cut pounded meat into 6-inch squares.

If salt pork is used, trim off rind and blanch in boiling water 2 or 3 minutes. Mince together the pork and potatoes, put about 1½ tablespoons on each square of meat, roll and secure with twine. Dust with salt and pepper; be sparing of the salt if you have used salt pork in the filling.

Heat butter or oil in a heavy skillet and brown the meatrolls thoroughly. Pour the wine over them, cover the pan, and cook over low to moderate heat 20 to 25 minutes; turn the meatrolls once or twice so they will cook evenly. Remove, allowing the pot juices to drain back into the cooking pan, and place the meatrolls on a warm platter. Stir 1 tablespoon butter into the simmering pot juices, scraping the pan while you stir; pour this over the meat as a sauce.

Serves 6 to 8.

## Meat Loaves and Patties

Few people pause to reflect that many of the conveniences, genuine and spurious, that we enjoy in culinary practice today are relatively new. Among these is the meat grinder. It was not until the late 1920s that chopped meat became ground meat. Before that time, few markets kept chopped meat on hand. When it was ordered, the butcher took out an honest piece of chuck or flank meat and reduced it to tiny bits with the rhythmic swings of a pair of heavy cleavers, one in each hand, their blades thunking with a steady clop-clop on his chopping block. That custom, of course, has gone, and we are today in danger of being engulfed in a flood of anonymous ground meat generically called "hamburger."

Meat chopped the old-fashioned way certainly has a better flavor than that passed through the blades of a mechanical grinder, which macerate the tissues and reduce its cooking characteristics. It is also difficult to load chopped meat with the suet and cereal fillers that are present in so much of the "hamburger" bought ready ground. Let me suggest that when you want to cook meat loaves or meat patties, indoors or out, you buy stewing beef or chuck and chop it the old-fashioned way. Or grind it, if you must; you'll still get a better-tasting dish.

## MEAT LOAF WITH VEGETABLES

| | |
|---|---|
| 3 pounds chopped or ground meat | ¾ can tomato paste or 1½ cups tomato juice or ¾ cup dry red wine |
| 1 pound pork fat, salt pork, or fat bacon | 1 tablespoon salt |
| 2 large potatoes or 1 cup rice | ½ teaspoon pepper |
| 2 large sweet onions | large pinch powdered oregano or basil |
| 3 carrots | butter |
| 3 dry biscuits or 4 slices bread | |

If chopped, the meat should be minced very fine, together with the pork fat or trimmed and blanched salt pork or bacon. Grate the potatoes, onions, and carrots; crush the dry biscuits or bread fine. Reserve ⅔ cup of bread crumbs. If you are using tomato paste, mix it with ¾ cup water; if wine is used, add ½ cup water to it. Combine all ingredients and seasonings except the butter and reserved bread crumbs and mix well. (If you like a firm meat loaf, add a raw egg.)

Spread a thick layer of butter on the bottom and sides of a Dutch oven and dust this liberally with the reserved bread crumbs. Pack the meat mixture into the pan, pushing it firmly into contact with the sides. Close the oven, bury it in coals, cook 3 to 3½ hours. When you open the oven you will find that in cooking the meat mixture will have pulled away from the sides, and the crumbs will have formed a rich, thick crust on the loaf.

**Pots and Pans on a Bed of Coals**

To cook in a sheepherder stove or kitchen oven, use a pan with a tight-fitting cover. Cook 1½ to 2 hours in a sheepherder oven, 2 hours at 375 degrees in the kitchen range.

Serves 10 to 12.

### MEAT LOAF WITH MUSHROOMS

This recipe can be prepared with either wild, cultivated or canned mushrooms; for information on uncultivated mushrooms, see page 254.

| | |
|---|---|
| 4 pounds meat; game, or beef chuck or flank | ½ cup milk |
| | 1 egg |
| ½ pound (approximately 2 cups) fresh mushrooms, or 1 large can mushroom "bits and pieces" | ⅛ teaspoon freshly ground white pepper |
| | ½ teaspoon salt |
| 2 cups unsalted cracker crumbs | thin slices of blanched salt pork or fat bacon |

Chop the meat very fine or pass through a grinder, using the coarse blade. If fresh mushrooms are used, parboil 1 to 2 minutes in boiling water, then chop coarsely. Canned mushrooms should be well drained. Unsalted cracker crumbs are most readily prepared by rolling oyster crackers with a rolling pin. Salt pork and bacon are blanched by putting in boiling water 2 or 3 minutes; this reduces their saltiness and removes part of their fat.

Combine all ingredients and seasonings except for the slices of salt pork or bacon, and blend thoroughly. Line the bottom and sides of a Dutch oven with the slices of pork or bacon, reserving enough to cover the top of the meat loaf. Press the meat mixture firmly but gently into the pan; do not pack tightly. Cover its top with slices of pork or bacon.

Close the Dutch oven and bury in coals, cook 3 to 3½ hours. The meat loaf can be removed intact from the Dutch oven, when cooked, by sliding two pancake turners between meat and pan on opposite sides and lifting free. To cook in a sheepherder oven or kitchen range, use a pan with tight-fitting lid; cook 1½ to 2 hours in the sheepherder oven, 2 hours at 375 degrees in the kitchen range.

Serves 10 to 12.

## Meat Patties, or "Hamburgers"

If you have forgotten what was said about grilled hamburgers, or any grilled chopped meat, go back to page 5 and refresh your memory. Meat cooked on grill or spit must be seared to hold in the juices that give it flavor; and by its very nature, ground or chopped meat cannot be seared properly. It is difficult enough to cook ground or chopped meat over the quick, dry heat of open coals even when using a pan, but the following method gives the most satisfactory results.

| | |
|---|---|
| 3 pounds chopped or ground meat; game or beef | 1 cup dry red wine |
| | bacon drippings or cooking oil |
| 6 to 8 pounds of cracked or crushed ice | salt, pepper |

Line a deep bowl with half the ice and put the meat in it in one chunk. Cover the meat with the remaining ice and let stand 45 minutes to 1 hour. Remove meat and squeeze out of it as much water as you can with your hands; don't press it between boards or wring it in a folded cloth. Blend the wine thoroughly with the meat; form into 12 patties of approximately equal size and ¾ to 1 inch thick. In a heavy skillet, bring bacon drippings or oil to high heat. Put two or three patties at a time into the pan; don't overcrowd. Cook on one side for 3 minutes, turn and cook for 3 minutes on the other side. This timing produces a rare meat patty; add 2 minutes for medium, 3 minutes for well done, but cook the full period on one side, turn to finish cooking, then remove from pan, and place on a paper towel to drain. Season after cooking, not before.

You can cook meat patties this way indoors, using very high heat, but the spattering when the moist, cold meat hits the hot fat in the pan is pretty messy. The method does not work in a covered pan. Still, it's your kitchen wall, if you want to clean it up afterwards.

Makes 12 large patties.

## Stews

Among the Dutch oven's many virtues is that its bottom makes a big stewpot when used uncovered on top of coals. Stews cooked outdoors not only seem to taste better, they are economical and a trouble-free dish to prepare when cooking for a crowd, in camp or in your own backyard. You have already encountered stews on pages 45, 53, and 59, and in later sections you will find stews for fowl, fish, and small game. See the index for detailed listings.

### BIGOS: POLISH GAME STEW

2 to 3 pounds of the meat of any large game animal, cut in very thin slices or strips; substitute beef or lamb

2 pounds sauerkraut

1 small sweet onion

2 apples

3 or 4 juniper berries (omit if the meat is game)

1 cup dry white wine

1 tablespoon flour

4 teaspoons butter

Brown the sliced meat lightly over medium heat in a heavy pot or deep skillet, using about 2 teaspoons of the butter. Wash the sauerkraut in three changes of cold water and drain well. Chop the onion and apples fine, mix them with the sauerkraut. Unless the meat is wild game, crush the juniper berries and add them to the mixture. Build up the pot by putting a 1-inch layer of the kraut mixture on the bottom, then a layer of meat, and alternate layers of kraut and meat, topping off with a layer of kraut. Pour the wine over the mixture in the pot. Cover and cook over medium to low heat 35 to 40 minutes.

Drain the liquid from the pot into a saucepan. Blend the reserved butter with the flour and add to the simmering pot juices, stirring into a thin, smooth sauce. Pour this over the mixture in the big pot. Let stand 5 to 10 minutes before serving.

Serves 6 to 8.

## STEW WITH POTATO DUMPLINGS

| | |
|---|---|
| 3 pounds of game or beef cut in 1-inch cubes | 2 teaspoons salt |
| | large pinch of pepper |
| 5 large potatoes | 2 cups milk |
| 1 sweet onion | 1 cup bread cubes, about ½ |
| 6 cloves | inch, lightly browned |
| 2 cups water | |

Peel and mince one potato, cover it with 2 cups water in a small saucepan, and start it cooking. Let it boil briskly until you're ready for it, which will be about 10 minutes. Peel and mince the remaining potatoes, put them in a bowl, and cover with cool water. Let them stand until ready, too.

Peel the onion and stick the cloves into it. Put meat and onion in your stewing kettle, cover with cold water, add the salt and pepper. Cook gently over medium heat until the meat is tender, 35 to 45 minutes, depending on the kind of meat you're using.

Heat milk to the boiling point, but do not let it boil. Mash the cooked potato into it, adding ½ teaspoon salt. Drain the pieces of raw potato, reserving the water. Put the pieces of potato into a fold of cloth and twist it to squeeze the potatoes dry; add the water from this process to the water in which the potato pieces soaked.

Mash the raw potato pieces into the milk mixture and blend into a smooth paste. Drain off the water in which the potatoes soaked, preserving the starch that has settled to the bottom of the bowl. Add 2 tablespoons of this starch to your mashed potatoes and blend well. Turn the potato mixture out onto a board lightly rubbed with flour, pat the potatoes into a smooth layer ¼ inch thick. Cut into 3-inch squares. Put a bread cube in the center of each square and fold the corners of each square up to form a dumpling. (The purpose of this is to avoid that uncooked doughy blob that sometimes remains in the center of dumplings; you can get the same effect by using a pitted prune or two or three raisins.) Handle the potato dough as lightly as possible; a gentle hand here pays off in fluffy dumplings. That's why you pat the dough thin instead of rolling it.

With a slotted spoon, lift the meat and onion from the pot onto a warm platter. Drop the dumplings into the simmering stock a few at a time, and let them dance in the liquid for 20 minutes. Serve the stew in deep bowls, some meat topped with a few dumplings and a portion of the broth ladled over all.

Serves 8 to 10 generously.

### SAUSAGE STEW

This might also be called Hunter's Consolation, or First-Day Stew, since it uses neither flesh, fish, nor fowl.

| | |
|---|---|
| 1 cup dry beans of any kind: pinto, red, navy, lima | 3 or 4 fresh ripe tomatoes or 1 #2 can of tomatoes |
| 2 large chorizo sausages or 6 smoked link sausages or a big ring of Polish sausage | 2 or 3 small sweet onions |
| | ½ teaspoon summer savory |
| | 1 tablespoon salt |
| ½ cup rice or 2 large potatoes peeled and diced | ¼ teaspoon pepper |

Soak the beans 1 to 2 hours in warm water, drain, put in pot and cover generously with cold water. Bring to simmer over gentle heat, and cook 30 to 45 minutes before adding the sausage, rice or potatoes, the tomatoes cut in coarse pieces, the onions sliced or quartered, and the seasonings. Simmer until the beans are soft, the rice or potatoes tender. The stew should be fairly liquid.

Serves 8 to 10.

### GAME POT PUDDING

A pot pudding is a sort of shotgun wedding between meat loaf and scrapple, or if you prefer, between hash and mush. Into it go all scraps and trimmings, shreds of flesh scraped off bones, pieces of heart, brains—whatever hasn't found a home in some other dish.

| | |
|---|---|
| 2½  to 3 pounds scraps and trimmings of meat; or flank or neck meat chopped fine | 1  cup corn meal or hominy grits |
| 1  pound fat bacon | 1  teaspoon salt |
| | ¼  teaspoon pepper |
| | ¼  teaspoon sage or oregano |

Put all the meat into a big pot of cold water; if you have some bones with shreds of meat clinging to them, put in bones and all. Bring to a simmer, skimming off any froth or scum rising to the surface during the early minutes of cooking. Simmer until the meat is very tender, and falls from any bones included. Add water sparingly. When done, strain the pot liquid, returning 1½ pints (6 cups) to the pot. Bring to a boil while separating meat from bones and chopping up any big pieces of cooked meat; your biggest pieces of meat should be no larger than a man's thumb. Return the meat to the pot and add corn meal or hominy grits a tablespoon at a time, stirring as you do so. Add the seasonings. Cook until the mixture becomes very thick. Serve as a hot pudding with a gravy or sauce, or let cool, slice, and sauté the slices lightly.

Serves 6 to 8.


## SAUERBRATEN

Like oysters, Sauerbraten is an acquired taste. It is also the perfect method of preparing such unruly cuts of meat as the brisket from an old elk or superannuated mule deer, or a bear. This is also the perfect dish to serve guests who say they don't care for wild game; you can tell them the meat is beef or lamb and they'll have to believe you. You can also make Sauerbraten from beef brisket and tell your guests they're eating venison or bear or bull moose, and they can't prove otherwise.

**Pots and Pans on a Bed of Coals**

| | |
|---|---|
| 4- to 5-pound chunk of boneless brisket, flank or chuck | 12 peppercorns |
| salt | 1 onion |
| 1 pint vinegar | ½ cup raisins |
| 1 pint water | ¼ teaspoon powdered ginger or 8 crushed gingersnaps |
| ½ cup sugar | 1 cup sour cream or 1½ cups buttermilk |
| 2 or 3 bay leaves | |

Rub meat with salt, let stand 15 minutes. Heat 1 pint water to boiling, remove from heat, pour in 1 pint vinegar. Dissolve ¼ cup sugar in this mixture, add the bay leaves, and crack the peppercorns and add them. Put the meat in a crock or deep enameled pot, and pour the liquid over it. Quarter the onion and add it. The meat should be completely covered; if the specified liquid is not enough, mix additional vinegar and water and add to the vessel. Cover the container with a cloth and set in a cool place for 4 days. Do not refrigerate.

At the end of 4 days remove the meat from the marinade and wipe dry; reserve the marinade. Heat a lightly greased pan and sear the meat until it is browned on all sides. Strain the marinade and pour 1 cup over the meat; reserve the remaining liquid. Cover the pan tightly and cook over medium-low heat 3 to 4 hours, until the meat is tender to a fork or knife blade. Check the pot as the meat cooks and add extra liquid if needed. When the meat is cooked, remove to warm platter and slice.

Dissolve the remaining ¼ cup sugar in 1¼ cups of the reserved strained marinade and add to any liquid remaining in the pot. Add the raisins and ginger or gingersnaps. Bring the pot liquid to the boiling point, but do not boil. Remove from heat, stir in the sour cream or buttermilk, pour over meat, and serve.

Serves 10 to 12.


## SPAGHETTI WITH GAME

Few dishes are better suited to being cooked and served outdoors than a hearty *pasta asciutta* with a sauce rich in the flavor of wild game. This is also a method of extending a limited supply of venison or other game meat to serve a large group. And it is a cook's delight on cookout or in camp, for the sauce can simmer indefinitely and the pasta can be cooked in 10 minutes or so when everyone's ready to sit down and eat.

| | |
|---|---|
| 2 to 2½ pounds any game meat, or beef | 2 bay leaves |
| ¼ cup fine olive oil or peanut oil | ¼ teaspoon crushed dry basil or several sprigs fresh basil |
| 2 cloves garlic | salt |
| 3 large sweet green (Bell) peppers | 1 cup chopped fresh mushrooms or drained canned mushrooms |
| 1 can tomato paste diluted with 1 can water | 2 pounds spaghetti, macaroni, or other pasta of your choice |
| 6 large ripe tomatoes or 1 #2½ can tomatoes | |

Chop the meat into a fine mince and brown in the oil over brisk heat in a deep heavy skillet. Peel and mince the garlic and add to the meat when browned. Peel and seed the peppers, remove pith, chop coarsely, add to the meat. Combine the tomato paste with an equal quantity of water and add, then chop the ripe tomatoes over the pot to preserve their juice and add (or add the canned tomatoes, cutting the solid portions coarsely). Tie the bay leaves together with a long thread, so they can later be located and removed. Add them and the basil; if fresh basil is used, mince it very fine. Simmer for a minimum of 30 to 45 minutes—the sauce can simmer as long as suits your own convenience if you will just add a bit of liquid when it begins to cook dry. Taste and add salt as necessary.

Ten minutes before dishing-up time, add the mushrooms to the sauce. In a deep pot bring 3 to 4 quarts of water to a brisk, rolling boil. Add 1 teaspoon of salt per quart. Put the spaghetti into the boiling water a little bit at a time, stirring frequently to keep it from sticking. After it cooks 5 minutes, test for doneness by fishing out a single strand and cutting off an inch from one end; the pasta is done when no white line of uncooked starch is visible in its center. Do not cook it beyond that moment, but quickly pour a quart or two of cold water into the pot to stop the cooking. Then drain off the water, put the spaghetti into the pot with the simmering sauce, stir a few seconds, and serve.

Pass grated Parmesan or Romano cheese and let each individual sprinkle his own serving. And forget the legend that Italians don't drink wine when eating pasta—it's nothing but a legend. A good Chianti or Barolo adds zest to your pasta.

Serves 10 to 12.


## Variety Meats

This is the polite name given to edible animal innards, or lights, such succulent morsels as kidneys and sweetbreads. The heart, liver, tongue, and brains also fall into the "variety" category, but I have dealt with these in Chapter I. Consult the index. What I have not covered in any detail are three variety meats, two polite, and a third that is largely ignored, the "fries," or testicles.

It's best to revert to the spit or kabob skewer when cooking kidneys or sweetbreads outdoors. They need no elaborate treatment or saucing, just frequent basting with butter or bacon drippings and a dusting of salt and pepper after they come off the coals.

Kidneys should be cleaned well and all membranes removed, then split almost through and threaded on the spit or clamped into a basket grill in the form of a butterfly. Sweetbreads must be washed in cold water, tubes and membranes removed, then plunged for about 1 minute into boiling water to firm them up so they will stay on the spit or skewer. Sweetbreads are usually cooked whole. Neither kidneys nor sweetbreads should be overcooked—8 to 10 minutes over bright coals with frequent basting will do the trick when spit-cooked, 3 to 4 minutes per side on the grill.

"Fries," or testicles, are often called mountain oysters or prairie oysters. Except for those from three small animals, the beaver, muskrat, and opossum, fries from all animals are very delicately flavored. That they contribute to the virility of the consumer is, sadly, only a legend.

Fries from small animals should be skinned of their membranous covering, rolled in flour, dipped in beaten egg, rolled in bread crumbs, then sautéed gently in butter until brown.

Fries from larger animals should be skinned, split in half lengthwise, and soaked in Marinade #1, page 30 for an hour or so. The big fries are best when rolled in a mixture of flour and corn meal and cooked in deep fat until the coating is a dark brown. Or they can be dredged in flour with a bit of salt and pepper mixed into it, placed in a well greased Dutch oven or double skillet, and buried in coals for 45 minutes to 1 hour. Lemon wedges are usually passed with a platter of fries, but the Green Sauce on page 32 is more exciting.

## Stretching and Salvaging

At one time or another, almost every camp cook faces one of three problems—and sometimes he faces all three. The first problem is to stretch scanty rations to serve a greater number than expected; the second is to utilize leftovers in an appetizing fashion; the third is to correct a bad guess made when a tough piece of meat stays tough even after being cooked. The dishes that follow will help the harried chef to cook his way out of any corner.

### CASSOULET OF GAME

In modern usage a cassoulet is thought of as a single specific dish, such as preserved goose cooked with white beans and sausage. Originally, this name was given any casserole-type dish of meat and beans. Dutch ovens cook wonderful cassoulets.

| | |
|---|---|
| 1½ to 2 pounds of precooked meat of any kind | 2 onions, peeled and quartered |
| 2 cups white beans | 4 medium tomatoes, quartered |
| 4 thick slices bacon | 1 tablespoon salt |
| 6 small link sausages, cut in two | large dash pepper |

Slice the meat very, very thin; if not paper thin, at least no thicker than cardboard. Soak the beans 1 to 2 hours in warm water; drain, cover with fresh cold water, add salt, and simmer over gentle heat for 30 to 40 minutes. Add liquid as needed to keep the beans covered.

When the beans have cooked the indicated time, sauté the bacon until it begins to brown. Remove, and sauté the sliced meat very lightly. Spoon a 1- to 1½-inch layer of beans into the Dutch oven. Add several slices of meat, a slice of bacon, a pair of sausages. Build up the pot with alternate layers of beans and sausages, topping with a layer of beans. Stud the layers with chunks of onion and tomato.

Pour all the fat from the skillet and all the liquid left in the bean pot over the layers of beans and meat. Cover the Dutch oven and cook on top of the coals for 30 minutes, or until the skins of the beans in the top layer begin to curl. A cassoulet can, of course, be cooked in a sheepherder stove (20–30 minutes) or kitchen oven (30 minutes at 350 degrees), using a covered casserole dish. Since the saltiness used in this dish determines its final flavor, taste and adjust seasoning just before serving.

Serves 10 to 12.

### BASQUE SHEPHERD'S PIE

Conventionally, a shepherd's pie is sliced cooked mutton in gravy, topped with a covering of mashed potatoes, and warmed in the oven. In the American West, Basque sheepherders flout convention with a vastly improved version.

1 to 1½ pounds cooked roast meat; lamb or mutton is traditional, but any meat can be used
thin slices of bacon or salt pork
3 thin slices lemon
2 small sweet onions
4 ripe tomatoes

1 cup fine bread crumbs (sourdough or sour French bread is best)
flour
large pinch paprika or cayenne
salt
flour
2 cups light milk or meat stock

Slice the meat very thin. Blanch the bacon or salt pork (trim rind off salt pork first) by putting into boiling water for 2 or 3 minutes. Cover the bottom of a Dutch oven or deep pan with a tight-fitting lid with slices of bacon or salt pork. Put the lemon slices on the bacon, then a layer of thin onion slices, then a layer of thin tomato slices, then a layer of bread crumbs. Sprinkle with flour, cayenne or paprika, and salt, then put on a layer of meat slices. Build the pot with alternate layers of onion and tomato covered with bread crumbs dusted with flour and seasonings, and slices of meat. Top off with a layer of bacon slices dusted with bread crumbs. Pour in the stock or milk. Cover the Dutch oven and bury it in coals to cook for 1 to 1½ hours.

Sheepherders, cooking in smaller quantities than given in the above recipe, usually put their pies in the sheepherder oven after breakfast, when the coals are dying. Then, when they return to their wagons at noon, their lunch is waiting. If speed is your need, though, the pie can be cooked in 40 minutes in the sheepherder oven over bright coals, in an open pan; in the kitchen oven, 35 to 40 minutes at 375 degrees.

Serves 6 to 8 generously.

## HASH PATTIES

Cynics will call this a retread of a retread, but it's really a pretty fair way to get rid of last night's hash at breakfast. We'll assume the hash you want to use up was made the time-honored way, with cubes of meat, potato, and onion.

| | |
|---|---|
| 2 to 3 cups cold hash | fine bread crumbs or unsalted |
| ½ cup milk | cracker crumbs |
| 1 egg | bacon drippings |

Chop the hash very fine indeed. Beat milk and egg together and blend with the chopped hash. Form into thin patties, roll in bread crumbs, and sauté in bacon drippings until golden brown on both sides.

Serves 4 to 6.

## HOT POT or HOTCHPOTCH

This is really nothing but hash under an assumed name, wearing a false beard to disguise it further. It can be made from any leftover meat you're trying to get rid of.

| | | | |
|---|---|---|---|
| 12 | thin slices precooked meat | ¼ | teaspoon cayenne or ⅛ |
| 2 | large sweet onions | | teaspoon Nepal pepper |
| 2 | large potatoes | 6 | drops Tabasco Sauce |
| 1½ | cups milk | 1 | tablespoon butter |
| 1 | teaspoon salt | | |

Peel the onions and potatoes and slice as thinly as the meat. Butter a deep skillet, begin with a layer of potatoes on the bottom, then a layer of onion, then meat, and build up the pot in alternate layers until all ingredients are used up. Mix milk and seasonings and pour over the layered pot. Dot the top with dabs of butter. Close the skillet and cook over low coals 20 to 30 minutes. No liquid should be added, but additional dots of butter should be placed on top and the dish dusted with a scanty sprinkling of pepper just before serving.

Serves 6 to 8.

# IV

---

# Small Game—
# An Infinite Variety

URBAN AND SUBURBAN RESIDENTS can no longer take a few steps
away from their doors and pot a rabbit or squirrel for the pot; but as
rabbit and squirrel retreat from civilization, other small animals
adapt to it. Raccoons and opossums especially thrive close to home-
lined suburban streets, and though few think of the coon in terms
of dinner, our ancestors ate him, as well as muskrats, porcupines,
woodchucks, and other small animals which we ignore today. Almost
all marshy, wet areas, and the banks of creeks and streams, harbor
muskrats. Woodchucks can be found within a drive of an hour or two
of even the most populous centers. And there is always the butcher
shop, where rabbits are sold by the pound. Chickens, Rock Cornish
game hens, and turkeys are also sold in butcher shops, and these
birds make suitable substitutes for small game in most recipes.

The pattern of this chapter is similar to that of Chapter III;
that is, recipes traditionally associated with a certain species of small
game will call for that species as first choice, but will indicate suitable substitutes. And small game species can in almost all cases be
substituted for each other.

### Small Game—An Infinite Variety

Most small game is even leaner of flesh than the larger wild animals; the small creatures are usually busier and more active. Even on rabbits raised by commercial breeders fat is noticeably lacking. This makes preparation for the pot as important with small wild animals as with the bigger ones. If brought down in the field, they should be bled and drawn at once, and cooled quickly, not stuffed into an airless game bag or the rubber-lined pocket of a hunting coat where they will stay hot and their flesh will soon sour.

Hanging is an important step in the preparation that should not be ignored; small game animals should be hung unskinned in a cool place for two or three days. Marinating is essential when the animal is to be grilled or spit-roasted; basting is also essential when these cooking processes are used. In cooking whole carcasses, a moist stuffing improves flavor and helps moisturize the flesh. Small game animals should be seared quickly over bright coals, then the cooking completed either over medium coals or further from the coals than the carcass was placed for searing. Braising or stewing is suggested for older and larger animals.

When any small game species requires special steps in its cleaning, these are given in association with the recipes.

### Beaver

Weight is your best indication of a beaver's age; young animals weigh fifteen pounds or less, older beaver up to about twenty. The tail should be removed during the skinning and cleaning, and cooked separately from the carcass. The method used in cooking bear paws, page 38, is very satisfactory for beaver tail. In cleaning beaver, be sure to remove the musk kernels under the animal's forelegs where they join the body, and to cut away the flesh for two or three inches around its genitals.

## BRAISED BEAVER

14- to 16-pound beaver (also
   suitable for raccoon, large
   muskrat, old and outsized
   rabbits)
Marinade #1
cooking oil

salt, pepper
large pinch of basil or thyme
3 or 4 carrots
cornstarch or flour and butter
   for thickening (optional)

Cut the animal into serving-sized pieces and marinate 2 to 3 hours. If handling an animal over 14 to 16 pounds in weight, parboiling for 15 or 20 minutes before marinating is advisable. After marinating, drain the pieces well and wipe dry. Reserve the marinade.

Rub each piece generously with cooking oil and brown lightly in a lightly greased skillet. Sprinkle with salt, pepper, and the crushed basil or thyme. Mix ½ cup of the marinade with ¼ cup warm water and pour into the skillet; close skillet and cook over low heat 30 minutes. Peel and slice the carrots into long strips, then add them to the pan and cook another 20 to 30 minutes, until both carrots and meat are tender. Turn the pieces occasionally to brown evenly. The pot juices may be used as a sauce or gravy; thicken them, if desired, with a scanty sprinkle of cornstarch, or with a roux made by blending 1 teaspoon flour with 1 teaspoon butter and flaking this into the simmering juices.

A small beaver can be cooked whole in a Dutch oven, using the method of handling and seasoning given above; after adding the carrots, bury the oven in coals for 1 hour. In a sheepherder stove or kitchen range, use a closed roasting pan; cook about 40 minutes in the sheepherder oven, 45 to 50 minutes at 375 degrees in the kitchen oven.

Serves 10 to 12.

## Muskrat

Our pioneer forefathers called the muskrat "mushsquash" or "mooshrat," and because the animal was plentiful and easily trapped, muskrats were a staple of the diet of settlers taking up land in marshy areas and along streams.

Most muskrats weigh six to eight pounds; big ones run up to twelve pounds. Since the animal's musk glands are in its abdomen, their flesh does not absorb the musky order associated with their burrows if the cavity is washed with salt water and wiped well at once after cleaning. Flesh bordering the genital area should also be cut away. The tail and first joints of the legs are removed before cooking.

When a muskrat colony took up residence in a dike protecting some tideland property we owned in California's Sacramento-San Joaquin Delta, old-time residents advised, "Get Old Pete to bring his traps and clean 'em out before they ruin the dike." Old Pete, we found, was a tideland squatter living in a cabin on stilts on one of the bay's marshy islands. When we found him, the cabin was draped with drying muskrat skins. Pete's income came from the sale of these skins; his diet, apparently, was largely the animals he trapped.

Pete was surprised to learn that none of us in the group visiting him had ever tasted muskrat, and promised each of us a pair from his next trapping. "The little ones are good fried like chicken," he said, "but the old ones are better cooked with paprika." True to his promise, Pete delivered muskrats and recipe, the directions written in a flowing Spencerian copperplate.

"Cut two muskrats into quarters and dip the pieces in milk. Mix two tablespoonsful of paprika with a little fine minced fresh parsley and about a spoonful of flour, a little pinch of salt and pepper. Roll the pieces in this and brown over a hot fire in a pan with a little grease.

**88**

Grate most of an onion into the pan and pour a cup or so of hot water over the meat, then put on the lid and cook until the meat is done."

The cooking time, we found, was about 30 to 35 minutes, and the meat should be turned occasionally.

Two 6-pound muskrats serve 8.


## Opossum

Zoologists tell us that the possum is an almost unchanged survivor from prehistoric times, with amazing adaptability and the ability to multiply under the most adverse conditions. Today's possum is proof enough. Until the early 1900s the opossum was found only in the southeastern U.S., but when the country took to wheels after World War I, migrants from that area took along a pair or two when they moved, to have something to remind them of home in new surroundings. Now, the possum is found in almost every state.

Though formidably armed with claws and very efficient teeth, the possum prefers to play dead when hard-pressed or when it encounters man. It can easily be taken alive, maintaining its feigned swoon even when picked up and handled. Since the possum's eating habits are unpredictable and frequently disreputable, the best possum to eat is one that has been taken alive. Penned closely and fed for a week or two on vegetables, bread and table scraps, the animal's flesh is purged of foreign flavors. If you must eat a possum whose diet you have not supervised, its carcass should be soaked 8 to 12 hours in lightly salted water; this is almost as effective as controlled feeding.

A possum is not skinned, but is gutted, dipped in boiling water, and scraped clean like a pig. Before dipping, though, remove the small red glands under each foreleg and at the end of the rib cage along the backbone. Head, feet and tail are removed before cooking. The time-honored way of a cook in possum country is to bake the animal with persimmons that are just on the green side, but sweet potatoes or a mixture of persimmons and sweet potatoes are almost as frequently used.

### POSSUM AND SWEET POTATOES

| | |
|---|---|
| whole possum, about 15 pounds; substitute suckling pig | ¼ teaspoon garlic powder |
| | ¼ teaspoon cayenne |
| | 1 cup flour |
| 8 or 10 sweet potatoes | ½ teaspoon salt |
| 1 tablespoon sage, or 1 tablespoon prepared dressing spices | 1 egg |
| | ½ cup brown sugar or 1 cup molasses |

Before cooking, wash the possum inside and out with a rag dipped in warm salted water; about 1 teaspoon salt to 1 cup water.

Powder the sage or dressing spices, mix them and the other seasonings (except the brown sugar) with the flour; beat the egg lightly and mix the spiced flour with it to form a thin paste. Brush the possum's body with this paste. Dust the sweet potatoes with brown sugar, or dip them in molasses, after they are peeled. Put two or three of the potatoes into the animal's cavity, the rest around the possum, in the Dutch oven. Close the oven and bury it in coals 3 to 3½ hours. Remove the oven, drain off the fat that has cooked out of the possum, then place the oven on low coals 10 to 15 minutes and drain off the fat a second time.

If cooked in the sheepherder stove, use a pan with a tight-fitting lid, and cook 1¾ to 2 hours; midway during the cooking, drain off the accumulated fat in the pan. Timing for the kitchen oven is 2 hours at 400 degrees.

Should you want to try the persimmon stuffing often used, mash firm persimmons with parboiled sweet potatoes, season with ginger, and brown sugar or molasses, and beat an egg into the mixture. Stuff the animal with part of the mixture, use the rest to place around it in the cooking pan.

A 15-pound possum will serve 10 to 12.

## Porcupine

Porcupines are highly edible, with a soft flesh that is much like that of the grey squirrel in flavor. Skinning a porky is no real problem—chiefly it's a matter of wearing heavy gloves to avoid his barbed quills. Since his diet is largely resinous, the porcupine should be marinated before being cooked.

Our good neighbors in Arcata, California, for many years were Del and Yvonne Harrit; with them we shared abalone, mussels, salmon, steelhead, elk, venison, and other goodies. The porcupine recipe that follows was adapted by Yvonne from one she created for squirrel.

| | |
|---|---|
| 8- to 10-pound porcupine; substitute squirrel or rabbit | 1 teaspoon garlic salt |
| ½ cup garlic-flavored red wine vinegar | cooking fat: 1 tablespoon bacon drippings and 3 tablespoons solid vegetable shortening |
| ½ cup salt | |
| 1 gallon cool water | 1 bay leaf |
| 1 cup pancake flour mix | |

Add the wine vinegar and salt to 1 gallon cool water and marinate the porcupine meat, cut into serving pieces, for 2 hours. Drain and blot dry.

Mix pancake flour and garlic salt and dredge the meat thoroughly. Bring the cooking fat to high heat and brown each piece of meat on all sides; there should be about ½ inch of fat in the skillet to brown properly. With the skillet on low heat, add 1 cup water, cover, and cook 35 to 40 minutes, or until the meat is tender. Put the bay leaf in during the last 15 minutes of cooking.

Serves 6 to 8.

## Rabbit

Except for a bit more firmness in the flesh and a heightened flavor, there is no difference between wild and tame rabbit. All rabbits can be grilled, spit-roasted, pan-fried, stewed, or cooked by any other method you choose, if properly prepared by marinating. Wild or tame, rabbits are very lean and well-muscled, and the marinating process should not be omitted unless the animal is to be stewed or prepared as Hassenpfeffer.

Very young rabbits have claws that can be bent easily between your fingers; older animals will have worn-down, horny, split claws and their pads will be much tougher. Young rabbits have a very narrow split in their upper lip; the split widens as the animal ages. The ears of young rabbits are very soft and flexible; with aging the ears grow stiff and thicken.

A rabbit is dressed by circling the skin just in front of the hips and peeling it off toward the head, in one piece. The head and fore-paws are then cut off, the hindquarters skinned in similar fashion and the hind paws cut off. When skinned, the intestines are easily removed; usually the liver and heart are saved. If the animal was brought down with a shotgun, pellets should be dug out with the tip of a thin-bladed knife. Then the carcass is washed inside and out with a rag dipped in salted water, 1 teaspoon of salt to a quart of water, and wiped dry.

Recipes given for rabbit are also suitable for squirrel and most other small game, as well as for most fowl, including chickens.

### BROILED RABBIT

|  |  |
|---|---|
| 2 whole rabbits, cleaned; substitute squirrel, fowl | strips of pork fat, salt pork, or fat bacon |
| Marinade #2 | salt, pepper |

Marinate rabbits 1½ to 2 hours, turning occasionally. Drain and blot dry, reserve marinade. Using the larding needle, string strips of fat into the hind legs, along each side of the backbone, and on the breast. Trim off any protruding bits of fat. Split the breastbone and flatten the carcass, or after splitting the breastbone, split the backbone lengthwise with a cleaver or fine saw.

Sear the carcass bone side down for 1 to 2 minutes, turn and sear the skin side 1 to 2 minutes. Cook skin side down, brushing with marinade liquid, for 10 minutes. Turn and cook 10 minutes bone side down, basting frequently. Do not season until cooking is completed.

Serves 4.

### GERMAN-STYLE RABBIT

2 small rabbits; substitute squirrel, any small game, fowl
¼ cup flour
1 teaspoon salt
large dash black pepper
cooking oil or fat (lard is traditional)
4 cups pitted prunes, soaked 15 minutes in warm water

1 cup tiny pearl onions
1 bottle (11 ounces) beer or ale
bay leaf
1 teaspoon cornstarch or 1 teaspoon flour and 1 teaspoon butter

Cut rabbits into serving pieces. Mix flour, salt, and pepper by shaking in a paper bag; put a few pieces of rabbit at a time into the bag and shake briskly to coat with the seasoned flour. Use enough cooking fat to cover the skillet's bottom ¼ inch. Bring to high heat and brown the pieces of rabbit quickly but thoroughly. Pour off any oil left in skillet. Put the prunes and onions in the skillet, pour in the beer, add the bay leaf. Additional beer or ale may be needed to cover the pieces of rabbit.

Cover the skillet tightly and cook 1 to 1½ hours over very low coals. Remove rabbit pieces, prunes, onions; discard bay leaf. Let the pan juices simmer gently while you stir in 1 teaspoon cornstarch to thicken them, or blend 1 teaspoon flour and 1 teaspoon butter into a smooth paste and flake it in small bits into the simmering juices. Stir well, and cook until all flour is blended into juices. Serve on individual warmed plates or in a bowl with the sauce poured over the rabbit, prunes, and onions.

Serves 4 to 6.

### RABBIT IN RED WINE

| | |
|---|---|
| 2 small rabbits; substitute squirrel, any small game, fowl | 2 cups dry red wine |
| | 1 cup cool water |
| | 2 cups sliced or coarsely |
| ¼ pound butter | chopped mushrooms, fresh or |
| 3 tablespoons flour | canned |
| ½ teaspoon salt | |
| ⅛ teaspoon Nepal pepper or ¼ teaspoon cayenne | |

Cut the rabbits into serving pieces. Knead together half the butter, flour, and seasonings and rub each piece of rabbit well with this mixture. Bring the remaining mixture to high heat in a skillet and brown the pieces of rabbit to a light tan. Mix the wine and water, pour into the pan, add the mushrooms. If canned mushrooms are used, substitute the liquid from them for an equal quantity of the water.

Cover skillet and cook over low coals 1 hour, or until rabbit is tender. In a Dutch oven, bury in coals 1½ hours; in a sheepherder stove, cook in a tightly closed pan 45 minutes to 1 hour; in the kitchen oven, 50 to 55 minutes at 375 degrees.

Serves 6.

### HASSENPFEFFER

For a very senior rabbit, toughened by age and life's vicissitudes, this method of preparation is perhaps the wisest choice. Though

**94**

traditionally associated with rabbit and hares, Hassenpfeffer will also render edible other small game animals in the grandfather age group.

| | |
|---|---|
| 2 rabbits, cut in serving-sized pieces | 2 cups cider vinegar |
| 2 medium-sized onions | 2 cups hot water |
| 4 or 5 whole cloves | 1 teaspoon salt |
| 5 or 6 cracked peppercorns | ¾ cup sour cream or 1 cup buttermilk |
| 3 bay leaves | |

Peel the onions and cut into thick slices. Spread onion slices, cloves, peppercorns, and bay leaves on the bottom of a small crock or enameled pan. Mix the vinegar with hot—not boiling—water, and dissolve the salt in it. Place the pieces of rabbit on top of the onion and spices and pour the vinegar mixture into the container. If it does not cover the meat completely, mix additional vinegar and water and add to the container. Cover the top of the container with a piece of cloth and place in a cool spot and let it stand 3 days. Once a day, shift the meat around so each piece will be penetrated by the marinade.

When cooking time arrives, lift out the pieces of meat, letting the marinade drain back into the container. Wipe the meat dry, then brown each piece on all sides in a lightly greased skillet. Strain the marinade, add 1½ cups to the pan, and let simmer over low coals until the rabbit is very tender, 35 to 40 minutes. Remove the meat from the pan to a warm platter. Stir the sour cream or buttermilk into the simmering marinade, scraping the bottom of the pan as you stir. When the sauce is smooth, pour over the meat.

Serves 6.

### CAMP-STYLE RABBIT STEW

Even in a stew, very old rabbits should be marinated before going to the pot. Use Marinade #2, page 30, for tough old animals. Young rabbits will not need this treatment, but should be soaked 30 minutes in lightly salted water before cooking.

| | |
|---|---|
| 2 rabbits cut in serving-sized pieces; substitute other small game animals or fowl | 1 teaspoon salt |
| | dash pepper |
| | 3 potatoes |
| 2 tablespoons butter or bacon drippings | 4 carrots |
| | 2 onions |
| *bouquet garni* in cloth bag: bay leaf, celery tops, thyme, parsley, 2 whole cloves | 8 to 10 cold biscuits |
| | bacon drippings |

Brown the pieces of rabbit quickly but thoroughly in hot fat in the stewpot. Add cold water to cover the meat completely, and put in the *bouquet garni,* salt, and pepper. Simmer over low coals until the meat begins to get tender, then peel the vegetables, cut in chunks, and add them to the pot. Cook 20 to 30 minutes; the carrots will be the last to reach tenderness, and can be your guide as to when the stew is done. Add only enough extra water to keep all ingredients covered. Fish out the pieces of meat when all ingredients are cooked, and slip out the bones; cut large pieces of meat into two or three bite-sized chunks, and return meat to pot. At this time, also take out the *bouquet garni* and discard it.

Split the biscuits and brown them in very hot bacon drippings. Arrange the biscuits on warmed serving plates or in shallow bowls, and ladle the stew over them.

Serves 8 to 10.

### STIFADO: GREEK RABBIT STEW

There is a legend that this rabbit stew saved a Greek village from being ravaged by bandits. In the first house the brigands entered to loot, the housewife was cooking *Stifado;* the bandit chief, inhaling the stewpot's aromas, offered to leave the town unmolested if he was given the stewpot and its contents.

1 or 2 rabbits; substitute other small game animals, fowl, or lamb

2 to 3 tablespoons cooking oil; olive oil is traditional

tiny onions equal in weight to the meat used

½ cup red wine or ¼ cup wine vinegar mixed with ¼ cup water

1 can tomato paste

3 cloves garlic

1 tablespoon pickling spices; the mixture should include allspice, pieces of cinnamon bark, mustard and dill seed, bay leaf, a chili pod, cloves, cardamom, and caraway seeds

Heat oil very hot and sear the pieces of rabbit lightly. Put the onions in and stir until they are gently browned. Add cold water to cover the meat and onions and let come to a simmer over low heat. When the liquid begins to bubble gently, add tomato paste, wine, garlic, and the spices. Cook very, very slowly for 1½ to 2 hours. If the liquid needs replenishing, add more wine or vinegar mixed in equal parts with water. Stir occasionally.

Two rabbits serve 6 to 8.

## Raccoon

Known as the midnight raider, especially in camps, the raccoon is one wild animal that thrives close to civilization. His numbers are actually increasing. Although omnivorous, raccoons are very sensitive eaters. Long before it was officially announced that the cyclamates used as artificial sweetners are hazardous to health, raccoons knew this; pet coons that had acquired a taste for bottled pop habitually refused soft drinks in which cyclamates were used.

Our ancestors ate coons regularly, whether from choice or from necessity history does not say, but today there is a certain prejudice against the raccoon as food. Certainly nothing in a raccoon's eating habits would taint his flesh; he insists on fresh food and does not eat offal. (His habit of washing his food, incidentally, has no bearing on the cleanliness of his ways, but is necessary because raccoons have no saliva glands and wash their food to moisten it.)

Large raccoons can be exceedingly tough; any over fifteen pounds are best left alone. The smaller ones are tasty when roasted, if marinated before cooking and cooked slowly with moist heat.

## ROAST RACCOON

| | |
|---|---|
| whole raccoon, 15 pounds or under; substitute any small game animal | 2 or 3 carrots |
| | 2 bay leaves |
| | 1 pod mild chili pepper |
| Marinade #3 | salt |
| 1 large onion | cooking oil |
| 3 or 4 whole cloves | |

Marinate the animal 4 to 6 hours, drain, and blot dry inside and out. Reserve the marinade liquid. Put the coon in a large pot and cover with cold water to which has been added ½ cup per quart of the strained marinade. Stick the cloves in the onion, quarter the carrots, add them and the bay leaves, chili pod, and salt to the pot. Cover and simmer slowly for 1½ to 2 hours. Remove the raccoon, drain, blot dry.

Brush the animal inside and out with cooking oil. Put in a Dutch oven and bury in coals 1 hour, or cook in a closed pan in a sheepherder oven for 45 minutes; in the kitchen oven for 1 hour at 300 degrees. Potatoes or sweet potatoes, carrots or turnips, onions, or other root vegetables are often added to the roasting pan during the final cooking.

A 15-pound raccoon will serve 10 to 12.

## Rattlesnake

Nothing is repulsive about rattlesnakes as food except the mental block resulting from the thought of dining on man's ancient enemy, the snake. My own squeamishness was overcome as a matter of professional necessity, when as a cub reporter I was assigned to eat and describe the grilled rattlesnake served by a museum as a publicity stunt. This was a good many years ago, before canned rattlesnake occupied a niche in the exotic-foods sections of grocery stores and before the proliferation of rattlesnake hunts in the South and Southwest, where the meat of the captured reptiles is served as an aftermath of the hunts.

The rattlesnake is a very clean creature. He does his own hunting, kills his own game, and eats it while fresh. His venom is confined to a pair of sacs in his jaws, and these are cut off and discarded with the head when the animal is cleaned. The flesh is rather like a fatty, coarse-textured crabmeat. If you choose to serve rattlesnake from the can rather than killing your own, the meat should be lightly grilled before serving.

| | |
|---|---|
| rattlesnake, cut in 2-inch sections | salt, pepper |
| butter | toast rounds or crackers |

Grill over medium coals, brushing with butter, turning often so the meat will cook evenly. Cook 10 to 15 minutes, depending on size. Canned rattlesnake that has been boned can be tossed in a hot skillet with butter. Serve with salt and pepper and toast rounds or crackers.

## Squirrel

In most states squirrel is restricted from being sold, even by commercial breeders who operate game farms. This is a far remove from the day when bounties were paid hunters for killing squirrels —in 1749, the colony of Pennsylvania paid out 8,000 pounds sterling in bounties at the rate of threepence per squirrel tail. (To save you the trouble of figuring it out, the bounty represents more than 600,000 squirrels killed in that colony in a year.)

If you want to enjoy the nut-sweet flavor of the bushytails, you must go to the woods on crisp autumn days and bag your own, or you must have a hunting friend who will share his bag with you. If you have neither hunting skill nor friends, rabbit or chicken can be substituted in squirrel recipes.

Young or old, squirrel requires marinating, for the tiny muscles of this busy animal's legs and back are almost like wires. To tell the age of a squirrel, look at its teeth and claws; the younger the animal, the sharper both will be. Another sign will appear after the animal has been skinned. Squirrels are fierce fighters, and the marks of battle can be seen as lines on the inner surfaces of their pelts. To be safe, treat all squirrels as though they were middle-aged.

To skin, circle the carcass above the hips and peel skin off like a glove, cut off the head and paws; then peel skin off hindquarters, cutting off brush and paws. There are small glands, like hard kernels, under each foreleg and along the backbone above each hip; these must be removed. So must shot pellets, if the animal had been taken with a shotgun.

### SQUIRREL POT PIE

This is not a pie with a pastry crust, but a pastry topping can be substituted for the one given. You will then cook the pie in the oven, rather than in a Dutch oven, spider, or skillet.

3 squirrels; substitute rabbit, other small game, fowl
Marinade #2
2 slices bacon or salt pork, about ½ inch thick
2 tablespoons flour
1 teaspoon salt
½ teaspoon freshly ground black pepper
1 onion
1 teaspoon cornstarch or 1 teaspoon flour and 1 teaspoon butter
6 to 8 biscuits, or 1½ cups coarse dry bread crumbs

Cut the squirrels into serving-sized pieces and marinate 1 to 1½ hours. Drain and blot dry.

Chop the bacon or salt pork coarsely and sauté it in a skillet until it begins to brown. Mix the flour, salt, and pepper and dredge the

**100**

meat pieces, coating each piece thoroughly. Brown in the skillet with the bacon. Pour hot water over the meat, covering it completely, cover and simmer over slow heat for 45 minutes, or until the pieces of meat are tender. Remove the meat pieces to a hot platter, draining the pan juices back into the skillet.

Bring the liquid to a rolling boil. Chop the onion fine or grate it, and add to the pan liquids. Cook 5 minutes, until the onion is tender. Test and adjust seasoning. Sprinkle cornstarch into the liquid, or blend flour and butter into a smooth paste and flake into the pan, stirring to a smooth gravy. Return the pieces of meat to the pan a few minutes. Remove from heat, split the biscuits, and top the dish with them, or sprinkle a thick coating of coarse dry bread crumbs over the top.

Serves 4 to 6.

### SQUIRREL SOUP

When the squirrels have been smarter than the hunters, this soup is a good way to extend their flavor so that more can enjoy it.

| | |
|---|---|
| 2 squirrels; substitute rabbit, other small game, fowl | ¾ cup rice |
| | ½ teaspoon salt |
| 3 quarts cold water | ¼ teaspoon pepper |
| ¾ teaspoon salt | 2 or 3 hard-boiled eggs |
| 1 medium-sized sweet onion | flour |
| 2 stalks celery, including leaves | butter |
| 3 or 4 large sprigs parsley | |
| ⅛ teaspoon powdered thyme or 1 sprig fresh thyme | |

Cut the squirrels into serving-sized pieces or quarters, put into a deep pot with cold water and salt. Simmer over very gentle heat, skimming off any froth or scum that rises to the top. When no more rises, mince the onion, celery, parsley, and thyme and add them to the pot. Cook 1 to 1½ hours, or until the meat slips from the bones. Using a slotted spoon, take out meat pieces and remove bones, cut meat into small dice, and return to pot. Add rice, salt, and pepper. Shell eggs, separate yolks and whites, chop whites coarsely and add to pot. Mash the yolks with a quantity of flour equal to their bulk and a quantity of butter equal to their bulk. Stir this into the soup a little at a time. Test and adjust seasoning. If you feel called to extend the soup further, sweet corn and green peas may also be added.

Serves 6 to 8.

## Woodchuck

Here is another vegetarian animal that deserves a better fate than to be used merely as a target for long-range marksmen. Woodchucks, which sometimes reach a weight of five or six pounds, are lazier than most small game, their flesh softer and somewhat fatter. In cleaning a woodchuck for cooking, be sure to remove the sacs under each forearm and the four sacs spaced along its backbone.

### WOODCHUCK FRICASSEE

1 large or 2 small woodchucks; substitute squirrel, rabbit, other small game animal, or fowl
Marinade #1
4 tablespoons flour
½ teaspoon Nepal pepper or ¼ teaspoon cayenne

3 tablespoons bacon drippings
1 cup minced onion
1 cup boiling water
bay leaf, powdered
large pinch powdered sage
1 teaspoon salt

Cut the meat in serving-sized pieces, marinate 3 to 4 hours, drain and wipe dry. Mix flour and pepper and rub it well into the meat. Heat bacon drippings in a deep skillet and brown the meat. Add the minced onion and cook until it begins to brown. Pour boiling water into the pan, scrape the bottom and sides well, then add water to cover the meat. Sprinkle in the powdered bay leaf, sage, and salt. Cover pan and simmer 45 minutes to 1 hour over gentle heat, without adding further liquid unless the pan gets almost completely dry. When done, the liquid should be thick, like a cream sauce. Taste and adjust seasoning before serving.

One large chuck will serve 4; two small chucks, 6 or 8.

## Small Game Stews

Three great stews have been created in the American South, all originally based on small game. All of them have suffered from "innovations" and "creative improvements" dreamed up by those who can't bear to see any great dish served in its traditional form. The following recipes are all more than a hundred years old, and present the three stews in original form.

### BRUNSWICK STEW

A Brunswick Stew must contain either squirrel or rabbit and ham. It must also contain corn, lima beans, okra, rice, and tomatoes. The ham should be the hard-cured, well-smoked, long-aged country type, which in its uncooked state can be cut only with an axe or a saw. You can, of course, add other ingredients. Chicken is a frequent optional addition. So are green beans, peas and potatoes. But these are extras, and a true Brunswick Stew need only have in it the items listed in the first two sentences of this paragraph.

| | |
|---|---|
| 4 squirrels or 3 rabbits; a plump chicken or two is optional | 2 sprigs parsley |
| | 1 sprig fresh thyme |
| | 2 cups whole-kernel corn |
| 1½ pounds ham cut in ½-inch dice | 6 ripe tomatoes |
| | 2 cups okra sliced in ½-inch rounds |
| 1 gallon cold water | |
| 1½ tablespoons salt | 1½ cups lima beans |
| 1 teaspoon pepper | 2 cups rice |
| 1 bay leaf | 1 tablespoon butter (no substitutes) |
| 1 pod hot red pepper | |

Cut the animals into serving-sized pieces, put in a big pot with the diced ham, and add cold water, salt, and pepper. Bring to a slow simmer. Put the bay leaf, pepper pod, parsley, and thyme in a cloth bag and add to the pot. Let simmer until the meat begins to become tender. When the hind leg of a squirrel or rabbit can be pierced with a fork, it is time to add the remaining ingredients.

Fresh vegetables should be put in at intervals so that each will be done perfectly and none overcooked. Put the corn and lima beans in first—wait 5 minutes and add the rice—then wait another 5 minutes before putting in the okra and quartered tomatoes. Then, cook 10 to 15 minutes longer, remove the bag of herbs, and stir in the butter to smooth the juices and marry the flavors.

You can, of course, use canned or frozen vegetables, but the stew will be deficient in flavor. Since canned vegetables are pre-cooked, they can be added all at once. Frozen vegetables are all blanched, which is the equivalent of quick parboiling, so they can be added frozen and cooked until they are hot. When using either canned or frozen vegetables, add the rice first and let it cook 5 to 7 minutes before putting in the vegetables.

If possible, avoid adding water to this stew as it cooks. A proper Brunswick Stew should be almost thick enough to be eaten with a fork, while all ingredients except the tomatoes retain their shapes and identities.

Serves 12 to 16.


## KENTUCKY-STYLE BURGOO

The Burgoo, thought to have originated in the Caribbean, belongs now to Kentucky. Like the Derby with which it is associated, Burgoo has traditions. A Burgoo must contain three meats and eight vegetables, as given below in the ingredients list. You can call any stew made without these components a Burgoo, but then it's like a martini made without gin. It might taste good, but it's not the genuine article.

1 rabbit, two if very small, cut into small pieces
1 pound veal or baby beef cut in ½-inch cubes
1 pound "side pork" or salt pork cut in ½-inch cubes
½ cup bacon drippings
1 gallon cold water
2 bay leaves
6 whole cloves
1 hot red pepper pod
1 clove garlic
1½ cups fresh corn
1 cup fresh lima beans or dried limas soaked 1 hour
1 cup coarsely diced carrots
2 cups coarsely diced potatoes
2 cups coarsely diced onion
1 cup okra cut in ½-inch rounds
6 ripe tomatoes, quartered
1 cup green beans cut 1 inch long
2 tablespoons brown sugar or sorghum
1 tablespoon salt

Heat the bacon drippings in a big stewpot; brown all meats lightly in the hot fat. (If salt pork is used it should be trimmed and blanched by putting into boiling water for 2 or 3 minutes.) Pour in cold water and bring to a simmer over gentle heat. Put the bay leaves, cloves, pepper pod, and garlic in a cloth bag and add them to the pot. Cook until the meat begins to get tender, 45 minutes to 1 hour. Consult the recipe for Brunswick Stew, page 104, for the order in which the vegetables should be added and the intervals between addition of each, and for the method of using canned or frozen vegetables. When all vegetables are in the pot, remove the bag of herbs, stir in the brown sugar or sorghum and salt, and simmer 10 to 15 minutes before dishing up.

Serves 12 to 16.

## JAMBALAYA

Less traditionbound than its cousins, this stew of the Mississippi Delta region was originally based on rabbit or squirrel, smoked meats, rice, okra, and tomatoes. Over the years, carefree additions became the rule, and today's Jambalaya is generally a shrimp dish. If you wish, add shrimp, chicken, sausage, or almost any other meat to the original recipe that follows.

## Small Game—An Infinite Variety

1 squirrel or rabbit
1 cup coarsely diced bacon
1 pound coarsely diced ham
1 pound any other meat,
   including but not limited to
   chicken, beef, veal, and
   shrimp
1 gallon cold water
2 cups rice
1 large onion, minced

2 sweet green (Bell) peppers
   coarsely diced
2 stalks celery, diced fine
4 large red ripe tomatoes,
   quartered
¼ teaspoon powdered thyme
⅛ teaspoon powdered basil
   generous dash (8 to 10 drops)
   Tabasco Sauce
1 teaspoon salt

Cut the squirrel or rabbit into small pieces; sauté the bacon cubes and in the fat they yield brown the meats used. Put cold water into the stewpot, bring to a simmer, and cook 30 to 45 minutes, until the meats begin to get tender. Add remaining ingredients and seasonings, cook until the vegetables are completely done. Taste and adjust seasoning before serving; a Jambalaya should be mildly spicy, but not overseasoned.

Serves 12 to 16.

# V

---

# Waterfowl and Reed Birds

No BREED OF CHEF is more fixed in his beliefs or more vocal in defense of them than the one who specializes in wildfowl cookery. What may well be the oldest written recipe for wild duck was found a few years ago on an Egyptian papyrus roll written about 5000 B.C. for a duck stew containing raisins, honey, and cinnamon. From that day on, cooks have sought the perfect way to cook wildfowl. There are differences of opinion that start from the moment the shotgun trigger is pulled and continue to the time the birds reach the table. Some hunter-chefs like to draw birds at once, in the field; others leave the cavities untouched during a period of hanging. Some advocate dry plucking, some want birds to soak in hot water first. Some cooks immerse ducks and geese in hot salted water before cooking, others hold that such soaking spoils the flesh. All of them advance unanswerable arguments in support of their fixed positions. My own follow.

Opponents of field-drawing claim that exposing the opened cavity to air causes too-rapid deterioration of the bird's flesh. Exposure to even smoggy air will do far less harm than will the juices leaking from shot-torn intestines. Opening the vent and removing the intestines prevents a bird's meat from being tainted. The airless rubber-lined "game pockets" of most hunting coats do more harm to birds than anything else. Whether drawn or left intact, birds kept warm in contact with the hunter's own body will usually be spoiled, even on cold days, if left in the pocket more than an hour or two. The J- or S-shaped wire carriers or the split leather belt thongs that allow the bird to dangle from the hunter's belt are cumbersome and inconvenient, but infinitely to be preferred to the game pocket.

Arguments over dry and wet plucking are rather pointless, because now a small rubber-fingered wheel is available, that can be used with an electric drill to whisk feathers off in seconds, once the light touch the wheel requires has been mastered. And any poultry shop has a commercial plucking wheel they will use on your game birds for a few cents apiece. Those committed to wet-plucking will cling to it, in any event—but remember that aged birds should not be plucked until the end of the hanging period.

Differences of opinion in cooking are chiefly between the school that holds to heavy, smothering sauces and that which claims that no sauce is the best sauce. Somewhere between the two lies truth. Underseasoning has its dangers because at times the uncertain diets of most wild birds can add strange flavors to their flesh that moderate saucing will make palatable. The best sauces are still based on the birds' own juices, caught in a drip pan or roaster. Most recipes calling for excessive seasonings and oversaucing date from the time when nearly all fowl served at table was wildfowl; these heavy sauces were designed to relieve and give variety to palates tired of the sameness of wild duck, pigeon, plover, quail, or partridge, day after day and week after week. Under present conditions, there is little likelihood that this problem will recur.

In the years of game bird plenty only the breasts were offered to guests at a dinner. To do that today, the guests would almost be forced to bring their own birds. In deference to modern bag limits, many recipes that utilize only the choicest parts of game birds have been omitted from this chapter; only a couple of outstanding ones are included. By sagacious selection of recipes, it is still possible to serve a party of friends a game bird dinner.

## Waterfowl

Ducks and geese, the most hunted waterfowl, fall generally into three classes. There are the shore, shoreline, and shallow-water feeders, geese, mallard, pintails, and teal. These are generally vegetarians. There are the vegetarian deep-feeders: canvasback, redhead, scaup, and ringneck. Finally, there are the fish-eaters: mergansers, scoters, and their kin, readily identifiable not only by plumage but by bills that have pronounced teeth. The vegetarian species are preferable for eating, but the oily flavor associated with the fish-eaters can be eliminated or minimized by proper precooking.

Age as well as species determines what handling is required before cooking. The most positive guide to age of ducks and geese is the breastbone; the younger the bird, the more flexible this bone. The bill is another indicator of age; it is more flexible in young birds. The skin of the feet and legs thickens and roughens with age, and the claws grow tougher and become split and broken. Thickness of pinfeathers also helps determine age—the thicker they are, the younger the bird, and very old ducks and geese will have coarse hairlike feathers among the pinfeathers.

Vegetarian ducks, unless very old, need only to be hung. The fish-eating species require marinating instead of hanging. Four to five days hanging in a cool place is usually adequate for ducks, but a day or two longer will benefit geese. Twitching out a few breast feathers each day after the second full day of hanging will give you an idea of how aging is progressing; when the feathers come out with ease, the bird is ready to be cooked. Freezing preserves, not ages, and is not a substitute for hanging. Birds once frozen cannot be hung; indeed, they should not even be thawed, but cooked with extended timing to compensate for their frozen condition

Waterfowl carry much more fat on their bodies than do most wild birds, and as is the case with most animals, it is the fat that holds offbeat flavors. Fish-eaters, even after marinating, should be cooked on a rack so that the fat that drains from the body in cooking will be kept away from the bird. Nor should the juices from this type of duck be used as a base for any sauce prepared to accompany them.

There are as many opinions on how long to cook a duck as there are on how best to set a string of decoys. Some insist on serving a 6-minute bird, which is roughly the equivalent of cooking a turkey over the flame of a cigarette lighter. A more sensible timing is 12 minutes on a grill; 20 to 25 minutes on a revolving spit; 30 to 40 minutes in the slow, gentle heat of a Dutch oven; 12 to 15 minutes in the quick dry heat of a sheepherder stove; and 15 to 18 minutes at 375 degrees in the kitchen oven. For teal, reduce times one third.

These timings will deliver to the table a bird with moist pink juices, but its flesh will be cooked. Too long in the oven, and your decoys will taste better than your duck; too short a time and you will not eat the bird, you will drink it. For geese, extend the timings given above by one third if you want birds that are completely cooked, but still moist and tender.

### WILD DUCK WITH PAN GRAVY

This recipe is suitable for young vegetarian ducks. Stuffings traditionally used for different species are: mallard, pintail, redhead, ¼ onion and ¼ apple; teal, ringneck, a stalk of celery and a piece of bacon; canvasback, a stalk of celery and ¼ of an apple.

| | |
|---|---|
| 1 whole duck, cleaned and plucked; if not aged by hanging, marinate 1½ to 2 hours in Marinade #1 | salt, pepper |
| | 2 tablespoons dry red wine |
| | 1 tablespoon butter |
| | 1 tablespoon flour |
| | 2 tablespoons brandy |

If the duck has been marinated, wipe dry. Rub the cavity very lightly with salt and pepper and put in the stuffing you select. Pour the wine into the cavity and close with a stitch or two, or use small skewers. Have the Dutch oven hot, with a rack on its bottom. Lay the bird breast up on the rack, close oven, bury in coals, and cook 30 to 40 minutes. (You will probably be cooking more than one bird at a time, but the cooking time does not change.) In a sheepherder oven, cook 12 to 15 minutes in a closed pan; in the kitchen oven, 15 to 18 minutes at 375 degrees. Outdoors, you can brown the bird's skin on the grill or spit after removing it from the Dutch oven; indoors, remove the pan's cover for the final 3 or 4 minutes of cooking.

Remove bird and rack from the pan. Tilt the pan on its side for a moment to allow the fat to rise, and skim off as much as possible with a spoon or rubber-bulbed basting tube. When the fat has been skimmed, put the pan over high heat and stir the juices well, scraping the bottom. You should have ¾ to 1 cup of pan juice—if there is not this much, add red wine. Knead the butter and flour into a smooth paste and flake bits of it into the simmering pan juice while stirring. When smooth, dash in the brandy, remove from heat, stir 1 or 2 minutes to marry the flavors, serve the pan gravy over the halved duck. The stuffing is discarded.

One duck serves 2; allow 1 teal per person.

## SPIT-ROASTED WILD DUCK

Suggested for young vegetarian ducks, small wild geese, or domestic duckling. Ingredient quantities are for one duck. For teal, cut the quantities about one fourth; for a goose, increase one third.

| | | | |
|---|---|---|---|
| 1 | whole duck, aged by hanging or marinated in Marinade #1, for 1½ to 2 hours | ½ | cup cider vinegar |
| | | 1 | tablespoon butter |
| | | ⅛ | teaspoon sugar |
| | | ¼ | teaspoon freshly ground black pepper |
| ½ | green cooking apple | | |
| ⅛ | teaspoon cinnamon | 1½ | tablespoons currant jelly |

If the duck has been marinated, drain and blot dry; if it has been hanging, wipe the cavity with a cloth dipped in lightly salted water.

Cut the apple into large dice, sprinkle with cinnamon, and put into the cavity. Close cavity with thread or small skewers, spit the bird, and cook 20 to 25 minutes. Baste often, using a liquid prepared by bringing the vinegar to boil in a small pan and stirring into it the butter, sugar, and pepper. (If margarine is used as a substitute for butter, avoid the "soft" margarines; these contain preservatives that prevent them from blending with acids such as vinegar and wine.) Catch drippings from the spitted bird in a pan. When the bird is done, remove to a warmed platter. Skim excess fat off the drippings, and combine over low heat with the currant jelly to make a sauce that is served with the duck.

Cooking time should be decreased one third for teal, increased one third for geese. Results similar to spit-roasting can be obtained by cooking birds in the sheepherder stove on a rack in an open pan; 8 to 10 minutes for teal, 12 to 15 minutes for other ducks, 18 to 20 minutes for geese. Similar timing will apply to the kitchen oven at 400 degrees.

One duck serves 2; allow 1 teal per person.

### GRILL-ROASTED WILD DUCK

Any wild duck, even a well-marinated fish-eater, responds to this method of cooking, as do domestic ducklings and small geese. Ingredient quantities are for one duck. For teal, reduce one fourth; for geese increase one third.

| | | | |
|---|---|---|---|
| 1 | whole duck, aged by hanging or marinated 1½ to 2 hours in Marinade #1 | ¼ | teaspoon garlic salt |
| | | ½ | cup peanut oil or other light cooking oil |
| 1½ | tablespoons butter | ½ | cup dry red wine |

A marinated bird should be drained and wiped dry; a bird aged by hanging should be wiped inside and out with a rag dipped in lightly salted water. Using a heavy-bladed knife or poultry shears, cut the bird's ribs along the backbone on one side, then snap the breastbone so it will lie flat on the grill grid. Mix the butter and garlic salt and rub over the bird, on both sides. Mix the oil and wine together for basting. Cook skin side down for 2 to 3 minutes, bone side down 6 to 8 minutes, and skin side down again 4 to 5 minutes, basting frequently throughout. The basting liquid tends to separate, and should be kept well mixed. This cooking method can be approximated in the kitchen range under the broiler, with the duck on a rack in the broiling pan. Timing and basting procedures given above will be approximately the same. Cooking times for teal should be reduced one third; for geese, extended one third.

A duck will serve 2; allow 1 teal per person.

## WILD DUCK BIGARADE

This is one of the great classic sauced duck dishes; it is as well suited to domestic duck and duckling as to wild birds. Its preparation is not as complicated as a glance at the recipe might make it appear, and the results are worth the effort. Ingredient quantities are given for the use of breasts and legs from 2 ducks, which will serve 4. However, a more generous serving would be these pieces from 3 ducks, and if 3 are used, increase other ingredient quantities one half.

breasts and legs from 2 ducks
(avoid fish-eaters)

Marinade:
¼ cup finest light olive oil, or peanut oil
1½ tablespoons lemon juice
½ teaspoon salt
⅛ teaspoon freshly ground black pepper
2 tablespoons chopped shallots
1 bay leaf
pinch of powdered thyme

For the sauce:
1 whole orange, unpeeled

1 pint boiling water
dash of Angostura or Peychaud bitters
2 tablespoons Cointreau or Triple Sec
1 tablespoon meat essence (BV, Bovril, etc.) or 1 cup game stock previously reduced one half by boiling

For the pan:
3 tablespoons butter (no substitute)
1 tablespoon lemon juice

**Waterfowl and Reed Birds**

Skin the pieces of duck and marinate 2 hours; turn frequently, stirring the marinade. While the duck pieces are marinating, prepare the sauce.

Peel the orange very thin, not allowing any white pith of its inner membrane to remain on the peel. Cut the skin into matchstick-sized pieces. Bring water to a boil, toss in the pieces of peel, remove from heat, let steep 5 minutes. Strain and reserve the liquid, discard the peel. Return the liquid to a simmer, but do not boil. Add the juice of ½ the orange (about 2½ tablespoons), the bitters, and the liqueur. Stir well, remove from heat, and set aside.

Take the pieces of duck from the marinade and drain the liquid clinging to them back into the bowl, but do not wipe the pieces dry. Strain and reserve the marinade. Cook the pieces of duck 3 minutes to each side on the grill, or under the broiler. Baste frequently with the marinade as the duck pieces cook. No matter how well done you like duck, do not overcook at this stage; the pieces are done when they feel firm to the pressure of a knife butt.

In a deep, heavy skillet melt the butter; when it foams and begins to darken, dash in the lemon juice and stir vigorously. Remove from heat, put in the duck pieces, and let stand, turning occasionally, while you complete the sauce.

Bring the previously prepared sauce base to a simmer; do not allow to boil. If meat essence is used, mix it with an equal quantity of very hot water. Add meat essence or reduced broth to the sauce base and stir thoroughly. Pour the sauce over the duck pieces in the skillet, and stir well while simmering over gentle heat 2 or 3 minutes. Serve quickly, dividing the sauce among the plates.

Serves 4, luxuriously.

**DUCK BREASTS IN WINE**

Over the years it's become my conviction that Charles Kinsley, Sr., of San Francisco knows the first name of every duck migrating on the West Coast's flyways. This is the only way to explain why they respond as they do to his calling. Charley is also a creative cook, as witness:

breasts of 2 large ducks
¼ cup butter (no substitutes)
3 tablespoons flour
scanty pinches of salt and pepper
1 cup brandy

1 cup dry red wine
1 bay leaf, stems removed, powdered
1 teaspoon fresh thyme, minced fine

Skin the breasts and coat them with softened butter. Mix flour, salt, and pepper, and roll the breasts in this until thickly coated. Grill 3 minutes per side. Do not overcook. Timing is the same for outdoor grill or kitchen range broiler.

Put the breasts in a heavy, prewarmed skillet. Warm ½ cup of the brandy, pour over the breasts, and light. When the brandy burns out, add the wine, bay leaf, and thyme. Simmer over gentle heat 20 to 25 minutes. Lift out the breasts with a slotted spoon, allowing the liquid to drain back into the pan; put the breasts on warmed serving plates. Over high heat, bring the pan liquid to a rolling boil, stirring well and scraping the pan's bottom. Dash in the remaining ½ cup brandy, remove from heat, stir a minute or two, then divide the sauce over the breasts.

Serves 2.

### GINGERED DUCK

This method of marinating and grilling will make even one of the fish-eating ducks palatable.

2 whole ducks
½ cup soy sauce
4 tablespoons lemon juice
2 tablespoons orange juice
1 tablespoon poultry seasoning (these prepared mixtures usually contain a few flakes of dried parsley, thyme, cracked

peppercorns, cloves, mustard-seed, and a shred of mild red pepper pod)
1 teaspoon powered ginger
½ cup medium-dry sherry
¾ cup flour
½ cup cooking oil

With a heavy knife or poultry shears, split the ducks in half by cutting the ribs along one side of the backbone and cleaving the breastbone. Mix all ingredients except flour and cooking oil and marinate the duck halves for 1½ to 2 hours, turning occasionally. Drain the pieces when removing, catching the liquid in the marinade bowl. Wipe the duck halves dry. Dust with flour, coat with cooking oil, then dust again with flour. Cook on the grill 10 minutes per side, bone side down first, and baste generously with the strained marinade liquid while cooking. Timing under the broiler of the kitchen range is the same.

Serves 4.

### STEWED DUCK

A stew enables you to serve four with a lone bird; it can also be made with leftover pieces of roast duck.

| | |
|---|---|
| 1 whole duck, cooked 8 to 10 minutes in a sheepherder stove or kitchen oven, or grilled 3 to 4 minutes per side on the grill; or 4 to 5 cups of cut-up leftovers | 2 cups green peas |
| | 4 cups game stock or chicken broth |
| | 1 teaspoon salt |
| | ⅛ teaspoon Nepal pepper |
| 2 cups pearl onions | ½ to ¾ teaspoon cornstarch, or 1 teaspoon flour and 1 teaspoon butter |
| 6 small carrots, peeled and diced | |

A whole duck cooked for stewing should be underdone, using the timing given at the beginning of this recipe. The meat is then cut into small dice. Leftover meat used in stewing should also be diced.

Put all ingredients and seasonings to simmer over gentle heat. Time your cooking by the carrots, which will be the last ingredient to become tender. Thicken the liquid by adding cornstarch a little at a time and stirring until thickened to your taste; or blend flour and butter into a smooth paste and flake into the pot, stirring until all flour dissolves. Then cook an additional 2 or 3 minutes to eliminate any starchy taste. Adjust seasonings, then ladle the stew over hot biscuits, boiled rice, or mashed potatoes.

Serves 4 to 6.

## ROAST GOOSE

Only young, tender wild geese or domestic ones, should be cooked by the recipes given for duck. Older, tougher geese are best roasted, with a moist stuffing, and our attention in this section focuses chiefly on this method of cooking. Prepare the goose by hanging to age, or by marinating 3 to 4 hours in Marinade #1 or #2, page 31. If you have an old gander that promises to be exceptionally tough, parboil in lightly salted water, 1 teaspoon salt per quart, for 30 to 45 minutes. Birds aged by hanging should be wiped with a cloth dipped in salted water; birds marinated or parboiled should be wiped dry after being thoroughly drained.

Geese have more natural fat than other wildfowl, and domestic geese are, of course, fatter than wild ones. Before cooking, the skin of a goose should be pricked with a sharp fork at the base of each wing, the bottom tip of the breast on each side, the back of the legs, and the joint where thigh meets back. Pockets of fat form at these points during cooking, unless the skin is pierced to allow this fat to escape. The long neck should be cut off close to the body, with a flap of breast skin left to be drawn over the back and secured with skewers, to close the front cavity. The oil sac and gland at the base of the tail should be removed, and it is customary to cut off the almost meatless wing tips.

Young geese can be spit-roasted, but this method is not recommended for older birds, which should be cooked in a Dutch oven, or in a tightly closed pan in a sheepherder stove or kitchen oven. Timing for a stuffed goose in the Dutch oven is 40 minutes per pound; in the sheepherder stove, 25 minutes per pound; in the kitchen oven, 30 minutes per pound with the temperature at 375 degrees for the first 15 minutes and 275 degrees thereafter. Birds cooked in the Dutch oven will be more tender than those cooked in other ways, but will not have a crisply browned skin; this can be done on the grill, turning the bird often. In sheepherder and kitchen ovens, remove the pan cover during the final 10 to 15 minutes of cooking. A rack should be used in the pan in which a goose is cooked.

## Waterfowl and Reed Birds

An 8-pound stuffed goose serves 10 to 12.
Three traditional stuffings are given for your roast goose.

### CELERY-ONION STUFFING

4 slices bacon sautéed very
soft
2 small sweet onions
3 or 4 stalks firm green celery
1 small turnip

3 cups coarse dry bread crumbs
1 tablespoon salt
1 tablespoon Hot Pepper
Vinegar, page 163

Prepare the goose according to procedures beginning on page 117. Chop the bacon, onions, and celery and grate the turnip. Mix with bread crumbs and seasonings. Stir Hot Pepper Vinegar into ¾ cup lukewarm water and moisten the mixture. Fill the cavity loosely —do not pack in the stuffing. Close cavity with skewers or by sewing. Truss legs, loop a string around wings at the tips, and pull close to body. Pass the string under the back, never over the breast. Cook by the method you prefer and the timing required.

### POTATO STUFFING

2 cups hot mashed potatoes
1 cup coarsely crumbled corn
bread, preferably made from
white stone-ground corn meal
½ teaspoon freshly ground black
pepper

1 tablespoon salt
3 teaspoons powdered sage
2 teaspoons onion juice, or 1
teaspoon onion salt dissolved
in 1 teaspoon dry white wine

Prepare the bird according to procedures beginning on page 117. Combine all ingredients and seasonings, mix well, and fill the cavity loosely. Close cavity with skewers or by sewing. Truss legs, loop a cord around the wingtips, and pull under the back to hold wings close to body. Cook by the method of your choice and the timing required.

**118**

## SAUSAGE STUFFING

| | |
|---|---|
| ½  pound country-style sausage | 2  tablespoons powdered sage |
| 3  large onions | large dash black pepper |
| 6  slices dry bread | generous pinch of nutmeg |
| 1½  teaspoons salt | 1  egg |

Prepare the goose according to procedures beginning on page 117. Sauté the sausage in loose pieces and drain well on paper towels. Peel the onions and bake in a dry, covered pan 15 to 20 minutes. Crumble the bread coarsely. Combine all ingredients and seasonings, mashing the onions during the mixing. Beat the egg lightly and blend into the dry ingredients. Stuff the bird, filling the cavity loosely; close cavity with skewers or by sewing. Truss legs, and loop a string around the wingtips and under the back to draw the wings close to body. Cook by the method of your choice with the timing given on page 117.

It is assumed you will be familiar with the seasoning of the country sausage used, and will adjust salt, pepper, and sage quantities accordingly—these quantities are based on the use of a mild commercial country-style sausage, not the hot sausage featured by some farmers or butchers. It is assumed that the bread you use will not be the soft commercial squoosh loaf, which tends to dissolve into an unpleasant paste when used in a dressing. Several national firms and many local ones now distribute a variety of breads made from hard-wheat flour without chemical additives. If you cannot find genuine bread in your local stores, bake a batch of Sourdough Bread by the recipe on page 268 and use it.

## ALSATIAN-STYLE GOOSE

| | |
|---|---|
| 1  whole goose aged by hanging or marinated 2 hours in lightly salted water, 1 teaspoon salt per quart of water | 2  quarts sauerkraut |
| | 8 to 10  small smoked link sausages |
| | 2  cups Rhine wine |
| thin slices of pork fat, salt pork, or fat bacon | salt, pepper |

## Waterfowl and Reed Birds

If salt pork is used it should be trimmed and blanched in boiling water 1 minute. Sauté the pork fat, salt pork, or bacon in the Dutch oven until transparent, then remove and reserve. Brown the goose lightly in the fat left in the pan, rolling it to get its skin a uniform golden tan. Remove to a warm platter.

Wash the sauerkraut in 2 changes of cold water and drain well. Cover the bottom of the Dutch oven with a layer of slices of the partly cooked pork fat, salt pork, or bacon, then put a 1-inch layer of drained kraut on the bacon. Put in the sausages and cover them with a 1-inch layer of kraut. Lay the goose on the kraut and use the remaining kraut to bury it completely. Pour 1 cup of wine over the kraut, then close the oven and bury it in coals for 2 to 2½ hours. Open the oven, remove the kraut into a large colander so that its juices will drain back into the pan. Lift out the goose, put it on a warm platter, and arrange the sausages beside it. Take out the remaining kraut. Discard the fat on the pan's bottom. Heat the juice in the pan, stir in the remaining cup of wine. Let simmer 5 minutes, and taste and adjust seasoning, adding salt and pepper as needed. Put the kraut in a deep bowl and pour the hot pan juice over it. Slice the goose and sausages on the platter and serve.

An 8-pound goose serves 10 to 12.

## WILD GOOSE FRICASSEE

There are always leftovers from a roast goose: the wing tips, neck, heart, gizzard, liver, and bits and pieces of meat clinging to the skeleton. There is also flavor in the bones themselves. A fricassee puts them all to use.

leftovers from roast goose:
  meat, trimmings, neck, liver,
  gizzard, bones, skeleton
1 gallon cold water
2 bay leaves
1 sprig thyme or ½ teaspoon
  crushed thyme
1 sprig basil or ¼ teaspoon
  crushed basil

3 cloves
1 large onion, quartered
4 tablespoons goose fat or
  bacon drippings
3 tablespoons flour
salt, pepper

Put all parts of the goose, edible or inedible, into a large pot with a gallon of cold water. (If the gizzard has not been cleaned, cut and clean it.) Add the herbs and onion and bring to a simmer over gentle heat. Cook 1 to 2 hours, until the meat falls from the bones, then strain the contents of the pot through a sieve or cloth. Discard bones and skin, and chop all edible meat into small dice. Return liquid and diced meat to the pot and simmer briskly 30 to 40 minutes, to reduce the liquid by one third to one half. Heat the goose fat or bacon drippings in a skillet and sprinkle it with the flour, stirring to form a light tan paste. Add ½ to ¾ cup of the pot liquid to the browned flour, over medium heat, stirring until well blended. Put this thinned paste into the pot liquid, stirring to blend. Add salt and pepper to taste. Serve over any starchy base—split toasted biscuits, bread cubes, rice, noodles, spaghetti, potatoes.

Serves 6 to 8.

## WILD GOOSE GUMBO

Use this method on an exceedingly tough goose or other game bird or small game animal.

| | |
|---|---|
| 1 whole old goose | ½ cup chopped celery |
| 2 bay leaves | 2 cloves garlic, minced very |
| 2 tablespoons salt | fine |
| 2 pounds fresh okra | 1 large onion, minced |
| 2 tablespoons goose fat or | 1 green (Bell) pepper, cleaned |
| bacon drippings | and minced |
| 3 tablespoons flour | 1 can tomato paste |

Remove legs and wings and cut the goose carcass in quarters. Put in a deep pot and cover with cold water—at least 3 quarts—and add bay leaves and 1 tablespoon salt. Bring to a boil, skim off froth that rises to the top, and reduce to simmer. Cook 2 to 3 hours, until meat falls from bones. Strain and reserve the pot liquid. Strip all meat from bones, discard bones, skin, gristle, and any inedible bits of meat. Dice meat fine.

Slice the okra in 1-inch rounds. Heat goose fat or bacon drippings in a deep, heavy skillet and sauté the okra until very crisp. Remove okra to plate with pieces of goose meat. Sprinkle flour over the fat in the skillet, stirring as it browns to form a smooth roux. Add 4 cups of strained pot liquid to the skillet, stirring into the browned flour to form a gravy. Add celery, garlic, onion, and pepper, blend well, and let simmer. Mix the tomato paste with 2 cups of the warm pot liquid, add to the contents of the skillet. Return the okra and meat to the skillet, simmer 15 to 20 minutes. The gumbo's liquid portion should be the consistency of heavy cream when the dish is ladled out over boiled rice in soup bowls.

Serves 10 to 12.

### STUFFED GOOSE NECKS or SAUSAGES

Near the southern tip of California's big Lake Almanor lies a vest-pocket-sized body of water called Round Valley Lake. Because it is so near the better-known and better-publicized Almanor, Round Valley Lake seldom has more than a dozen fishermen on it at any given moment. It not only contains some of the biggest black bass west of the Mississippi, but is on the big Central Valley flyway, and furnishes stopover facilities for a lot of ducks and geese early in the wildfowl season. Nick Bath operates the boat and cabin rental facilities at Round Valley Lake, and at the right time can be persuaded to cook up a few Stuffed Goose Necks for fortunate hunters.

| | |
|---|---|
| 2 goose necks, the skin intact and carefully plucked, plus 1 cup of raw goose meat | 1 hot red pepper |
| | ½ teaspoon sage or oregano |
| | 1 teaspoon salt |
| 1 clove garlic | ½ cup rice flour |
| 1½ cups chopped sweet onion | ⅓ to ½ cup goose fat or bacon drippings |
| 6 to 8 peppercorns | |

Parboil the unskinned necks 20 minutes, then roll back the skin very carefully and remove it intact without tearing or cutting. Return the necks to the pot and add the cup of meat; simmer 45 minutes to

1 hour, until the meat will slip easily from the neckbones. Put meat, garlic, onion, peppercorns, pepper pod, sage or oregano, and salt through meat grinder twice, using the finest blade. Blend with the rice flour. Turn the neck skins so they are skin side out, tie one end with heavy twine, and stuff them with the meat mixture. Tie the open end. In a heavy skillet over gentle heat, melt the goose fat or bacon drippings. You will need enough to fill the pan to a depth of ½ inch. Sauté the stuffed skins very slowly, turning with tongs as they cook to avoid puncturing the skins. Cook 35 to 45 minutes, until the skin is brown but not crisp. When cooked, hang in a cool place over a shallow pan, and let drip for 2 to 3 hours.

When all loose fat has drained away, the stuffed skins, or sausages, are ready to eat. They can be sliced and eaten cold, or made into sandwiches, or warmed in a lightly greased skillet. Stored in the refrigerator, wrapped in foil or plastic film, they will keep 3 to 4 weeks. These make a very unusual hors d'oeuvre; top a round cracker with a ¼-inch slice of the stuffed neck plus a slice of stuffed olive or pickle. Slices are also good with fried eggs, as a breakfast meat.

## Mudhens or Coots

Few wildfowlers pay much attention the the mudhen, as the black, coarse-fleshed coot is usually called. They are looked on as trash birds, totally inedible. Mudhens are found on most waters that attract ducks; they are both numerous and voracious, and will occasionally damage farm crops. When mudhens appear in crop-damaging numbers, farmers thin them out; this was the situation in the San Joaquin Valley of California in the early 1920s. L. A. Sischo, a market-hunter who supplied ducks (quite illegally, of course) to the private homes, clubs, and restaurants in San Francisco during those heedless, free-wheeling years, created a dish to utilize the wasted and unappreciated mudhens.

So popular did Sischo's mudhen recipe become that it is still being served forty years later in the area where it was first cooked. Judge D. Oliver Germino of Los Banos, replying to my query for this book, very kindly refreshed my memory of the recipe and confirmed the continuing popularity of the dish at sportsmen's dinners. Having dined well many times on Sischo's mudhen stew, my suggestion is that the next time you go duck hunting, you drop a few mudhens and try it for yourself. On its home ground, the dish is called:

## PORTUGUESE DUCKS

24 mudhen breasts; they are quite small, and 6 should be allowed per person. The birds are not cleaned; an incision is made down the breastbone and the breasts skinned, then cut from the bone with filleting slices

Marinade:
1 quart red wine vinegar mixed with 1 quart cool water
12 crushed peppercorns
1 large onion, grated or chopped fine

1 tablespoon salt

Sauce:
1 quart dry red wine
1 quart cold water
3 sweet onions
6 ripe tomatoes
3 sweet green (Bell) peppers
3 stalks celery
2 cups sliced mushrooms
½ teaspoon nutmeg
1 tablespoon salt
½ teaspoon pepper

Marinate the breasts 24 to 36 hours in a cool but not refrigerated place. After 8 hours, add 1 pint cool water to the marinade. Stir occasionally and be sure the breasts are always completely covered. Let them drain for at least 1 hour on folded cloth or paper towels before cooking. The marinade is discarded.

Mix all the ingredients of the sauce cold. The onions are peeled and sliced and tomatoes quartered over the cooking pot so all their juices will go into the mixture. Seed the peppers and remove the pith, then slice into ½-inch strips, cut the celery into coarse chunks, and slice the mushrooms fairly thin. Put in the seasonings and mudhen breasts and simmer very, very slowly 45 minutes to 1 hour, until the breasts are tender. All ingredients should cook completely covered by liquid; if more is needed, add wine and water mixed in equal parts. A somewhat thicker sauce can be achieved by adding 1 can tomato paste. The breasts are usually served in a deep dish with enough sauce to cover them generously, and thin slices of lemon floated on top. Thick-sliced sour French bread and fresh butter make the rest of the meal.

Serves 4.

## Marsh and Reed Fowl

The most prominent members of this rather exclusive family are his highness the woodcock and the shifty-flying jacksnipe, but the family includes all members of the snipe and curlew group. Once relatively plentiful, they are growing increasingly rare as bulldozers destroy their marshy haunts. Seasons on most of these birds are short and bag limits small, and they may not be sold commercially in most states. These birds are unique in their flavors, and if you want to enjoy them, you must bag your own.

Life spans of these birds are short, so their age is not a factor in preparing them for the pot, or in cooking them. They need not be hung to age, though a day or two in a cool place before they are plucked and cooked will improve their flavor. Whether you utilize the trail (the lower intestine) by leaving it in the bird or adding it to the sauce is up to you. If you have an aversion to its use you will lose the pungency added to the bird's flavor by its retention.

Any cooking method given for one of the marsh birds is suitable for use with all of them. Methods of cooking marsh birds can also be used with small upland game birds such as doves and pigeons, and recipes for doves and pigeons used with marsh birds; see pages 130–132 and 141–143.

### BAG-BRAISED JACKSNIPE

2 or 3 birds should be allowed per serving; in this particular recipe, quantities of ingredients vary according to the number of birds you are cooking

1 small brown paper sack for each bird cooked
bacon drippings
flour, salt, pepper

Dip the bags in warm bacon drippings until they are well impregnated. Drain until loose fat is gone, then put a bird into each bag and tie the neck closed. Put the bagged birds on a rack in a Dutch oven, close the lid, put on bright coals for 25 minutes. In a sheepherder oven, cook 12 to 14 minutes in a closed pan; in the kitchen oven, 15 minutes at 400 degrees. Don't try to substitute foil for paper sacks. It will not work. The foil will not absorb the hot bacon fat essential to the cooking process, and it steams the birds, making them soggy rather than crisp.

Heat bacon drippings very hot in the skillet; mix flour with the seasonings; to each tablespoon of flour, use about ⅓ teaspoon salt and a large dash of pepper. The seasoned flour should be rubbed on in a thin coat. Take out the birds, cut the bags open, and quickly roll each bird in seasoned flour, then sauté in the very hot bacon fat until a rich brown crust forms on its outside.

Allow 2 or 3 birds per serving.

### GRILL-BROILED JACKSNIPE

2 or 3 birds should be allowed per serving; the quantity of ingredients required will vary

with the number of birds cooked
butter, salt, pepper

Wipe the plucked, drawn birds with a cloth dipped in lightly salted water, 1 teaspoon salt per quart of water. Put the birds between the folds of a lint-free cloth on a firm surface and press down hard on them with a rolling pin or the side of a heavy cleaver to flatten them and crack their breastbones. Brush the birds with melted butter and grill over bright coals 4 minutes per side; brush with butter as they cook. Season to taste only after removing from the grill.

An alternate method of preparing is to cut the birds' ribs close to the backbone along one side, spread open, and snap the breastbone between the fingers. Start the birds cooking bone side down and cook 3 minutes per side, basting frequently. Season after removing from the grill.

## WOODCOCK WITH BRANDY

4  woodcock
⅓  cup butter (no substitutes)
¼  cup brandy
¼  cup meat extract mixed with
   ½ cup water, or reduce 1 cup
   of meat stock to half its
   original volume by boiling

juice of 1 lemon about 3
   tablespoons
scanty pinch of salt
small dash of Nepal or cayenne
   pepper

Quarter the woodcock, reserving the trail if it is to be used. Flatten the birds by pressing them under the heel of a hand on a firm, flat surface. Heat the butter in a heavy skillet and cook the pieces over medium heat, 4 minutes per side. If the trail is used, chop fine and add to the pan, stirring into the juices. Warm the brandy in a heavy saucer and light it, let burn 1 minute, then pour into the skillet; douse the flames by stirring briskly. Pour in the meat extract and lemon juice at once, and add the seasonings. Stir well, cover the skillet, remove from heat, and let stand 5 minutes before serving. Caution: do not let the sauce boil up after the brandy has been added.

Serves 2.

# VI

---

# Upland Game Birds

A DUCK IS A DUCK and a goose is a goose wherever either one of them flies or swims, but in some areas of the upland game bird field no such solid certainty exists.

A quail is a quail, except where it's called a bob white or a partridge. Grouse is called partridge in parts of New England; in Texas it becomes a prairie chicken; in Kansas, a sage hen; in Northern California, a ruffed grouse; in the Pacific Northwest, a timber grouse; and still further north, in Alaska, the grouse is a ptarmigan. Actually, the grouse of England is technically a ptarmigan, and in France, the grouse becomes a hazel hen.

In spite of the disparity of names, regional differences in plumage and shades of color, and minor variations more meaningful to ornithologists than to cooks, the grouse is a grouse wherever it is found and by whatever local name it is called. And a quail is still a quail in the pot, regardless of its subspecies status or regional title. So, to keep things straight from here on, translate "grouse" or "quail" into whatever it's called where you live or hunt—in this section these two birds will be called only grouse and quail.

No aliases are encountered among other upland game birds. Doves, pigeons, pheasants, turkeys, and chukkar all answer to their proper name wherever they're encountered, even though there are subspecies with minor differences of plumage. Moreover, birds of the same size can readily be interchanged in recipes. Doves and pigeons, pheasants and chukkar, respond to the same type of treatment in cooking. While on the subject of substitutes, chicken can stand in for pheasant, Rock Cornish hens for quail, domestic turkeys for wild. Any necessary variation in cooking processes or preparation will be noted in individual recipes.

In preparing smaller upland birds for cooking, it is usually wiser to age them a day or two in a cool place than to marinate. Then cook them in a manner that will put some fat and moisture into their sparsely fleshed bodies. Larger birds such as pheasant need either aging or marinating, if they are to be cooked by the dry processes of spit-roasting or grilling. In birds to be sauced, hanging is preferable to marinating. The very large birds, such as turkey, are difficult to age by hanging, and should be marinated.

Some hunters insist on overhanging pheasant. The long hanging period of pheasant and grouse is a custom imported from Europe; extended hanging is often called the "English way" of aging. The custom began as a matter of need, not of taste. It was propagated by profiteering butchers, hunters, or whatever.

Wildfowl shooting in most European countries is done on private lands, by invitation or for a fee, and the birds brought down belong to the landowner. The squire sells some birds to the hunters, but the bulk are sold to London clubs, restaurants, and hotels. This custom began several centuries ago, long before refrigerated transportation. Game birds traveled by wagon from estate to buyer, and when they reached London, they were already aged. Thus, the custom of eating game birds in varying degrees of putrescence, encouraged by the arbiters of fads and fashions, became fashionable.

The "English way" consists of hanging a grouse or pheasant by the bill until the bill pulls free of flesh and the bird falls to the floor. Birds hung this long do acquire a flavor, but it's the flavor of decay, not of grouse or pheasant. Zealous adherents spread the cult of the overaged bird, and scorn those who question its validity. No one who has blunted his teeth on a tough pheasant will argue against some hanging, but three to six weeks, as our British cousins would say, is a trifle much.

In a cool, well-ventilated place, small birds need hang only a day or two; quail, perhaps three to four. Grouse and pheasant will become tender in five days; turkey in a week. During periods of high humidity, the hanging time should be reduced. When a breast feather can be pulled from its mooring without resistance, the bird is ready to be cooked.

Whether small or large, upland birds are lean of flesh. When cooked over direct coals, on grill or spit, they must be basted often. Barding, which means enclosing the entire carcass in a thin sheet of unseasoned pork fat, is one of the secrets of cooking upland fowl in the open. Flaming the carcass with brandy or whiskey not only tenderizes, but also adds flavor while searing. If you must cook old birds on grill or spit, it is wise to marinate them or to braise them first and then finish up over direct heat.

In cooking wildfowl, as with any game, your objectives are twofold: to preserve the integrity of the bird's own flavor, and to render its flesh chewable. Everything else is extra, but often these extras are too enjoyable to be overlooked.

## Doves

Recipes and processes for cooking doves and pigeons are interchangable; so are those for marsh birds beginning on page 125. With shortened cooking time, these recipes can also be used for squab.

### SPIT-ROASTED DOVES

Individual taste plays such a large part in determining what you do to roast your doves or other small birds on the spit that basic procedures and suggestions are given here instead of repetitive recipes.

Small birds, spit-cooked, need the protection of an outer sheath or covering during the first stages of cooking, or the skin and flesh will be bone hard and tasteless before the bird is completely cooked. The most commonly used outer coverings are pork fat, very thin slices of bacon or blanched salt pork, grape leaves, cabbage leaves, fig leaves, and moist green cornhusks. When any of the nonfat coverings is used, the birds should be brushed with a light coating of oil or butter before they are wrapped. Notice that neither parchment cooking paper nor aluminum foil is mentioned. The paper burns when used for this purpose, and if you missed earlier remarks on the use of foil in cooking over coals, you will find them on page 20.

Cooking time for doves and birds of equivalent size on the spit is 3 to 4 minutes with the protective sheath and an additional 2 to 3 minutes after it is removed, to brown the skin crisply. Bright coals should be used. Salt birds after cooking.

### DOVES FRIED IN DEEP FAT

| | |
|---|---|
| 12 doves, plucked and drawn | 2 tablespoons butter |
| cooking oil, preferably a neutral oil such as peanut oil | 1 tablespoon flour |
| | 1 cup heavy cream |
| 1 cup milk | ½ teaspoon salt |
| ½ cup flour | ⅛ teaspoon pepper |

Into a heavy deep skillet put enough oil to cover the bottom to a depth of 2 to 2½ inches. Bring to high heat. Dip the birds in milk, then roll them in flour mixed with salt and pepper. Drop the birds into the hot fat, one or two at a time, so that cooking temperature is not lowered suddenly. Do not overcrowd the pan. Turn the birds to brown evenly. Cooking time will be about 3 minutes. Spread paper or cloth toweling on a warm platter, transfer the birds to this as they finish cooking. Pour off the fat in which the birds cooked, but do not scrape the pan. Chop the hearts and livers taken from the birds, and the trail, if it is to be used—some cooks fry the birds with the trail left in—and return the pan to low heat. Put in the butter and when it is hot, sauté the chopped bits. When they are nicely browned, sprinkle the tablespoon of flour into the pan and stir to form a light tan paste. Add enough to the milk used in dipping the birds to bring it back to 1 full cup, and pour this and the cream into the skillet, stirring vigorously to combine it with the flour-butter roux that you have formed in the pan. Do not allow mixture to boil up. When the gravy is smooth, taste and adjust seasoning. Pour the gravy over the doves and serve.

Serves 4.

## Grouse

Having already covered the aliases under which this bird travels, there remains only a brief note to add here. Unlike their small cousins, grouse attain what is by ornithological standards a respectable age. You will want to use young birds for spit-roasting or grilling, and use a moist, tenderizing process when cooking older specimens.

To judge the age of a grouse, hold the bird in your palm and press its breastbone with the thumb of your other hand; in a young bird, there will be a resilient "give" to the breastbone. Legs of young grouse are plump, and the legs of older ones elongated and more muscular. The skin on the legs darkens with age and grows rough, and the claws get blunted. Finally, the eye circle grows a deep red as grouse age.

### GRILLED GROUSE

| | |
|---|---|
| 1 bird per person; use young birds | butter, salt, pepper |

Split the birds up the back, cutting the ribs close to the backbone on one side with a sharp knife or poultry shears. Flatten the carcass by pressing it with a firm hand onto a flat surface, to break the breastbone. Brush well with butter on both sides. Grill over bright coals skin side down 4 to 5 minutes, basting the upper side with butter; turn and cook bone side down for 4 to 5 minutes with frequent basting. Season only after removing from grill.

## GROUSE WITH CABBAGE

This recipe is designed for old birds.

| | |
|---|---|
| 4 grouse | 2 or 3 carrots |
| thin slices of pork fat, salt pork, or fat bacon plus one slice about ½ inch thick | bay leaf<br>sprig of fresh thyme or a generous pinch of powdered thyme |
| 1 medium-sized firm young cabbage | salt, pepper |

Truss the birds, putting a folded piece of cabbage leaf into the cavity of each, along with a sliver of pork fat or bacon. Cut the cabbage into slices 1 inch thick. Line the bottom of a Dutch oven with a layer of thin slices of pork fat, salt pork, or fat bacon; if salt pork is used it should be trimmed and blanched in boiling water for 1 minute. Put slices of cabbage on the fat to cover the bottom of the oven. Cut the carrots into thick rounds and stud the cabbage slices with these; dice the thick slice of meat and sprinkle a few pieces on the cabbage. Wrap the birds in thin slices of fat and put them breast up on the cabbage. Crumble or pound the bay leaf, mince the thyme if fresh, and sprinkle the herbs over the grouse and cabbage slices in the pot. Sprinkle scantily with salt and pepper. Separate the leaves of the remaining slices of cabbage and drape them over the grouse. Close the oven and bury in coals for 1 hour. When the oven is opened, tilt it to spoon up accumulated pan juices, pour these over the top of the birds, close the oven and let it stand 15 minutes on dark coals. Serve the birds on top of the cabbage, include some pieces of carrot with each serving. Discard the fat covering the birds and lining the pot, as well as the stuffing in the birds' cavities.

Serves 4.

## GROUSE WITH GRAPES

This recipe is designed for old birds.

| | |
|---|---|
| 4 grouse | bunch of tart, firm-fleshed grapes |
| ¾ cup butter | such as Malaga, Alicante, or |
| 12 to 15 grape leaves, washed and blotted dry | Muscat, seeded; allow about a dozen grapes per bird |
| 1 cup brandy | ¼ teaspoon salt |
| 1 cup chicken stock or broth | |

Rub the carcass of each bird with a light coating of butter, put a folded grape leaf into the cavity of each, and wrap each bird with grape leaves, tying them on with string. Rub a light coating of butter on the bottom and sides of a Dutch oven or a deep skillet and warm the pan. Put in the birds breast up. Warm the brandy, pour it over the birds, and light. When the flames die, close the Dutch oven or skillet tightly and put on medium coals for 15 to 20 minutes.

Open the pan, remove the grape leaves from the birds, add any remaining butter, and the warmed stock or broth. Distribute the grapes evenly over and around the birds in the pan and sprinkle with salt. Cover the pan and cook over medium coals 25 to 30 minutes. To cook in a sheepherder oven, use an open roasting pan and cook 10 minutes before removing the leaves and adding the broth, then cover the pan and cook an additional 15 minutes. In the kitchen range, use an open pan and cook 20 minutes at 375 degrees before removing leaves and adding broth, then close the roasting pan and cook 20 minutes more at the same temperature. Serve a portion of the pan juices with each bird.

Serves 4.

## STUFFED SPIT-ROAST GROUSE

This recipe is for young birds only.

| | |
|---|---|
| 4 grouse | ¼ teaspoon salt |
| 2 cups fine dry bread crumbs | large dash of Nepal pepper or |
| ¼ cup minced fresh parsley | larger dash of cayenne |
| 1 sprig fresh thyme or 1 | 2 tablespoons butter |
| teaspoon powdered thyme | ½ cup dry red wine |
| ½ teaspoon celery seed | butter for basting |

Combine the bread crumbs with the herbs and seasonings. Melt the butter in the wine over very low heat, and use this to moisten the dressing. Stuff each bird, close the cavities by sewing or with small skewers, truss the legs. Cook on revolving spit over medium-bright coals 15 to 18 minutes, basting generously with butter. Should you want to use older birds in a stuffed-bird dish, use the above stuffing, butter the birds heavily inside and out, cook in an open roasting pan in the sheepherder oven for 10 to 12 minutes; in the kitchen range, 15 minutes at 400 degrees.

Serves 4.

## Pheasant

Since a pheasant is about the size of a young frying chicken, many cooks look on these birds as fodder for the skillet. Actually, the skillet can be the pheasant's worst enemy. The grill and spit can be the bird's enemies, too, unless in using them you select young birds and prepare them properly for cooking.

It's easier to identify a young pheasant than it is most other wild-fowl. In a young bird the first wing-tip feather is pointed, and as the bird ages this feather grows round at the tip. In their tender years, cock pheasants have short, rounded spurs. Young pheasant of both sexes have light gray legs, soft breastbones, pliable beaks. With age the legs grow dark and roughen, the breastbone and bill become firm and hard. The claws also indicate age—the older the bird, the more rounded, blunt, and split the claws will be.

We have already covered, on page 129, the aging of these wild-fowl. Let the bird's age determine the method by which it is to be cooked. Reserve the grill and spit for young and tender birds, and never fry a pheasant as you would a chicken. If your soul yearns for fried chicken, buy one and fry it, and reserve more suitable methods of cooking for pheasant.

### PHEASANT IN SOUR CREAM

This recipe is particularly suited to old birds.

| | |
|---|---|
| 2 pheasants | 1 pint milk |
| ½ pound butter | ½ pint sour cream |
| ½ cup flour | salt, pepper |

Cut the pheasant into serving pieces. Rub each piece with butter and roll in flour. Melt all of the remaining butter in a deep, heavy skillet and sauté the birds very gently at low heat until their skin turns a light tan. Sauté—not fry—8 to 10 minutes. Beat together the milk and sour cream, pour into the skillet, and stir to blend with the butter in the pan. Close the skillet tightly and let cook very slowly. Do not allow the contents to reach boiling heat or the milk will curdle. At the correct low temperature, cooking time will be 45 minutes to 1 hour, depending on the age of the birds. When the legs are tender, the birds are done. Taste and adjust seasoning of the sauce before serving, and serve each portion generously covered with sauce.
Serves 4.

### GRILLED PHEASANT

| | |
|---|---|
| 2 pheasants, use only young, tender birds | 3 tablespoons butter |
| ¼ to ½ cup milk | salt, pepper |
| 2 cups very dry, very fine bread crumbs | |

**136**

Open the birds by cutting the ribs along one side of the backbone with a sharp knife or poultry shears. Press flat, breaking the breastbone. Dip each bird in milk and press firmly into the bread crumbs to coat thoroughly. Heat butter and sauté lightly until a crust forms on the birds. Remove to grill and cook over bright coals breastside down 4 to 5 minutes, basting with butter from the skillet; turn and cook 5 to 7 minutes, continuing to baste. Season after cooking.

Serves 4.


## HUNTER-STYLE PHEASANT

On a late fall fishing trip to Chiquita Lake in the California Sierras, in about 1940, Dolf Martinelli, who produces some very superior olive oil in his plant in Madera, California, introduced me to this cacciatore-style pheasant.

| | |
|---|---|
| 2 pheasants; select young birds | 1 small sweet onion |
| ½ cup finest light olive oil | ½ sweet green (Bell) pepper |
| ¼ cup dry red wine | 6 to 8 small button mushrooms |
| 2 or 3 small red ripe tomatoes | salt |

Wipe the birds inside and out with a cloth dipped in lightly salted water, about 1 teaspoon of salt per quart of water. Wipe dry, then rub a thin coating of oil on the birds, inside and out. Mix the remainder of the oil with the wine. Quarter the tomatoes and onions, cut the pepper into coarse chunks, halve the mushrooms lengthwise, and sprinkle with a very scanty pinch of salt. Soak these ingredients in the oil-wine mixture 10 to 15 minutes. Drain, letting the liquid return to the bowl. Divide the tomatoes, onions, peppers, and mushrooms between the two birds, putting them loosely in the cavities. Close crop and belly cavities by sewing; it is important that both be tightly closed.

Grill the birds breast down for 15 minutes over low coals, basting with the leftover oil-wine mixture. Turn and cook 15 minutes more, continuing to baste. Finish with the birds breast down on the grill for 10 minutes.

**137**

**Upland Game Birds**

To cook on the spit, the coals should be low and cooking time 40 to 45 minutes, with constant basting. In a sheepherder oven, put the birds in an open pan over very low coals, and baste frequently; cooking time 30 to 40 minutes. In the kitchen oven, use an open pan, baste often, and cook 50 minutes at 275 degrees.

The secret of this style of cooking is to close the cavities well, and use very low heat; the extended cooking time allows fragrant steam from the stuffing to penetrate the bird's flesh.

Serves 4.


### PHEASANT WITH VEGETABLES

| | |
|---|---|
| 2 pheasants; age not important if cooking time is not a factor | 1 cup coarsely diced carrots |
| | 1 cup coarsely diced turnips |
| ½ cup dry gin | 1 cup coarsely minced onion |
| pinch of salt, dusting of pepper | 2 cups game stock, chicken |
| ¼ pound butter | stock, or broth |
| 2 stalks firm green celery, cut in 1-inch pieces | 1 teaspoon salt |

Rub the birds inside and out with gin and dust lightly with salt and pepper. Put them breast up in a warm Dutch oven, warm the gin, and pour it over the birds and light it. Let it burn out. Put the pan on low coals, and melt the butter. Cook the vegetables in the butter 10 minutes, stirring occasionally. Pour in the warmed broth or stock, add salt. Close the Dutch oven and bury it in coals. For a young bird, cook 45 minutes to 1 hour; for old, tough birds, extend the cooking time to 2 hours. You cannot overcook in the Dutch oven. If a sheepherder oven is used, cook in a tightly closed pan, 30 to 40 minutes for young birds, older birds until they test tender at the legs. In the kitchen oven, follow procedure for the sheepherder oven and cook at 275 degrees until the bird tests tender. Serve a portion of the broth and vegetables with each half-bird.

Serves 4 very generously.

**138**

## RUSSIAN-STYLE PHEASANT

If you must cook a pheasant just brought down, or if you encounter a tough old cock that you fear will defy any other method,
here's your answer. It's not included just because it will tame an
ancient bird, though. It's an unusual and delicious dish in its own
right.

| | |
|---|---|
| 2 pheasants | ⅛ teaspoon salt |
| thin slices of pork fat, salt pork, or fat bacon | large dash freshly ground black pepper |
| ¾ cup orange juice | 1 tablespoon meat extract |
| 1 cup undiluted grape juice | (BV, Bovril, etc.) or ¼ cup |
| ½ cup red port | concentrated meat stock pre- |
| ½ cup very strong green tea | pared by reducing ½ cup |
| ¼ cup butter | stock one half its original |
| 3 cups walnut meats—halves are best | volume |

Cover the breasts of the birds with thin slices of pork fat, salt
pork, or bacon; if salt pork is used, trim off rinds and blanch in
boiling water 1 or 2 minutes. Truss the birds' legs. Mix strained
orange juice, grape juice, port, and tea; keep the mixture warm,
but do not heat even to a simmer.

Melt half the butter in a Dutch oven over low coals and sauté the
walnut meats for a minute or two, turning them and stirring so they
will brown evenly. Put the trussed birds into the pan on top of the
walnut meats. Pour the liquid mixture into the pan over the birds,
close the Dutch oven, and bury in coals for 1 hour, or longer if you
wish.

When you lift out the birds, remove and discard fat or bacon. Melt
remaining butter in a heavy skillet and brown the birds, turning to
allow them to tan evenly. Transfer to a heated platter. Strain the
liquid from the Dutch oven into the skillet, stir in the meat extract or
stock. Taste and adjust seasoning with salt and pepper as needed.

Pour this sauce over the birds on their platter, or pass separately to be poured over individual portions after the birds have been carved. Serves 4.

### SAUCED SPIT-ROAST PHEASANT

| | |
|---|---|
| 2 pheasants; use young birds only | 1 cup mushroom buttons, fresh or canned |
| livers from the pheasant | ¼ cup onion pulp scraped or grated fine |
| 2 tangerines, peeled and broken into sections | 2 tablespoons flour |
| pork fat or salt pork in thin strips for larding | 4 juniper berries |
| ¼ cup butter | 2 cups Marsala |

Score the livers lightly with the tip of a sharp knife; put a liver and the sections of one tangerine into the cavity of each bird. Lard the birds with strips of fat in the backs, breasts, and legs. If salt pork is used, blanch the strips in boiling water for 1 minute. Spit-roast over bright coals 15 to 20 minutes, until the skin is brown and crisp.

In a Dutch oven or a deep heavy skillet with a tightly fitting lid, sauté the mushrooms gently in the butter, adding the onion pulp as the mushrooms cook. Parboil fresh mushrooms 1 minute in boiling water. Push the mushrooms to the sides of the skillet, sprinkle flour in the center of the pan, and stir until the flour is browned. Crush the juniper berries in the bottom of the pan, pour in the Marsala, stir until smooth. Put the pheasants in the pan, spoon the sauce over them, and close the pan. Put over very dark coals for 20 to 25 minutes. This dish can be cooked in a sheepherder stove by using a roasting pan with a tightly fitting lid, and preparing the sauce in a separate skillet; pour the sauce over the birds in the roasting pan, cover pan, and cook 15 minutes.

Serves 4.

## Pigeons

Though yesterday's massive flights of wild passenger pigeons belong to history, there are places where varieties of these small game birds fly in quantity today—the passes in Southern California's Tehachapi Mountains, along the Arizona-Mexico border, and in northern Mexico. And commercial breeders are always ready to supply a pigeon for your pot. Remember that recipes tagged for doves and reed birds are also suitable for use in cooking pigeons, and vice versa.

### FIELD-COOKED PIGEONS

| | |
|---|---|
| 8 pigeons | ¾ cup brandy |
| ½ pound butter | scanty pinch of salt |
| 1 small sweet onion, minced very fine | dash of freshly ground black pepper |

After plucking and drawing, split the birds up the back, remove backbone and ribs, heads, and legs. Heat butter to foaming in heavy skillet over bright coals. Flatten the birds and drop them split side down into the butter; cook 2 or 3 at a time so as not to crowd the pan. Cook 3 minutes, turn, cook 3 to 4 minutes; drain butter back into pan, put birds on warm platter. When all the birds have been cooked, sprinkle the onion over the butter remaining in the skillet. As the onion begins to brown, dash the brandy in the skillet and let the mixture boil up. Remove from fire, stir in salt and pepper to taste. Pour the sauce over the pigeons and serve.

Serves 3 or 4; an allowance of 3 birds per person is more generous.

### PIGEON POT PIE

When Passenger pigeons in migration darkened the skies across most of the central U.S., this is the pot pie that appeared regularly on dinner tables; many pioneer families were saved from starvation by it. Traditionally the pie is cooked in a spider, using a precooked top crust of a pan-sized biscuit baked earlier in the same utensil. Since spiders are relatively rare, even among dedicated outdoor chefs, plain biscuits and the Dutch oven are used in the recipe that follows.

| | |
|---|---|
| 6 or 8 pigeons, plucked and drawn | ½ teaspoon salt |
| thin slices of pork fat, salt pork, or fat bacon | large pinch of pepper |
| 2 cups minced green onions, including tops, or sweet onion | 2 cups chicken broth, veal broth, or meat gravy |
| 1 cup parsley, minced fine | 2 tablespoons butter |
| 6 hard-boiled eggs | 2 tablespoons flour |
| | 1 pan-sized biscuit, or 6 to 8 small biscuits |

Line the bottom of the pan with thin slices of pork fat, salt pork, or bacon; if salt pork is used, trim off rinds and blanch in boiling water for 1 or 2 minutes. Bring the fat up the sides of the pan 3 to 4 inches. Sprinkle a generous coating of minced onions over the fat in the pan. Cut the pigeons into quarters, rub the pieces lightly with butter, and roll each piece in the minced parsley to coat it well. Lay the pieces of pigeon in the pan. Dice the eggs coarsely and sprinkle the pieces on and around the pieces of pigeon. Dust lightly with salt and pepper. In a separate pan, bring the broth to a simmer. Knead the flour and butter into a smooth paste and flake bits of it into the broth. Stir until all flour is dissolved. (Alternatively, you can melt the butter in a pan and sprinkle it with flour, stir into a golden-tan paste, and pour in the broth, stirring it until smooth.) You want a sauce or gravy about the consistency of heavy cream. If gravy is used, do not prepare a thickened sauce; just thin the gravy with a little hot water. Pour the sauce into the pan, close the Dutch oven, and bury in coals 45 minutes to 1 hour. Remove from coals, uncover, and top with a single pan-sized biscuit split in two or with regular-sized biscuits. Ladle into deep bowls, serving a portion of the crust with each helping.

This pie can be made with a pastry crust topping in either a sheepherder stove or kitchen range. Use a deep casserole-type pan and when all ingredients except the top crust have been added, cook uncovered for 30 minutes in the sheepherder stove, or 45 minutes at 350 degrees in the kitchen oven. Then spread the pastry crust over the pan, slashing it to vent steam. It may be necessary to add more broth or gravy when the pie is cooked this way. Once the crust is in place, return it to the oven and cook until nicely browned.

Serves about 6.

## Quail

Simplicity should be the keynote when cooking quail, for the nutlike flavor of these small birds needs little embellishment. Quail have a bit more fat than most upland birds, and it accumulates in the same places that it does on humans. So, to judge a quail's age, prod it at belly, breast, and backside. In young birds, the fatty deposits will be soft and yielding, while in older ones the fat will be firm, even hard. Flexibility of breastbone, condition of claws—blunted and split on older birds—and roughness of leg are other indications of age. Quail are readily available through commercial channels, while the quail's best domestic substitute, Rock Cornish game hens, will be found in nearly every supermarket freezer.

### GRILLED QUAIL

| | |
|---|---|
| 8 quail; young, tender birds | 1½ teaspoons paprika |
| ½ cup butter (¼ pound) | salt |

Split the birds along the backbone by cutting the ribs on one side with a sharp knife or poultry shears. (Some cooks like to remove both backbone and ribs.) Flatten the birds on a firm surface by pressing with the heel of a hand to break the breastbone. Knead the paprika into the butter until it is evenly distributed, and spread the birds generously on both sides. Cook breast down over bright coals for 3 to 4 minutes, basting once or twice with the remaining seasoned butter. Turn and cook 4 to 5 minutes with the bone side down, basting with more of the seasoned butter. Dust with a very scanty sprinkling of salt after taking the birds off the grill. A *roti,* or vertical grill, as described on page 16, is very handy for grilling small game birds in the fashion just described.

Serves 4.

### SPIT-ROAST QUAIL

This method really needs no formal recipe with its list of ingredients. You will need ½ teaspoon of butter for each bird cooked, and enough thin slices of pork fat, salt pork, or fat bacon for barding the birds. If salt pork is used, the rinds should be trimmed and the meat blanched in boiling water for 1 minute. To add an extra haunting of flavor to spit-roast quail, wrap them in grape, fig, or cabbage leaves. The best procedure is to knead a little salt and pepper into the butter to be used, wrap ½ teaspoon of the seasoned butter in a leaf of the same kind that will encase the bird, and place this in the cavity. Then, wrap the quail in a leaf—two if the leaves are small—and over this put the pork barding, covering the bird completely. Secure the outer wrapping with twine, spit the birds, and cook them 10 to 12 minutes over bright coals. Then remove the barding and leaf and cook another 3 to 4 minutes to brown the bird, basting during this final cooking period with drippings from the pan which you have foresightedly placed under the revolving spit.

Allow 2 quail per serving.

### QUAIL WITH MUSHROOMS IN WINE

| | |
|---|---|
| 6 quail; young or old birds can be used | 1 cup chicken broth or stock, or game broth or stock |
| ½ pound butter (no substitutes) | 1 stalk celery |
| ⅓ cup flour | pinch of salt, dash of pepper |
| 2 cups mushrooms, fresh or canned | juice of 2 oranges (about ½ cup) |
| 1½ cups dry red wine | |

Split the birds in half along breastbone and backbone. Rub lightly with butter, then roll in flour to coat each piece thoroughly. Divide the butter into two parts; use half in one skillet to sauté the quail very, very gently, about 4 minutes per side, until lightly browned. If necessary, cook in two batches, keeping those cooked first warm on a hot platter. With the remaining butter, sauté the mushrooms in a separate pan. Fresh mushrooms should be sliced lengthwise and parboiled 1 to 2 minutes before sautéeing; canned mushrooms need only be drained well and heated in the butter.

Arrange all the quail halves in the skillet in which they were browned, spread the mushrooms over them, and pour in the juices from the pan in which the mushrooms were cooked. Mix the wine and broth or stock, add a scant pinch of salt and a small dash of pepper, and pour over the mushrooms and quail. Lay the stalk of celery on top. Close the pan tightly and cook 30 to 40 minutes over very gentle heat. Remove the celery stalk, pour in the orange juice, cover the skillet and remove from heat after 2 to 3 minutes. Let stand 10 minutes before serving. A good service for this dish is to put a mound of boiled rice in the center of a warmed plate, circle the rice with three quail halves, put mushrooms on the rice, and ladle some pan juices over all.

Serves 4.

### QUAIL PIE

This improbable recipe dates back to covered-wagon days. It's been slightly updated, but in spirit remains the same. It stretches a little bit a long way, and it saves a lot of trouble for the cook.

| | | | |
|---|---|---|---|
| 4 | quail, young birds or old | ¾ | teaspoon salt |
| ¼ | cup butter | ¼ | teaspoon sugar |
| ½ | cup green peas or green beans | ¾ | cup milk |
| ½ | cup diced carrots | 2⅓ | cups chicken broth or game stock |
| ½ | cup minced onion | | |
| 1¼ | cups flour | ½ | teaspoon cornstarch |
| 2½ | teaspoons baking powder | | pinch of nutmeg |

Split the quail up the back, take out backbone and ribs and the leg bones, and quarter the carcasses. Rub the bottom and sides of a Dutch oven with a sparse coating of butter and brown the pieces of quail very lightly over medium coals. Remove and set aside on a warm platter. If fresh vegetables are being used, parboil them 3 to 4 minutes in lightly salted water and drain well. If canned vegetables are used, drain them well.

Sift together flour, baking powder, salt, and sugar. Stir these into the milk to make a smooth, lump-free batter. Combine the pieces of quail and the vegetables with this batter in the cooking pan, mixing them with a very light touch. Warm the broth or stock and stir into it the cornstarch, nutmeg, and the remaining butter. When the butter has melted, pour this liquid over the batter in the pan. Close the Dutch oven and bury in coals for 1 to 1½ hours. You can use a sheepherder stove or kitchen range, cooking the pie in a roasting pan or deep casserole-type pan with a tightly-fitting cover. In the sheepherder stove cook 45 to 50 minutes; in the kitchen oven, 55 minutes at 375 degrees.

As the cooking proceeds, the batter will separate from the solids in the pan, and rise to form a crust floating on top of them, while the pieces of quail and vegetables settle down to simmer in the bubbling juices. But please don't be tempted to open the pan and watch the process at work; if you do, it won't work. The pan must stay closed during the entire cooking period.

Serves 6 to 8.


## Turkey

The wild turkey, once so prominent a feature of the American scene that Benjamin Franklin proposed that it, rather than the eagle, be named our national bird, today is returning to places where he has not been seen for decades. After a long period of decline, extensive propagation and resettlement programs by state game departments have brought the turkey back to the point where it may now be hunted in about twenty states.

My own baptism in hunting this bird was supervised by Gene Schneider of Borger, Texas, who spends most of his spare hours seeking out new hunting spots. Gene's chattering cedarbox brought out the birds in a wooded area near Lake Marvin, which lies on the Texas-Oklahoma border.

A wild turkey is a streamlined fowl, no comparison to the deep-breasted one you buy in butcher shops. It has more leg than breast meat; the back carries as much flesh as the breast. Like the farmyard turkeys of forty or fifty years ago, the wild turkey needs preparation before being cooked. The Dutch oven does the best job of tenderizing the bird's too solid flesh. If you want to spit-roast a turkey, get a commercially bred bird, or better still a squab turkey.

A wild turkey's age can be told by the reticulation of the tom's wattles, which grow rougher with the years. Feet and claws are also good indicators; on old birds the leg-skin roughens and the claws break and split. Any wild turkey should be hung, after drawing but before plucking, for three to four days in a cool, dry place. After plucking, the carcass is wiped inside and out with a cloth dipped in water in which baking soda has been dissolved; about 1 tablespoon of soda to a gallon of water. Following its soda bath, wipe the carcass down with a cloth dampened in plain water, then plunge the bird into a pot of boiling water, remove the pot from heat, and leave the turkey in it 15 to 20 minutes. Drain well before cooking by any of the following recipes, which are as suitable for other large fowl such as guinea hens, sandhill cranes, or domestic turkeys as they are for wild birds.

### ROAST WILD TURKEY

12- to 15-pound turkey
2 cups coarse bread crumbs; the best stuffing mixture is composed of ¾ white home-baked or solid French or sourdough bread and ¼ cornbread
1 cup bacon or salt pork, blanched and diced coarsely
¼ cup minced parsley
½ cup chopped celery, including a few leaves
½ cup chopped nutmeats, walnuts or pecans
1 teaspoon salt
¼ teaspoon pepper
¼ teaspoon sage or oregano or a mixture of the two
½ cup melted butter
2 to 2½ cups dry white wine
1 egg

It's assumed that your wild bird has been prepared for stuffing as described in the paragraph preceding this recipe. Commercial birds do not need this preparation, of course.

Combine bread crumbs, bacon, parsley, celery, nutmeats, salt, pepper, and sage or oregano. Moisten them with the butter and wine, beat the egg lightly, and toss the stuffing ingredients while adding it. Stuff both cavities loosely—do not pack in the dressing. Close the cavities by sewing or with skewers and truss the legs loosely, and secure the wings close to the body by looping a length of cord around the first-wing joint and drawing it tight across the back of the bird.

Rub the bird with butter or oil. Put on a rack in the Dutch oven and pour about ¼ inch of water, or water and wine mixed in equal parts, into the pan. The liquid should not touch the bird. Close the oven and bury it in coals 3½ to 4 hours; 16 to 20 minutes per pound. Because of the extended cooking period required, the sheep-herder stove is not recommended. If you want to use the kitchen range, soak a 24-inch-square piece of clean white cloth in melted butter or peanut oil and drape this over the bird, in an open roasting pan with no rack. Tuck the corners of the cloth around the bird so they touch the pan's bottom. Cook 20 minutes per pound at 275 degrees, without basting; the cloth acts as a wick to pull up the pan juices and distribute them over the bird's breast as it cooks. In cooking a commercially produced turkey by either of the above methods, reduce cooking time 3 to 4 minutes per pound.

A 12-pound turkey will serve 8 to 10, and there will be leftovers.

## SPIT-ROAST TURKEY

To repeat, spit-roasting is recommended only for small turkeys, less than 10 pounds in weight, and the best birds for spit-roasting are the small squab turkeys weighing 6 to 8 pounds. If you want a larger quantity of meat than one provides, roast two. Spit-roasting is not recommended for stuffed turkeys. Instead, put a piece of pork fat or bacon in the cavity along with some pieces of celery and a sprig or two of fresh marjoram; or use the dried herb and roll the fat in it. Big birds to be spit-roasted should be barded, that is, covered with thin slices of pork fat or thin slices of salt pork blanched 1 minute in boiling water. Cooking time over bright coals will be 25 to 28 minutes per pound, with the barding removed during the final 8 to 10 minutes and the bird basted with butter in which a generous pinch of paprika has been mixed—the chemical reaction of the paprika to heat keeps the skin from getting leathery as it browns. After the bird is cooked, let it stand about 10 minutes before carving to allow the flesh to firm up and the juices to set.

## TURKEY HOT POT

When oldtime range cooks fed the hands with freshly killed wild turkey, this was the recipe they used. It doesn't really matter how old and tough a turkey is, this stew tames it. Even if the objective isn't to tame a tough wild bird, the Hot Pot is worth cooking for its own hearty good eating.

## Upland Game Birds

12- to 15-pound turkey
¼ pound butter
1 cup flour
1 teaspoon salt
2 large onions minced very fine
4 large red ripe tomatoes, or a #2 can of tomatoes

¼ cup bourbon or brandy or ½ cup sweet vermouth
2 teaspoons salt
½ teaspoon chili molido

Cut the turkey into about 20 pieces. Use part of the butter to grease the bottom and sides of your Dutch oven and melt the remainder in a heavy skillet over medium coals. Rub each piece of turkey thoroughly with the flour and salt combined, then brown the pieces lightly in the skillet before transferring them to the Dutch oven. Using the butter left in the skillet, sauté the onions until they begin to become transparent. Scald and peel the tomatoes (a nicety not practiced by range cooks, but one that adds to the attractiveness of the finished dish) and chop them over the skillet so the juices are retained. Cook until both tomatoes and onions are tender, and the tomatoes can be pulped with a fork. (Canned tomatoes, of course, need only be heated and large pieces broken up as they cook.) When the tomatoes are pulped, add the liquor, salt, and chili molido; simmer for 10 minutes, then pour the contents of the skillet into the Dutch oven over the pieces of turkey. Add hot water to cover. (If you have some chicken stock or broth on hand, it can be used instead of water.) Cover the oven and bury it in coals 1½ to 2 hours.

This dish can be prepared in the sheepherder oven or kitchen oven, using a tightly closed roasting pan. Cooking time in the sheepherder stove will be about 1 hour; in the kitchen oven, cook 1½ hours at 300 degrees. In both these alternative ovens you can test the turkey for tenderness.

Serves 10 to 12.

### TURKEY MOLE

This great classic dish of Mexico, with its subtle seasonings, evolved when cooking in that country was customarily done on a *parilla,* the equivalent of a sheepherder stove, which usually was located on the patio just outside the kitchen door. Other fowl can be cooked in mole sauce (pronounced *mo-lay*), but turkey responds best.

10- to 12-pound turkey, cut in pieces
1 to 1½ cups milk
¾ to 1 cup *masa de harina* or flour
2 to 4 cups lard or cooking oil
6 mild red peppers, fresh or dried
3 or 4 very hot small red peppers, fresh or dried
3 cups chicken or turkey stock or broth
½ teaspoon *cominos* (cumin)

1 cup raw *piñon* nuts or peanuts
2 tablespoons *masa de harina* or fine white corn meal
2 cloves garlic
2 large red ripe tomatoes or the equivalent in solid-pack canned tomatoes
½ teaspoon powdered cloves
1 teaspoon cinnamon
2 tablespoons bitter dark chocolate—*not* milk chocolate

Before beginning the preparation of the Mole, let's look at the ingredients, with some of which you may not be familiar. Peppers are the character-imparting ingredients, and the best Mexican cooks prefer the long, red Anchas or the reddish-purple Chimayos. Ripe Jalapeños would be third choice, with red-ripe Bell peppers a poor fourth. Mexican peppers in dried form are widely available today, especially the Chimayos. Sun-dried peppers should be parboiled in simmering water for 4 or 5 minutes before being used in the sauce. The small hot peppers called for can be Tepines, Pepines, or Japonais, all of which are very hot indeed, and available whole at most stores having a good selection of spices. *Masa de harina* is a corn meal ground nearly as fine as flour; indeed, it is the flour of Mexico. It is packaged commercially and distributed under that name; its green, white, and red carton or bag will be found in most supermarkets. If you cannot find it, use a fine-ground white cornmeal. Now, on with the cooking.

Dip the turkey pieces in milk and coat them heavily with the *masa,* corn meal, or flour, reserving 2 tablespoons, and set them aside

**151**

on waxed paper in a warm place for the coating to dry. This will take 30 minutes to 1 hour.

Heat enough lard or oil in your deep cooking pot to give you a 3-inch-deep pool of bubbling fat. Fry the unseeded, unskinned peppers in this fat for 5 minutes. Drain them, letting the oil drip back into the pot, then open the pods, discard the seeds, and scrape the pulp from the skins. Mash this pulp into a smooth paste. Deep-fry the floured pieces of turkey in the oil used to cook the peppers. Cook 6 to 8 minutes; the meat should be brown, but underdone. Drain the pieces and put them into a deep stewing kettle that can be tightly closed—the Dutch oven is ideal, but any deep casserole-type pan that can double as a top-of-stove or over-coals utensil will serve. Cover the turkey with broth or stock and simmer gently, with the lid on the pot, for 20 to 30 minutes.

Using a dry pan, without oil or grease, parch the *cominos* and nutmeats together, stirring them often so they will not scorch. Pound the seeds and nutmeats into a fine powder, using a mortar or rolling pin, or the blender if you're cooking indoors. Don't put them through a metal meat grinder, as the oil in the nuts will cause the meats to blacken. Using 2 or 3 tablespoons of the oil in which the peppers and turkey cooked, sauté the peeled garlic cloves until they are soft. Mash them with the oil into a smooth paste. Combine this paste with the pulp from the fried peppers and the seed-nut-meat powder, and blend it with the peeled tomatoes and their juices, using a potato masher. While blending, add 2 tablespoons of *masa* or cornmeal, the cloves, and the cinnamon. Spoon in enough of the fat in which the peppers and turkey cooked to bring this mixture to a thick liquid, the consistency of a heavy cream soup. Pour this over the slowly simmering turkey pieces, close the pot, and simmer gently for 1 to 1½ hours, or until the turkey meat is falling from the bones. Lift the bones from the pot, if you wish; some cooks do this, some don't.

Just before serving, stir in the chocolate. When it has blended with the sauce, dish up pieces of meat with some of the sauce onto warm plates. If only a portion of the dish is to be served, do not add chocolate to the portion reserved for future use. The sauce keeps well, refrigerated or frozen, but chocolate should be added only when the sauce is simmering a few moments before being served.

Serves 10 to 12 generously.

## TURKEY TERRAPIN

Another classic turkey recipe, this time from the southeastern U.S., is an old plantation dish, the regional equivalent to Turkey Mole. Its name refers to a style of cooking commonly employed in preparing the meat of the terrapin that was so prevalent in that area years ago.

| | |
|---|---|
| 4 cups dark meat of turkey, in small dice; or any dark meat of fowl or small game | 3 cups heavy cream (undiluted evaporated milk can be used) |
| 1 pair calf sweetbreads, cleaned and blanched | 1 teaspoon cornstarch |
| | ½ cup milk |
| 1½ pints water | 1 egg yolk |
| 1 tablespoon vinegar | 1 cup medium-dry sherry |
| 1¼ teaspoons salt | dash of cayenne or Nepal pepper |

Bring water to a brisk boil, add vinegar and 1 tsp salt, and drop in the sweetbreads. Cook 10 minutes and add the turkey meat. Cook 4 to 5 minutes, drain. Dice the sweetbreads. Warm the cream, but do not allow to boil. Mix the cornstarch with ¼ cup of the milk, beat the egg yolk with the other ¼ cup, and add both to the hot cream. Stir in the diced turkey and sweetbreads and cook 3 to 5 minutes without boiling. Add the sherry, pepper and ¼ tsp salt. Remove from heat, let stand 5 minutes, and serve over boiled rice, crisp dry toast, or split toasted biscuit halves.

Serves 6 to 8.

## Game Bird Giblets

Innards of wildfowl, especially those of wild ducks, carry unpredictable flavors. However, the proper treatment makes such nuggets as livers, hearts, and the less-desirable gizzards both edible and delicious. Preliminary to using hearts and gizzards, they should be scored lightly with a knife tip and parboiled in lightly salted water for 10 minutes, then drained well. Or they can be marinated in water to which has been added the juice of a lemon (about 3 tablespoons) or 2 tablespoons cider vinegar, for 45 minutes to 1 hour. As with giblets that have been parboiled, they should be well drained and blotted dry. The recipe for Turkey Terrapin works well with giblets. So does the following.

### GIBLETS IN WHITE WINE

3 to 4 cups of giblets: hearts, gizzards, livers; all pieces should be parboiled or marinated, and if any strange odors have been encountered when the birds were cleaned, the livers should be treated like the hearts and gizzards

3 tablespoons butter

2 tablespoons flour

½ teaspoon salt

1 cup dry white wine

2 cups chicken stock or broth

1 cup cooked rice

2 celery hearts or hearts of palm

sprig or two of parsley, a few celery leaves, sprig of fresh thyme or marjoram or a few flakes of dry thyme or marjoram

dash of freshly ground white pepper

Melt 1½ teaspoons butter in a skillet over gentle heat. Slice the giblets, rub them in flour and dust lightly with salt, then sauté gently until very delicately browned. Mix wine and broth and pour into the pan over the giblets, close pan and simmer softly 25 to 30 minutes, or until the gizzard pieces (which will be the last to get done) are tender.

In a separate skillet, using the remaining butter, warm the rice and coarsely chopped celery or palm hearts, sprinkled with the herbs and pepper. Cook just long enough to warm the rice and marry the flavors of the herbs. Serve with the giblet pieces stirred into the rice and the broth poured over them, or put a bed of rice on warmed

**154**

plates and strew giblet pieces on top of it, ladling some of the broth over each portion.

Serves 4 to 6.

## Game Bird Soup

When game birds were plentiful, many hunter-chefs served only the breasts, or the bird carcasses from which legs and wings had been removed. The less desirable legs and wings went into the soup pot, along with the necks, coarse back-skin and the picked skeletons. In preparing the following soup, do use the bird's bones for added richness.

2 to 3 cups of meat from wings, backs, legs, plus the necks, plus any coarse pieces of skin and the bones

*bouquet garni* of parsley, thyme, celery leaves, 2 or 3 whole cloves, a pinch of mustardseed

1 onion, minced

2 stalks of celery, minced

3 chicken bouillon cubes or 2 teaspoons bouillon granules or 1 tablespoon meat extract (BV, Bovril, etc.)

½ teaspoon salt
large pinch pepper
¼ cup medium-dry sherry

Reserve all pieces of edible meat that will be left in the soup, and chop them coarsely. Put wing tips, skin, and bones into a large bag with the herbs. Put the pieces of meat into the soup pot with 2½ quarts cold water, add the *bouquet garni* bag with the inedible portions, and simmer gently for 1 hour. Remove and discard the bag. Add the minced onion, celery, and bouillon cubes or granules or meat extract. (Read the labels of any meat concentrates you buy; some of these contain no meat, but are composed of salted hydrolized vegetable protein only.) Stir in salt and pepper, simmer 10 to 15 minutes, taste and adjust seasonings. Pour in the sherry, stir well, remove from heat. Let stand 5 minutes before serving.

Serves 6 to 8.

## Preserved Game Birds

You should check local game laws before preserving any game, for some states limit the time during which wild game may be in possession after seasons close. Nor are these laws uniformly interpreted; in some states they apply only to refrigerated or frozen game, in others to game preserved by any method at all.

Any type of upland game bird can be preserved, if you have jars with mouths wide enough to accommodate the carcasses. Preserving is not recommended for any duck except teal. For small birds, the standard pint wide-mouth fruit jar will be adequate, and will hold two carcasses of quail or teal, three or four doves, pigeons, or jacksnipe. Wide-mouth quart jars will take small pheasant and woodcock, and for bigger birds there are half-gallon wide-mouth jars available.

Recipe is based on 6 quail, using 3 wide-mouth pint jars; quantities should be increased for bigger birds and larger jars.

| | |
|---|---|
| 6 quail | ¼ cup each grated onion, |
| ½ cup cubed salt pork, rinds trimmed, blanched in boiling water 1 to 2 minutes and drained | carrot, and celery |
| | 3 cups dry white wine |
| | 1 teaspoon salt |
| | 6 cracked peppercorns |

Combine the salt pork and grated vegetables, spread the mixture on the bottom of a deep, heavy pot, and lay the birds on top of it. Pour in the wine; the birds should be completely covered, and additional wine added if needed. Add salt, bring to a boil, then simmer over gentle heat for 30 minutes. Add the peppercorns during the final 10 minutes of cooking—if peppercorns simmer too long they bring a bitterness to any dish. Remove the pot from heat and let stand overnight in a cool but not refrigerated place.

Sterilize the jars to be used by putting them into briskly boiling water 3 or 4 minutes; do not let them cool before using. Lift the quail from the cooking pot, without wiping or draining them, and put a

**156**

pair in each hot jar. Strain the pan juices and fill the jars to within ¾ inch of the top, being sure the quail are covered completely. If there is not enough juice, add wine to fill the jars. Close the jars but do not seal. Process 40 minutes in a pressure canner, 2½ hours in a water-bath cooker. Seal the jars at once when removed from canning bath, by tightening the lids. Set in a cool place. You can tell whether the jars are sealed, as each one will close itself with a loud "snap" and the lids will ring a light brilliant note when tapped with a fingernail. Jars that have not sealed will sound a dismal, dull "thud."

Birds processed this way will keep up to a year, which is far longer than recommended freezer storage time. In serving, the birds can be removed from the jars and heated in the liquid contents, or dried well and sautéed gently to warm them—or eaten cold just as they come from the jar. Chopped meat of processed game birds mixed with a parsleyed butter or herbed butter and spread on crisp toast rounds or crackers makes very fine hors d'oeuvres.

# VII

---

# Fresh-Water Fish

WITH TODAY's fast, refrigerated shipping facilities, it is indeed an isolated region that does not have fresh fish available. The fish may be fresh-frozen, but you can still cook it tastily.

In the smaller towns of inland areas, the choice may be limited to ready-cut fillets from the frozen food bin, or the semi-prepared products unblushingly called "breaded fish sticks" or "fish fingers." It is possible to cook respectable dishes with frozen fillets, but the "breaded" products are suitable for nothing but frying and some of them are not even fit to be fried. Under standards established by federal food regulations, any "breaded fish" product need only contain 40 per cent fish—the rest can be bread or fillers. Few of the "breaded fish" products exceed this minimum requirement. If you buy fish in frozen form, buy whole fish or unaltered fillets.

If you catch your fish, you learned long ago that all fish must be cleaned at once after being removed from the water, and "at once" does not mean after you've finished a half-day in a boat or wading a stream. Atlantic salmon caught in fresh water are the only fish that should not be cleaned until just before cooking. Most fishermen make a virtue of the necessity of cleaning their catch, but most fishermen have not bothered to learn the easy way to clean a fish. Many other-

**158**

wise expert anglers take five or ten minutes to do a job that should take at most thirty seconds.

Almost without exception, the tongue, gills, gullet, and intestinal cluster of fish form a single unit. Start to clean your fish at the head, not the vent. Open the fish's mouth wide and with the tip of a very sharp knife cut the narrow strip of gristle in back of the mouth at the top, where the gills join the head. There is a bony ridge back of the gill plate, between gills and shoulders of fish; run the tip of the knife along this ridge on both sides, cutting away skin and connecting membrane. Carry the cut from the top of the gill plates to the tip of the lower jaw.

At the tip of the jaw, inside the mouth, another strip of gristle joins jawbone and tongue; cut through this. Slit the belly from the anal orifice to the jaw in a shallow cut that extends only through skin and the thin layer of belly flesh. Slip a finger into the cut you made along the jawbone, hook the finger around the tongue of the fish, and pull. This pull will remove tongue, teeth, gills, and all intestines in one unit. A V-cut at the anal orifice frees the offal from the fish's body, and all that is left is to run a thumb along the blood-filled back vein at the top of the cavity, along the backbone, to clear out the clotted blood it contains. On large fish, you may have to slit the membrane to clear it, and on very large fish you may need a teaspoon to scoop out the blood.

Some anglers believe they are keeping their catch fresh by tossing the fish into a bucket of water after taking them off the hook. This is not so, unless the water is in a fish cage or live-well in a boat, where the fish will live. Water makes a dead fish slippery and hard to handle and softens its flesh; keep fish away from water until after they have been cleaned and are ready to be cooked.

If you buy your fish instead of catching them, look for these signs that indicate freshness: bright, bulging eyes; firm, reddish gills; flesh that springs back quickly when prodded. Scales of a fresh fish will be firmly attached to the skin and have a lustrous sheen. If you suspect a fish of being other than fresh, smell at the gills and the cleaning slit; these areas will be first to give off telltale odors. Very fresh fish have little or no "fishy" smell.

Although every ounce of flesh on the body of a fish is technically muscle, fish are not tough in the sense that red meat is, unless you make them tough by overcooking. In fish cookery your objective is not to tenderize, but to coagulate body juices. In attaining this objective, the sharp, dry heat from unadorned coals has no equal. This is not to suggest that fish should all be grilled over the hottest coals you can create. In grilling fish, time must be allowed for heat to penetrate to the bones at the thickest part of the body. If your coals are too bright, too close, the skin and outer layers of flesh will dehydrate, char, and harden, while the inner part of the backbone will remain underdone, even raw. Especially when whole stuffed fish are grilled, coals must be dark enough to cook the stuffing before burning the skin and outer layers of flesh. Frozen fish, too, should be cooked over moderate coals; start them on the grill while still frozen and extend cooking time to compensate for thawing.

Overcooking a fish anywhere—on the grill, in a skillet, a Dutch oven, a stewing kettle, or a roasting pan—will toughen the flesh. If you err in timing, undercook rather than overcook. A fish is done when there is still moisture at the center of its thickest part; cooking is finished between grill or pan and the table. In chowders and stews, fish pieces are done when they flake easily.

Your clues to the point at which a fish is done when grilled, spit-cooked, or fan-fried is the condition of its skin and the amount of moisture at its dorsal fin. As complete cooking nears, the skin of a fish begins to wrinkle and bubble—at this point, slip a knife or fork between skin and flesh along the cleaning slit and if the skin lifts readily, serve the fish. To test at the dorsal, slip a knife tip in along the fin and twist the blade; if no liquid flows, cooking is complete.

All fish are classified as being fat or lean. The classification is not clean cut; there are borderline cases, but it does give you a guide to the style of cooking best to use. Fish classified as fat are usually better grilled than pan-cooked, since grilling allows the fat to drain away. When you cook smaller specimens of the fat fish you may

**160**

want to retain the fat, but the results can be unpleasant when large fat fish are pan-cooked without being held up from the pan's bottom on a rack, to keep them from reabsorbing cooked-out oils which may develop an unpleasant rancid taste.

Fish classified as fat are eel, grayling, shad, sturgeon, and trout (the trout family includes salmon and steelhead). In the lean category are black bass, bream, carp, catfish, muskellunge, all panfish, pickerel, pike, suckers, and whitefish.

A general and important rule is that any fat fish too big to be sautéed whole in a 10-inch skillet, with only the head and tail removed, should be grilled or baked, and when baked should rest on a rack in the pan. In other words, a fish weighing over 2 or 3 pounds should not be cut into sections and pan-fried or sautéed. If you have been pan-frying steaks or fillets from big fish and are not convinced that this method damages their flavor, try rack-cooking and see what a difference it makes.

Remember, too, when you cook fish on the grill or spit, that fish oil dripping on coals creates a very objectionable smoke with an odor easily transferred to the fish itself. Use a drip pan to catch this oil, or clear all live coals away from the area directly beneath the fish being cooked. In baking or roasting big fish or sections of big fish, use a rack to hold the fish off the pan's bottom so the flesh will not reabsorb the oils. A rack also makes dishing up a baked fish easier—invert a platter and lay it on the fish, then turn platter, fish, and rack over and lift off the rack. If the fish is being served with sauce, slip off the top skin before putting the platter on the fish. When the rack is lifted off the other section of skin can be slipped free and your fish will remain unbroken.

A wire rack that will fit inside your Dutch oven, double skillet, or roasting pan is one of the few accessories necessary to fish cookery. A handy accessory is a basket grill for your spit. A flat basket grill enables you to use the roti, or vertical grill, described on page 16; the roti simplifies outdoor fish cookery since with it whole small fish and steaks from big ones cook on both sides at once.

Recipes cited in this chapter as being suited for a certain type of fish are certainly not restricted to that fish alone. Generally, recipes given for firm-fleshed game fish can be freely interchanged between species and are suitable for salt-water fish as well. You will find, though, that your rewards are greater if you substitute between fish closely related to each other in fat content and body structure.

## Sauces

What has already been said about the saucing of wild game to preserve the integrity of its own fine flavor can be applied with even more emphasis to fish. Sauces should point up natural flavors, not mask them. If you don't enjoy the delicate flavor of a trout or bass or one of the other countless varieties of fish, don't hide behind ketchup and steak sauce. Eat meat.

Facilities around an outdoor fire are generally too limited to allow preparation of sauces requiring a row of bowls and pans and a long list of ingredients, or sauces involving complex processes and precise timing. Such sauces are better left for indoor cooking. Like other foods cooked over coals, fish should acquire authority in the cooking and require only an added fillip of flavor for emphasis. Of course if you insist on frying all fish, indoors or out, you'll need sauces to break the skillet's curse. Those given here will serve that purpose, but they have other uses as well.

### SOUR LIME SAUCE

Origin of this sauce has been lost in antiquity, but it was very probably used by contemporaries of Blackbeard and Captain Kidd. It migrated north via the Florida Keys to the U.S.

2 cups fresh lime juice          1 teaspoon salt

Strain the lime juice and mix the salt with it. Put into a bottle, close the neck with a cloth, but do not seal. Let stand in a warm place for 3 weeks before using; shake the bottle every day or two as it ages. Use in sober moderation on plain baked or pan-cooked fish.

## HOT PEPPER VINEGAR

Native to the South and Southwest, this is often called "Pepper Sauce." It must be used very sparingly. One drop is a feast, two drops a banquet, three drops a bonfire, so use with caution. (More can be used prior to cooking.)

¾ cup (15 to 20) small, hot, red     1 cup grain vinegar
   and green peppers     ½ teaspoon salt

Bruise the peppers by putting them on a flat firm surface between two or three layers of cloth and tapping them lightly with the butt of a knife. Do not remove stems or seeds. Put the peppers into a jar, bottle, or crock; heat but do not boil the vinegar. Sprinkle the salt over the peppers and pour the vinegar over them. Let the container stand for two weeks, with its opening covered but not tightly sealed or corked. Shake occasionally during the aging period.

## WHITE WINE SAUCE

Serve this hot over fish that have been poached, baked, or pan-fried in butter.

3 tablespoons butter     ⅛ teaspoon dry mustard
1 tablespoon flour     1 cup dry white wine
½ cup fish stock or chicken stock     pinch of freshly ground white
½ teaspoon salt     pepper

Melt the butter over medium heat, stir in flour to make a thin roux; the flour should not be allowed to brown, but must be cooked long enough to eliminate its raw starchy taste. Add the stock, stirring briskly, until the sauce is smooth. Put in seasonings and wine, take from heat, let stand 5 minutes before serving.

**163**

## HERBED BUTTERS

Often a simple herbed butter is the best sauce to serve with fish that have been cooked in a simple, straightforward fashion without seasoning other than salt and pepper. Herbed butters can be used in your outdoor cooking for basting fish being grilled—be sure to put a half-teaspoonful in the cavity—and for pan-frying.

Margarine can be substituted for butter except where any of the acids such as vinegar, wine, or lemon juice is to be used. Most of the margarine sold today is modified by the addition of a silicone to prevent foaming when the fat is used for cooking; the silicone keeps the margarine from "marrying" with an acid in preparing such sauces as black, drawn, and maître d'hotel butter. The "soft" margarines contain other chemicals besides silicone which enable them to maintain their semi-solid consistency; they are useless for cooking when used in any process combining them with herbs and liquids.

Butter and margarine used in making compound or herbed butters benefit by being washed; the process is simply one of kneading them in a bowl of cold water and changing the water three or four times, then squeezing the water from the butter with gentle pressure. Only a few suggestions for herbed butters will be offered here; the variety available is limited only by your imagination.

To ¼ pound butter or margarine, washed, add:

a drained anchovy fillet mashed with 2 or 3 capers
fresh parsley minced very fine and a pinch of Nepal pepper or cayenne
1 teaspoon scraped onion pulp (or onion powder or juice)

1 teaspoon roasted fresh garlic mashed to a pulp and a drop or two of tarragon vinegar (garlic powder can be used)
¼ teaspoon each minced fresh thyme and marjoram and a drop or two of dry vermouth

After mixing, a compound or herbed butter should be allowed to sit for 30 minutes or more to bring about the marriage of flavors.

**164**

# Black Bass

Senior citizen of the numerous sunfish species, the black bass is sometimes called "green trout" in parts of the U.S. and is divided into the subspecies of smallmouth and largemouth. The difference between them is more important to the angler than to the cook.

Only one special precaution needs to be observed in cleaning black bass, and it is especially important when the fish being cleaned is one of the moss-backed old lunkers that lurk in warm southern waters. When cleaning any black bass weighing over 2 or 3 pounds, or smaller bass from warm muddy waters, all fins and the half-inch of skin around them should be cut away. These are the places where algae cling, defying washing, and it is these microorganisms that give the black bass an undeserved reputation for having a "muddy taste."

### BAKED STUFFED BLACK BASS

|  |  |
|---|---|
| whole black bass of 4 pounds or more, cleaned | ¾ cup soft bread crumbs |
| 1 tablespoon chopped onions or shallots | ½ teaspoon thyme or basil |
| | ¼ teaspoon nutmeg |
| ½ cup chopped mushrooms, fresh or canned | ¼ cup milk |
| | 2 tablespoons butter |
| | large pinch of salt |

Sauté the onions and mushrooms in a very lightly oiled skillet over low heat, until the onions are transparent. Fresh mushrooms should be parboiled for 2 to 3 minutes before being chopped. Canned mushrooms should not be cooked, but only heated; add them when the onions begin to become transparent. Combine the onion-mushroom mixture with the bread crumbs and seasonings, moistened with the milk. Rub the fish inside and out with butter and dust lightly with salt. Stuff, then close the cavity with a few stitches of thread or small skewers. Cook on a rack in a Dutch oven with a thin film of water on the bottom of the pan, but not enough water to touch the

**165**

fish; bury the oven in coals 45 minutes to 1 hour, depending on the size of the fish. In the sheepherder oven, with the fish on a rack in a tightly covered roasting pan, cook 25 to 30 minutes; in the kitchen oven, cook 35 minutes at 300 degrees.

A 4-pound fish will serve 4.

### PAN-FRIED BLACK BASS

| | |
|---|---|
| 4 whole fish of about ¾ pound each, heads and tails removed | corn meal |
| bacon drippings | salt, pepper |

Wipe the fish with a cloth dipped in lightly salted water, about 1 teaspoon of salt per quart of water. Rub lightly with bacon drippings and roll thoroughly in corn meal, dust a little salt and pepper into the cavities. Bacon drippings should be no less than ¼ inch deep in the pan, no more than ½ inch deep, and should be hot enough to brown a 1-inch cube of bread in 2 minutes, no hotter. Cook until the fish brown nicely on one side, about 4 minutes, then turn and brown the other side. Drain on paper before serving on heated plates.

Serves 4.

### BLACK BASS FILLETS IN WHITE WINE

When not busy with his radio station in Texarkana, Arkansas, Bill McDaniel can usually be found on one of his state's famous bass streams. A lazy fisherman who'd rather fillet than clean a fish, Mac likes to cook black bass this way.

| | |
|---|---|
| 12 fillets from bass of ¾ pound to 1 pound | 2 cups tiny pearl onions or 1½ cups minced onion |
| 3 tablespoons butter or cooking oil | 2 cups ½-inch dry bread cubes |
| 2 cups dry white wine | 1 tablespoon flour |
| 2 tablespoons brandy or bourbon | pinch of garlic salt |

**166**

Warm a deep, heavy skillet and rub it very lightly with butter or cooking oil. Wipe the fillets dry, dip them in white wine, lay them on the bottom of the pan. Warm the brandy or whiskey, pour over the fillets, and light it. When the flames die down, pour the remaining wine over the fish and poach over gentle heat 10 to 12 minutes.

While the fillets poach, melt the remaining butter in another skillet and sauté the onions until they begin to brown. Add the bread cubes and stir until they are very crisp. Remove both onions and bread cubes with a slotted spoon and reserve in a warmed bowl. Sprinkle flour over the butter left in the skillet and stir until it browns very lightly. Ladle wine off the poaching fish and mix with the flour, stirring into a smooth paste, then pour the wine still remaining on the fish into the paste, stirring vigorously. Add a pinch of garlic salt. Strew the onions and bread cubes over the fillets, pour the sauce from the second pan over all, and let simmer 2 or 3 minutes before serving.

Serves 4; 6 sparsely.

## Carp

In areas where gamier fish thrive, anglers look down their noses at the scavenging carp. In clear water, though, he is a wary fish and hard to catch, and a challenge on very light tackle. The carp is also a challenge to the cook, having soft flesh and indiscriminate eating habits that often give it a muddy or mossy taste.

This objectionable taste can be removed, or at least minimized, by proper handling. The instant a carp is out of the water, kill it and hang it by the lips and cut a half-inch oval of skin from the bottom of its tail, just back of the anal orifice. When no more blood flows from the cut, clean the carp and scale it, cut out all fins and the skin around them for a half-inch area, then scrub inside and out with a rough cloth dipped in lightly salted water—about 1 teaspoon salt per quart.

## Fresh-Water Fish

Carp should be cooked as soon as possible after they are out of the water. They are not customarily filleted, but are cut in thick slices across the body into a sort of steak. Carp is best when cooked in a sauce that is kind to its soft flesh and that makes its bones easier to slip out.

### CARP IN BEER

4- to 5-pound carp, bled and cleaned as described above
1 cup salt
2 medium-sized onions
1 lemon
1 bay leaf
6 cracked peppercorns
1 bottle (11 ounces) beer
1 tablespoon butter
1 tablespoon flour
1 teaspoon sugar
¼ teaspoon powdered ginger

Cut the cleaned fish across the body into 1-inch-thick slices. Spread the pieces liberally with salt, covering both sides, and let stand 30 minutes. Scrape off salt and wipe the pieces clean. Lay the slices in a large lightly greased skillet and over them place a piece of cheesecloth big enough to be doubled back on itself to form a bag or envelope. On the piece of cloth put the onions and lemon, both sliced very thin, the bay leaf, and the peppercorns. Fold the cloth over to close it as a bag, tie the ends. Pour the beer over the fish; if not enough to cover, add more. Close the pan and simmer very gently over low heat for 30 minutes. The flesh of the fish should flake easily when touched with a fork.

Remove and discard the bag containing the onions and lemon. Lift out the pieces of fish with a slotted pancake turner and slip them off to a warmed platter. Work the butter, flour, sugar, and ginger into a smooth paste and add this in small flakes to the pan liquids. Stir until smooth. Pour over the fish and serve. If a thicker, spicier sauce is wanted, use a half-dozen gingersnaps instead of powdered ginger; crumble them into the pan liquid and stir until they dissolve.

Serves 6 to 8.

## CARP IN TOMATO SAUCE

4- to 5-pound carp, bled and
    cleaned
1½  tablespoons butter
  6  shallots or small green onions,
    minced
  1  clove garlic, minced

  1  bay leaf
large pinch thyme
½  teaspoon salt
large dash pepper
  2  cups dry red wine
½  cup tomato paste
  2  tablespoons brandy

Butter the Dutch oven well. Heat the remaining butter in a skillet and sauté the minced shallots or green onions and garlic; add the bay leaf, thyme, salt, and pepper as they cook. When the onions are tender but not brown, blend the wine and tomato paste and pour over them. Simmer 15 minutes, stirring occasionally. Put the carp whole into the Dutch oven, strain the sauce over it, and add the brandy. Close the oven, bury in coals, and cook 1 hour. In the sheepherder stove, use a tightly closed pan and cook 30 to 35 minutes. In the kitchen oven in a tightly closed pan, cook 40 to 45 minutes at 325 degrees.

Serves 6 to 8.

# Catfish

A catfish will eat almost anything, as any angler will affirm, but its diet does not taint its flesh, which is almost invariably firm and sweet. Since catfish have fewer bones than most fish, they are favored for deep-fat frying; since the flesh is white and firm, it stands up well in stews and chowders. Because its body is so thick, the catfish is not an especially good choice to cook on the grill.

Customarily, catfish are skinned, an easy job if you go about it the right way. Pin its nose to a sturdy board with an icepick and circle the body behind the gills with a sharp knife, loosen a tab of skin, and grasp it with pliers. Pull with gentle but steady pressure toward the tail, and the skin will peel off like a glove. Head is then cut off, the entrails come out with a single quick pull. But avoid the sharp fins, which can inflict a nasty puncture.

Catfish are beginning to be raised commercially in farm ponds; they are readily available on the market, fresh or frozen.

### DEEP-FRIED CATFISH

A fish fry is to the South what a clambake is to New England and a barbecue to the Southwest. You need enough fish and fat to cook up a quantity sufficient to satisfy, in the idiom of the region, "ever how many who's there." The only ingredients needed to stage a fish fry are catfish in generous quantities, a big kettle of lard or other fat, and a sack of corn meal, to make Hush Puppies, the recipe for which follows.

The catfish should be in the 8- to 10-inch size range, but chunks cut from bigger fish are commonly used. The best fat for deep-frying is a mixture of two parts bacon drippings to one part lard. Heat the fat in a big, deep kettle until it will brown a 1-inch cube of bread in 40 seconds. Mix salt and pepper with corn meal and roll the fish in it; toss them into the kettle a few at a time so temperature of the fat will not be lowered abruptly. Three to 4 minutes cooks the fish thoroughly and browns the outside crisply. Drain on a stack of papers before serving. Have a crock of dill or sour pickles handy.

Allow about half a pound of fish per person. And there must be Hush Puppies.

### HUSH PUPPIES

True Hush Puppies can be cooked only in the same kettle of fat used to deep-fry catfish. Otherwise, they're nothing but corn pone.

| | |
|---|---|
| 2 cups stone-ground corn meal | 1½ cups boiling water |
| 1 teaspoon salt | kettle of hot fat in which catfish |
| 2 tablespoons bacon drippings or lard | have just been fried |

**170**

Mix the corn meal and salt, blend the fat into it. Stir in the hot water, adding a little bit at a time. Using an oversized spoon, drop spoonfuls of the batter into the kettle of hot fat. As the blobs of batter bob around, turn them to cook evenly. When the outside is a rich tan, they're done. Fish them out, drain on a stack of papers, break open and eat while steaming hot.

In later days, cooks have come to add an egg to Hush Puppy batter to make a lighter pone, but the eggless Hush Puppy is the traditional one.

Makes about 12 Hush Puppies.


## Eel

Like many fish, the eel commutes from fresh to salt water and vice versa. It does not matter from which kind of water you took him, or whether you bought him—as far as cooking is concerned, an eel is an eel is an eel.

Eels have a peculiarity which, together with their snaky look, have caused them to decline in popularity in recent years. They must be kept alive until the very moment they go into the pot. The eel man with his barrels of eels on a creaking wagon is seen no more on city streets; New York, Boston, and San Francisco are perhaps the only three cities remaining where fish dealers still offer eels for sale. Fishermen still take them, but few know how to prepare them, and consequently toss them back. Those who do keep and cook their catch are rewarded with meat that is rich and toothsome.

Preparing an eel for the pot requires that you overcome your squeamishness, for they should be skinned alive. Twist a wire around the eel's head just back of the gill bulge and make a circling cut two inches below the wire. Loosen a flap of skin, grasping it with a cloth to overcome its slickness, and strip off the skin with a long, firm pull. Take out the long intestine exposed when the skin is removed, cut the head off two inches back of the gills to avoid the gall sac, and cook the eel whole or in sections.

## EEL STEW

| | |
|---|---|
| 3-pound eel, skinned and cleaned, cut in 2-inch sections | 1 teaspoon minced fresh parsley |
| 1½ quarts cold water | ¼ teaspoon powdered basil |
| ½ teaspoon salt | 1 tablespoon butter |
| 2 tablespoons scraped onion pulp or grated onion | 1 tablespoon flour |
| | large pinch of pepper |

Remove as much fat from the eel meat as you can scrape off. Put the pieces in a pot with cold water, add the salt, onion, parsley, and basil, bring to a quick boil, then simmer 30 minutes over low heat, until the meat is tender. Skim off the fat that will rise to the top of the liquid. Knead the flour, butter, and pepper into a smooth paste and flake bits of it into the pot while stirring briskly. Cook 5 minutes after the last of the flour-butter paste has been added.

Serves 6.

## Grayling

Because they do not survive in any but clean, clear, cold water, the grayling have been driven by pollution from most of the streams in the north-central U.S. where they once swam. Today, only wilderness streams in Minnesota and Wyoming and in Alaska and Canada have grayling. Commercial fishermen are barred from taking and selling it, so its delicate flesh can be enjoyed only by those willing to take the time and effort to seek out the secluded spots it now inhabits. Any cooking method used in preparing trout is suitable for grayling. As a suggestion, cook grayling *au bleu,* using the recipe on page 184, to which the grayling responds dramatically.

## Lake Trout

Once the great commercial fish of the central U.S., the lake trout suffered near-extinction when men opened the waters of the Great

Lakes to the bloodsucking lamprey, and human pollution of these lakes has further diminished its numbers. Whether or not the lake trout or any other fish can survive in the Great Lakes depends on the success of belatedly begun efforts to clean up their waters.

There are other concentrations of lake trout, chiefly in a big arc that starts at Tahoe in the California Sierras and swings up into the Pacific Northwest into the clean waters of northern Canada. The Lake Trout bears many regional names: togue, mackinaw, kamloops, depending on where you are fishing. The lake trout is a large fish, its flesh somewhat coarser in texture than that of its smaller cousins. Lake trout is best cooked in a stew or chowder, or poached gently and used to make a very pleasant hash.

### LAKE TROUT HASH

| | |
|---|---|
| 3 cups precooked meat, coarsely flaked | ½ teaspoon vinegar |
| 1 cup boiled chopped potatoes | 3 tablespoons milk |
| ½ cup minced onion | flour |
| ½ teaspoon salt | cooking fat |
| ¼ teaspoon cayenne or ½ teaspoon paprika | |

Combine the flaked fish, potatoes, onion, and all seasonings. Moisten with the milk to bind it together and form into flat patties or spread it in a thin layer just a bit smaller than the bottom of the skillet you will use to cook it in. Dust both sides of the patties or patty with flour, heat the skillet with a scant coating of fat on the bottom, and pan-fry until crusty brown on one side. Turn and brown on the other.

Serves 4 to 6.

## Muskellunge

Deep-feeding denizen of northern lakes, the muskellunge is a game fish much prized by sport anglers. It is not available commercially.

**Fresh-Water Fish**

Generally, because they are bony, muskellunge are filleted and the fillets pan-fried or poached. However, small muskellunge are good candidates for being cooked whole, stuffed and baked.

### MUSKELLUNGE FILLETS IN CREAM

| | |
|---|---|
| 4 large, thick fillets, about ½ pound each | ¼ teaspoon salt |
| | 2 cups dry white wine |
| 4 tablespoons butter (no substitutes) | 3 cups cream (diluted evaporated milk can be used) |
| 1½ cups chopped onions | paprika |

Melt 3 tablespoons of the butter in a heavy skillet and sauté the onions until they become transparent. Dust the fillets lightly on both sides with the salt, and lay them on the onions. Pour the wine over the fish and let it simmer 3 to 4 minutes, then add the cream slowly. Cover the pan and cook over low heat 10 to 12 minutes. Just before serving, dot the tops of the fillets with the reserved butter and dust them with paprika.

Serves 4.

## Panfish

Ichthyologists tell us, quite seriously, that we may never know exactly how many species of panfish there are. Each species has as many different names as there are countries and regions within countries, and each species varies in size, shape, color, and characteristics in each locale. The perch family, for instance, encompasses both the three-inch sunperch that swims in Smith's Creek just outside town, and the two-hundred-pound Nile perch. Variously, the panfish group includes perch and the small sunfish, crappie, bream (brim), bluegill, punkinseed, redear, warmouth and so on down a long, long list.

**174**

## FRIED PANFISH

20 to 24 panfish, cleaned and scaled

8 to 10 pounds crushed ice
cooking fat

Bury the fish in ice 30 minutes before cooking, no matter how fresh they are. Heat cooking fat ½ inch deep in a heavy skillet; it should be hot enough to brown a 1-inch cube of bread in 1 minute. Pull the fish out of the ice, wipe dry, drop into the fat a few at a time. Cook no longer than 2 minutes on each side. Lift out and drain on stacks of paper before transferring them to hot plates. It is important to keep the level of fat constant and the temperature even. Fish cooked this way should be eaten as soon as they are cool enough not to burn the mouth. They should not be seasoned until after they are boned on your plate.

Serves 4 adequately.

## PANFISH IN CIDER

20 to 24 panfish, cleaned and scaled
1 large sweet onion
2 stalks celery
2 carrots
2 quarts sweet fresh cider

1 teaspoon salt
2 tablespoons flour
2 tablespoons butter
½ teaspoon chopped summer savory or flaked dried savory

Slice the vegetables very, very thin, the onion and celery across their grain, the carrots lengthwise. Bring the cider to a gentle simmer in a deep pot, add vegetables and salt, and cook 10 minutes. Put in the fish, cook an additional 10 minutes. Lift fish and vegetables out with a strainer or slotted spoon, divide them among warmed bowls. Strain the cider through a cloth and return 6 cups to the pot. Blend flour and butter into a smooth paste and add in flakes to the simmering cider. Stir in the savory and cook until the last traces of flour vanish, 3 to 4 minutes. Pour the thickened sauce into the bowls over the fish. Serve with side dishes of rice or boiled potatoes.

Serves 4 to 6.

## PANFISH WITH VEGETABLES

20 to 24 panfish, cleaned and scaled

salt, pepper

2 boiled potatoes, or 10 to 12 tiny new potatoes, boiled

2 onions, or 10 to 12 tiny pearl onions, parboiled 1 minute

3 tablespoons butter

3 cups fresh or frozen green peas, parboiled 1 minute, or

3 cups fresh or frozen green beans, cut in 1-inch lengths and parboiled 1 minute (canned peas or beans can be used; they need only be drained)

1 cup dry white wine

¾ cup light cream (diluted evaporated milk can be used)

Dust the cavities and outsides of the fish lightly with salt and pepper and set them aside while the vegetables are being prepared. If large potatoes are used, cut them in julienne strips after peeling; large onions should be thin-sliced. Heat 2 tablespoons butter in the skillet and toss the vegetables in the butter over medium heat. After they are butter-coated, spread them in a thick layer on the bottom of the pan. Put the fish on top of the vegetables, use the remaining butter to put a dot on each fish. Pour in the wine, close the skillet tightly, and cook 10 minutes over gentle heat. Open the skillet long enough to pour the cream over the fish, close it and cook 3 to 4 minutes more. Stir the fish and vegetables together to serve, and spoon the pan juices over them on their warmed platter or in individual bowls.

Serves 4 to 6.

## Pike, Pickerel

We have already considered one member of this large and varied family, the muskellunge. Now we come to the chain pickerel and the northern pike; we will include also the walleye, which is not a pike, but a perch, since walleyes are spiritually, at least, in the pike-pickerel group.

All the members of this family grow large; the chain pickerel is perhaps the smallest of them. All pike are bony fish, and are usually filleted for pan-cooking, or baked stuffed or unstuffed in a closed pan so that the steam from cooking makes the bones easier to separate from the delicately flavored flesh. None of the pike present any special cleaning or handling problems.

### SWEET & SOUR PIKE

| | |
|---|---|
| 8 fillets of about ½ pound each | cardamom seed, a few |
| salt | cracked whole allspice, a |
| 1 large sweet onion | sliver or two of cinnamon |
| 3 cups cold water | bark, and a few shreds of red |
| 1 tablespoon pickling spices; | pepper pod |
| use a packaged commercial | 6 whole cloves |
| mixture or prepare your own | ¾ cup cider vinegar |
| by stirring together, dry, small | ½ lemon, sliced very thin |
| pinches of mustardseed, | 1 tablespoon sugar |
| fennel seed, dill seed, | 6 cracked peppercorns |
| caraway seed, mace, a crushed | |

Dust the fillets lightly on both sides with salt and put them aside on a dish or platter; they should rest 10 to 15 minutes after salting. Cut the onion in quarters, put in a deep pot with water and bring to a boil, then reduce to a simmer. Cook 10 minutes, then add the fillets. Put the pickling spices and cloves in a cloth bag and drop in the pot. Add vinegar, lemon slices, and sugar, simmer gently for 30 minutes. Add the peppercorns during the last 10 minutes of cooking. Remove the pot from heat and let it cool naturally. Take out the fillets, whole if possible, and arrange them on the bottom of a flat shallow dish or a high-lipped platter. Strain the pot liquid over them to cover, let stand 24 hours.

There are several ways to serve the fillets. They can be drained and served cold; minced or mashed with a bit of the cooking liquid to make a canapé spread, or to fill the whites of hard-boiled eggs, or mounded high in parboiled mushroom caps as an appetizer, or served in a mound with crackers for spreading, as stuffing for onions or tomatoes.

Serves 8 as fillets; spreads about 30 canapés; stuffs a dozen eggs; serves 12 to 14 as a dip or spread.

## Shad

Most prized of the shad are roe-heavy females. Usually the roes are removed in their sac and cooked separately from the fish. Shad are usually cleaned from the back rather than the belly to make possible the removal of the roe sac without breaking it. Our interest is not in the roe, which is a by-product that can only be heated in butter, but in the fish itself. Shad is best served grilled, planked, or baked. It is a "fat" fish, and should be cooked by a method that will allow its oils to drain off.

### BAKED STUFFED SHAD

| | |
|---|---|
| 3- to 4-pound whole shad, or 2 smaller fish | ½ small onion, grated |
| ¾ teaspoon salt | ¼ teaspoon dill seed |
| ¼ teaspoon paprika | ½ teaspoon celery seed |
| 1 cup fine bread crumbs, very dry | 1 egg |

Wipe the fish inside and out and dust with the salt and paprika mixed together. Combine the bread crumbs, onion, dill seed, and celery seed; the dill seed should be bruised before adding. Stir the egg into the mixed dry ingredients. Put a tablespoon or two of the stuffing into the cavity, and close with small skewers or a few stitches. Spread the remaining stuffing in a thin coat over the outside of the fish. Cook on a rack in a Dutch oven with a thin film of water in its bottom; bury in coals 1 hour. In a sheepherder oven, cook on a rack in a closed pan with water on its bottom for 35 to 40 minutes; in the kitchen oven, using the same procedure, cook 45 minutes at 300 degrees. To serve, peel away the outer layer of stuffing and the skin. The stuffing in the cavity is also discarded. According to your taste, season with a few drops of Hot Pepper Vinegar or White Wine Sauce, page 163.

Serves 4.

## PLANKED SHAD, CAMP STYLE

| | |
|---|---|
| 3- to 4-pound whole shad | 2½ tablespoons paprika |
| 1 tablespoon salt | lemon wedges |

Any fish you cook planked should be cleaned from the back, leaving the belly skin and flesh intact. Mix the salt and paprika and rub generously over the inner surface of the fish.

Your board should be of a nonresinous wood and should be soaked in water at least an hour before it is used. The open fire should be allowed to die to a thick bed of coals. Using nongalvanized (black or blued) roofing nails, nail the fish to the plank, skin side next to the wood. Prop up the plank 18 to 24 inches from the coals with rocks or short stakes driven into the ground. Cooking time will be 20 to 25 minutes, and at the midpoint the plank should be turned end for end so that the heat will strike the fish evenly. Sprinkle with lemon juice before eating.

Serves 4.

## SHAD COOKED TO BE BONELESS

In America's early days, shad was an important food fish, and our forefathers probably got tired of picking the bones out day after day during the spawning run. Somewhere along the line, a clever Colonial cook evolved a method of cooking shad so the bones would be less of a problem. When prepared by this oldtime method, the bones are still there, but they're about like those in canned salmon, soft and chewable. In Colonial days the cooking was done in a spider but you get the same result in a Dutch oven.

| | |
|---|---|
| 3- to 4-pound cleaned whole shad | ½ cup minced celery |
| | ½ teaspoon fresh tarragon |
| 1 quart milk (use fresh milk only) | 1 teaspoon salt |
| | ¼ teaspoon cayenne |
| 2 cups fine dry bread crumbs | ½ cup dry white wine |
| ½ cup minced onion | |

Put the fish in the Dutch oven, pour in the milk, and bury in coals 2 to 2½ hours. Combine all ingredients and seasonings and moisten with 1 or 2 tablespoons of the wine. Open the oven, lift the top half of the fish along the slit opened for cleaning and spoon the dressing on, then let the top half drop back into place. Pour in the wine. Close the oven and bury it in coals for another 45 minutes. If you have roe that you do not want to cook separately, add it to the stuffing. In the sheepherder oven, cook in a heavy pan with a tightly fitting cover for 1½ to 2 hours for the first cooking and 20 minutes for the second. Use the same timing in the kitchen oven at 275 degrees.

Serves 4.


## Sturgeon

These prehistoric survivors grow to tremendous size in the ocean, and return to spawn in fresh water; they are common on both Atlantic and Pacific coasts in the big rivers that are relatively unpolluted. Streams north of Cape Cod on the east coast and north of San Francisco Bay on the west still harbor sturgeon, though not in the numbers and size of years past. Old records tell of sturgeon weighing 1200 pounds. Today, a sturgeon over 150 pounds is big.

Sturgeon yield a very fine but oily flesh. It is usually smoked, the lox of the delicatessen counter. Fresh sturgeon is usually sold by fish markets cut into steaks or roasts; when properly cooked, so the oil drains away and does not come into contact with the flesh, these are delicious. Sturgeon steaks are very good for grilling; they should be rubbed with salt and paprika, using 1 tablespoon salt to 2½ tablespoons paprika, and cooked over low coals, turning two or three times. Sturgeon should never be cooked in a skillet, nor baked in a pan without resting on a rack.

## BAKED STURGEON, POTATO SAUCE

| | |
|---|---|
| 8-pound roast, cut 4 to 5 inches thick | salt<br>Nepal or cayenne pepper |

Wipe the roast well; if any fat is visible on its surface, trim or scrape off. Dust with salt and Nepal or cayenne pepper. Put on a rack in the Dutch oven, bury in coals, and cook 1 hour. Your timing in the sheepherder oven will be 35 to 40 minutes over bright coals with the fish on a rack in a closed pan; in the kitchen oven, 45 minutes at 350 degrees. Ten minutes before serving, prepare the Potato Sauce:

| | |
|---|---|
| 1 cup milk | ¼ teaspoon freshly ground black pepper |
| 1½ cups cooked mashed potatoes | |
| 1 tablespoon butter | 1 teaspoon Hot Pepper Vinegar, page 163 |
| ½ teaspoon salt | |

Heat the milk and beat in the mashed potatoes, butter, and salt and pepper. The sauce should be almost the consistency of mayonnaise, if it is too thick, add a little more milk. Beat the Hot Pepper Vinegar into the sauce just before serving.

Serves 10.

## Suckers, Whitefish

Although they belong to different families, these two fish share characteristics which make them cook alike. Both are clean, when taken from clean waters, and both are bony, and coarser in flesh than most fresh-water denizens. Suckers and whitefish can be prepared by the method of rendering shad boneless, given on page 179.

## SUCKERBURGERS

The late Forest S. Townsley, who was first appointed to the Forest Service Ranger force by President Theodore Roosevelt in 1904, served as Chief Ranger at Yosemite National Park until his death in 1943. Forest enjoyed taking friends into Yosemite's high country, off the tourist trail, and enjoyed equally cooking and serving to them the suckerbergers he originated.

| | |
|---|---|
| 3 to 4 pounds of freshly caught suckers | ½ teaspoon nutmeg |
| | ¼ teaspoon salt |
| fat for deep-frying; ⅓ lard and ⅔ bacon drippings | 1 egg |
| | 2 cups coarse dry bread crumbs |
| 1½ cups chopped onion | |

Clean and skin the fish, removing head, tail, and fins. Have the fat heated until it will brown a 1-inch cube of bread in 30 seconds; there should be about 3 inches of fat in a deep kettle. Drop the fish into the fat, one or two at a time, and cook 5 to 8 minutes—they must be very crisp. Grind the suckers, bones and all, using the fine blade of a meat grinder, and passing through with them the onion and seasonings. Combine the ground mixture with the egg and bread crumbs and form into patties 1 inch thick. Cook these in the hot fat 2 to 3 minutes, until the outsides are browned. Drain well on a stack of papers before serving.

Serves 6 to 8.

## Trout

Somewhere, there is a trout stream each angler claims as his own. It may be a stream still untouched by civilization's pollution, where brook trout abound, or one of the West's brawling rivers where the husky steelhead leaps. It may be a river passing near a big city where brown trout have adapted themselves, or a tiny mountain creek where rainbows dance on the fishes' tails, or a frothing Northern river where a few of the speckled native trout abide. It may be a small lake above timberline where the exotic golden trout are found, or a big lake in whose depths sulk the red-jawed cutthroat or jut-chinned kokanee or kamloops.

When the angler turns outdoor chef, though, he realizes that a trout is a trout, and that all species can be cooked by any recipe that alters the fish's own flavor in only the most delicate fashion.

### TROUT AMANDINE

| | |
|---|---|
| 4 pan-sized trout, about 8 inches | 3 tablespoons butter |
| salt | ½ cup blanched slivered almonds |

Heat the butter until a 1-inch bread cube browns in 2 minutes— a very gentle heat is best for trout. Rub the cavities of the fish lightly with salt and sauté them 2 to 3 minutes per side, depending on size. Remove to warm serving plates and slip off their skins. If you want to be fancy, lift off each fillet and discard backbone and ribs. Spread the almonds in the butter left in the skillet and sauté until they are crisp, a light tan, not brown. Divide the butter and almonds over the fish.

Serves 2.

### TROUT BAKED IN CORN HUSKS

| | |
|---|---|
| 7- to 8-inch trout | corn husks soaked 2 hours in warm water |
| salt, pepper | |
| butter | |

**Fresh-Water Fish**

Dust the cavity of each fish lightly with salt and pepper, put ½ teaspoon butter in the cavity. Wrap each fish in five or six layers of wet corn husks and secure the ends of the husks with wire. (Do not wrap the husks in foil.) Bury in coals 30 to 40 minutes.

Allow 2 trout per person.


**TROUT AU BLEU**

Except for the patrons of the two restaurants in New York and one in San Francisco where this delicacy is featured, Trout au Bleu is reserved for the streamside chef who has access to the fresh, live trout needed to prepare this traditional dish.

| | |
|---|---|
| 7- to 8-inch live trout; recipe quantities are for 1 fish | 2½ tablespoons lemon juice or 2 tablespoons vinegar |
| 1 quart boiling water | |

Have the quart of water boiling before the fish is killed and cleaned, the lemon juice or vinegar standing at hand ready and measured.

Stun the fish and clean it quickly. Handle no more than is absolutely necessary, as the outside mucus coating the fish is essential to the success of the cooking process. *Do not wipe the fish at any time.*

Pour the lemon juice or vinegar into the boiling water the moment the fish has been cleaned, and slip in the fish at once. Boiling will stop. When it starts again, remove the pan from heat, cover it, and let it stand. A 7- or 8-inch fish will be cooked in 5 to 6 minutes; a smaller one in 3 to 5 minutes. The fish is ready to serve when its eyes pop white from its head. It is a mistake to try to cook more than two trout at the same time in one pan. And the cooking solution cannot be reused; fresh water must be boiled and the lemon juice or vinegar added each time a trout or pair of trout is cooked. Any firm-fleshed game fish can be cooked this way; just keep the size down to about 8 inches.

Allow 1 trout per serving.

## CRISP PAN-FRIED TROUT

small trout, 7 to 8 inches; adjust
   recipe quantities to the
   number of fish being cooked
bacon drippings
salt, pepper

milk
fine dry bread crumbs or
   unsalted cracker crumbs or a
   mixture of 2 parts corn meal
   to 1 part flour

Have ¼ inch of fat in the skillet, hot enough to brown a 1-inch cube of bread in 1 minute. Dust the cavities of the trout lightly with salt and pepper, dip them in milk and roll in the breading mixture. Cook 1½ to 2 minutes per side, just long enough for the breading mixture to turn to a deep brown. Drain on stacks of paper before serving on warmed plates.

Allow at least 2 trout per person; 3 is better.

## GRILLED TROUT

medium-sized trout, 10 to 14
   inches; adjust recipe
   quantities to the number of
   fish being cooked

butter
paprika
salt, pepper

Wipe the fish dry, rub the outsides with butter and put a small piece of butter, about the size of an acorn, into the cavity of each fish. Dust the cavities gently with salt and pepper. Use a small skewer or toothpick to close the cavity. Rub the outsides of the fish generously with paprika; the flavor will not be transferred to the flesh of the trout, but the chemical action of paprika to heat retards the cooking of the layer of flesh immediately under the skin and keeps it from getting dry and hard while the fish cooks through. Grill over medium-dark coals, 4 to 6 or 7 minutes per side, depending on the thickness of the fishes' bodies. If the heads have been removed, watch the backbone where the cut was made; when liquid stops oozing from it, the fish is done. It should be taken off the grill and will finish cooking during the time taken to serve.

Allow 1 medium-sized trout per serving.

## BAKED TROUT OR STEELHEAD

Very large trout, those weighing 4 pounds or more, are better baked than grilled, or cut into steaks and pan-fried. This is also true of the steelhead, the lordly sea-run member of the trout family found only in Western rivers. In recent years, anglers of the Great Lakes region have been giving the name "steelhead" to the coho salmon that have taken hold in those waters. Contrary to general belief, the steelhead is not a rainbow trout that has wandered out to sea, but a separate species of the trout family; many trout migrate between large lakes or the ocean and the rivers feeding them, but not all these migrating trout are steelhead.

Steelhead should not be cooked like small trout; they have a much higher fat content than trout, and even small steelhead should be grilled rather than pan-fried. Recipes for salmon, page 199, are all good for steelhead; so is the recipe for baked stuffed black bass on page 165, and all these recipes are suitable for large trout.

| | |
|---|---|
| whole large trout or steelhead, 4 pounds or bigger | ¼ teaspoon salt |
| | large pinch marjoram |
| 1 tablespoon butter | 2 tablespoons chopped chives, |
| 1 to 1½ cups coarse dry bread crumbs | or small green onions |
| | ¼ cup dry white wine |

Coat the trout's cavity with butter and rub a thin film on the outside. (If the fish is a steelhead, omit butter; its own fat will be sufficient.) Combine the bread crumbs, salt, marjoram, and chives or onions, and moisten with the wine. Stuff the cavity loosely—do not pack. Secure with skewers, or by sewing. Bake on a rack in the Dutch oven, buried in coals 8 minutes per pound for a fish under 5 pounds, 12 minutes per pound for larger fish. In the sheepherder oven, use a rack in a tightly closed roasting pan and cook 5 minutes for small fish, 7 to 8 minutes for big ones. In the kitchen oven, with the temperature at 350 degrees, cook 6 minutes per pound for fish under 5 pounds, 10 minutes per pound for bigger ones. It is not necessary to turn the fish being cooked in this style. And the only additional seasoning that should be used is a sprinkling of lemon juice after the skin has been slipped off.

Serves 4.

## POTTED TROUT

This old English method of "putting down" trout dates back to prerefrigeration days. Fish preserved in this manner make interesting hors d'oeuvres when crumpled on butter crackers or crisp thin toast.

| | |
|---|---|
| 10 to 12 small trout, 7 inches or under | 1 large sprig fresh marjoram or 1 teaspoon dried marjoram |
| 2 carrots | ¼ teaspoon salt |
| 2 small onions | ½ pound butter (no substitutes) |
| 1 quart cold water | |

Chop the carrots and onions coarsely, put them into cold water with the marjoram and salt, and cook until the carrot pieces begin to fall apart. Remove from heat, strain, and discard the solids. Let the liquid cool. Put the cleaned trout in the cool liquid, bring to a slow simmer over gentle heat, and cook for 10 minutes after the first bubbles appear. Remove from heat, let the fish cool in the liquid. When cool, lift them out, drain, slip off their skins and divide into fillets by running a blunt knife along the backbone and lifting off the top fillet, then lifting out the bones from the bottom half. Lay the fillets in an earthenware crock or tureen. Melt the butter and pour over them; the fish must be covered completely. Cook in the oven at 200 degrees for 15 minutes, remove from oven, and let cool naturally. If butter does not cover the fish when cooled, add more.

Without refrigeration, trout prepared this way will keep three to four weeks. Refrigerated, the terrine covered, they will keep twice that long.

Small pieces cut from these fillets, the excess butter scraped off, can be speared on cocktail picks as an hors d'oeuvre, or the fillets can be mashed with some of the butter into a smooth canapé spread.

# VIII

## Salt-Water Fish

FISH OF INLAND WATERS are affected by seasonal temperatures and geographical differences which often change their coloration as well as the taste and texture of their flesh. These influences are minimized in the ocean; its colder depths and more constant food supply produce fish that are generally firm and usually fat. Salt-water fish are candidates for baking, stew, and chowder. Most of them produce steaks that can be grilled, but beware the occasional maverick such as the albacore, which cannot be cooked well over direct heat.

In this chapter the strictly regional and the exotic have been avoided. You will not find bouillabaisse in it, for true bouillabaisse calls for fish not found in U.S. waters. Nor will you find the Fugu Stew, that strange, frequently fatal Oriental concoction made from the innards of the poisonous blowfish. You will meet neither the dogfish nor the shark, though both are eaten on occasion. Recipes generally are confined to the salt-water fish you are most likely to encounter, either as an angler or a customer of the fish market.

Trying to classify and enumerate even the most common salt-water fish from a culinary standpoint is an almost impossible job. There are too many species or varieties to deal with efficiently, so look to types of fish rather than names of species when you thumb through recipes for suggestions. In most cases, the recipes in this chapter are tagged to names of fish because a certain method of preparation or style of service has come to be associated with that fish, but in almost all recipes one type of fish can be substituted for another, though you should remember the fat-lean classifications.

Salt-water fish classed as fat are barracuda, bluefish, striped bass, halibut, mackerel, pompano, redfish, salmon, smelt, snapper, swordfish, tuna, and weakfish (sea trout). Those classed as lean are sea bass, bonito (albacore), codfish, flounder, haddock, all of the whitefish family except the Pacific candlefish, and whiting.

As with fresh-water fish, it has been necessary to make a few arbitrary classifications of species included in the salt-water category, especially among the anadromous fish. Both sturgeon and steelhead are placed in the preceding chapter as fresh-water fish, though they spend part of their lives in the ocean. In this chapter, for example, the striped bass is included as a salt-water fish in spite of successful experiments to habituate the striper in numerous big fresh-water lakes. And some may question the inclusion of octopus and squid in the salt-water fish category, but these celaphods are closer kin to fish than to the mollusks, crustaceans, and amphibians which are covered in a later chapter.

What was said beginning on page 159 about the selection and/or care, and the cooking of fresh-water fish applies without change to those from salt water.

## Albacore

This small tuna-type fish is known to Atlantic and Gulf fishermen as the bonito, but to compound confusion it is sometimes called bonito in Pacific waters as well. Ranging in size from 8 to 15 pounds, the albacore is as streamlined inside as out; its stomach and intestine form a straight line, and properly speaking the fish has no belly cavity. Albacore is not suited to grilling, or even to pan-frying; direct heat causes its flesh to become leathery and stringy. Cooked in a roasting pan or in a stew or chowder, the meat is delicate and tender.

### ALBACORE BAKED WITH OIL AND PEPPER

| | |
|---|---|
| 10- to 12-pound whole albacore | 1 tablespoon vinegar |
| 1½ to 2 teaspoons salt | ½ cup fine light olive oil or |
| ½ teaspoon Nepal pepper or 1 | peanut oil |
| teaspoon cayenne | |

Cut head, tail, and fins from the cleaned fish. Mix salt and pepper and rub generously over the body. Put the fish on a rack in a Dutch oven. Mix the vinegar and oil and pour into the bottom; the liquid should not touch the fish. Close oven and bury in coals 1½ to 2 hours, depending on size of fish. In the sheepherder oven, cook on a rack in a tightly closed pan, 45 minutes to 1 hour; in the kitchen oven, 50 minutes to 1¼ hours at 300 degrees. When cooking is complete the skin will slip easily off the flesh. Serve with lemon wedges, or with your choice of the sauces given beginning on page 16. The meat of albacore is especially good served cold.

A 10-pound fish will serve 12.

## Barracuda

Barracuda run to large sizes, and so are seldom cooked whole; it is more common to fillet them or to slice their bodies crosswise into steaks. Of the fish classed as fat, barracuda are relatively lean, and can safely be pan-fried. Grilling is better than pan-frying, however, and large sections cut as roasts and stuffed for cooking should be placed on a rack. Fillets or steaks poached in the oven or surface-cooked should be scraped free of fat.

## BARRACUDA STEAKS OR FILLETS

4 steaks of about ¾ pound each, cut 1 to 1¼ inch thick, or equivalent in fillets

2 tablespoons butter or peanut oil

¼ cup minced chives or small onions including tops

2 cups dry white wine

large pinch salt

1 cup light cream (diluted evaporated milk can be used)

dash of nutmeg, dash of cayenne

1 teaspoon arrowroot or cornstarch, or 1 tablespoon flour and 1 tablespoon butter

Melt the butter in a Dutch oven or deep skillet and sauté the chives or onions very lightly over gentle heat. Arrange the fish steaks or fillets on the chives, pour in the wine, and add a pinch of salt. Close the pan and poach over very low heat 12 to 15 minutes. Lift the fish pieces from the pan, allowing all liquid to drain back into the pan. Put the pieces of fish on a warmed platter or individual serving plates. With the pan over high heat, let the liquid boil until it is reduced ⅓ in volume. Remove from heat and stir in the cream, nutmeg, and cayenne; taste and adjust seasoning.

The sauce should not be thin and watery, but about the consistency of a thick creamed soup—if too thin it can be thickened by adding arrowroot or cornstarch while stirring over gentle heat, or by mixing the flour and butter into a smooth paste and flaking it into the simmering sauce. The simmering should continue until there is no trace of a starchy taste in the liquid. Pour the sauce over the fish.

Serves 4.

## Bluefish

An Atlantic fish prized by sports anglers, the bluefish is classed as "fat," but its oil is neither excessive in quantity nor objectionable to the taste. When served as steaks, the grill should be used rather than the skillet. The fish is perhaps best when stuffed and baked whole.

### BAKED STUFFED BLUEFISH

| | |
|---|---|
| 6- to 8-pound bluefish | ¾ cup small green onions, tops included, minced fine |
| salt, pepper | |
| ½ cup grated raw potato | ⅛ teaspoon thyme |
| ½ cup coarse unsalted cracker crumbs | ¼ teaspoon salt |
| | 2 tablespoons dry white wine |

Dust the cavity with salt and pepper. Combine potato, cracker crumbs, onion, and seasonings, moisten with the wine, and stuff the cavity loosely, closing with stitches or small skewers. Bake on a rack in the Dutch oven, with a thin film of water on the bottom of the pan. Bury the oven in coals 1 to 1¼ hours. In the sheepherder oven, with the fish on a rack in a tightly closed pan with a film of water on its bottom, cook 40 to 45 minutes; in the kitchen oven using the same technique, cook 50 minutes at 300 degrees.

Serves 6 to 8.

## Codfish

Once, most codfish wound up in the salt cask. Today they go to the freezer and emerge as a half-dozen different fish; the cod is also the fish chiefly used in the concoctions sold as "breaded fish fingers" or "fish sticks," which contain about 60 per cent bread or fillers. When you can get hold of a fresh codfish, or one of the immature codfish called scrod, it makes up into a marvelous chowder. Beware of over-cooking—a fresh cod toughens when cooked too long.

### CODFISH CHOWDER

| | |
|---|---|
| 2 pounds fresh cod cut in 2-inch cubes | bay leaf |
| | pinch of powdered thyme |
| 3 large potatoes, sliced very thin | 1 tablespoon fresh parsley, chopped fine |
| 2 large sweet onions, sliced very thin | ¼ teaspoon salt |
| ¾ cup milk thinned with ¼ cup water | large dash black pepper |
| | butter |

**192**

Butter a deep, heavy pot very generously and sauté the potatoes and onions until they begin to soften. Put in the pieces of cod and stir. Cook only 1 or 2 minutes, then add the milk and seasonings. Simmer—do not boil—for 10 minutes, stirring occasionally. Just before serving, float a big chunk of butter on the surface.

Serves 4 to 6.

## Flounder

This is the fish you will be served as "sole" in all but the small handful of restaurants that import genuine sole from abroad; it is also the fish you will be given when you ask for sole at most markets. The flounder and sole belong to the same family and respond to the same treatment in cooking. Incidentally, if you are forced to buy frozen "sole," avoid the breaded version; it contains even more bread than most packagings of frozen breaded fish.

### GRILLED FLOUNDER FILLETS

Adjust recipe quantities to the number of fillets being cooked.

| | |
|---|---|
| milk | salt |
| flour | lemon wedges |
| butter | |

Wipe the fillets dry, dip in milk, roll in flour. Grill 3 minutes per side over medium-bright coals, brushing with melted butter. Give the fillets a final brush of butter when they are on the serving plate, dust very, very lightly with salt, and serve with lemon wedges. Some people like to add a sprinkling of minced fresh parsley to the cooked fillets, or substitute the White Wine Sauce given on page 163. If the fillets are small, allow two per serving.

### FLOUNDER FILLETS IN TOMATO SAUCE

| | |
|---|---|
| 8 fillets, about palm-of-hand size | canned tomatoes, well drained |
| 3 tablespoons butter (no substitutes) | ½ teaspoon salt |
| | ¼ teaspoon sugar |
| 1 small sweet onion, grated or minced fine | ½ cup dry white wine |
| | ½ cup cool water |
| 3 ripe tomatoes, scalded and peeled; or 1 cup solid-pack | fine unsalted cracker crumbs or dry bread crumbs |

In a heavy skillet, melt the butter and sauté the onion until it begins to soften. Chop the tomatoes coarsely over the pan or a bowl to preserve their juice and add tomatoes and juice to the pan. If canned tomatoes are used, the juice left in them after draining will be just about the right quantity. Add salt and sugar; mix the wine with water and add it. Simmer 5 to 10 minutes, mashing the tomato pulp smooth with the stirring spoon as the sauce cooks. Slip in the fillets, cover the pan, and cook 10 minutes at a gentle simmer. Brown the crumbs lightly in an ungreased skillet or on a cookie sheet in the oven, and sprinkle thickly over the top of the dish just before serving.

Serves 4.

## Haddock

Like its close relative, the cod, haddock has in the past been chiefly associated with the smokehouse, from whence it emerges as finnan haddie. Like the cod, too, haddock travels to the frozen food bins under many aliases. And again like the cod, the haddock when cooked in its fresh state tends to toughen if overdone.

## DEVILED HADDOCK

| | |
|---|---|
| 8  fillets, about palm-of-hand size | canned tomatoes, well drained |
| 3  or 4 slices of bacon | 1  tablespoon chili molido |
| 1  small hot onion, minced | 4  or 5 whole cloves |
| 1  green (Bell) pepper, minced | 4  thin slices lemon, or 1 tablespoon fresh lemon juice |
| 3  ripe tomatoes, scalded and peeled; or 1 cup solid-pack | 2  tablespoons paprika |

Sauté the bacon in a heavy deep skillet, and set aside to drain on paper toweling. It should be crisply brown but not burned. Pour excess bacon fat from the pan, leaving only a thin film clinging to its bottom and sides. Sauté the onion and pepper until they begin to soften. Chop the tomatoes coarsely over the skillet or in a bowl to preserve their juices, and add to the pan. (If canned tomatoes are used, the juice left in them after draining will be just about the right quantity.) Add cold water to bring the level of all ingredients in the pan to about ½ inch. Stir in the chili molido, cloves, and salt. Let simmer 7 to 10 minutes, until the tomatoes are soft enough to crush into pulp with your stirring spoon. Add the lemon slices or juice and simmer 5 minutes. Rub the fillets generously with paprika and slide into the sauce. Close pan and cook gently 8 to 10 minutes. Just before serving, crumble the slices of bacon and sprinkle over the top of the dish.

Serves 4.

## PICKLED HADDOCK

Prepare this in advance to use as a canapé spread, or if you must go along with a food fad that seems to be losing some of its favor, as a "dip."

**Salt-Water Fish**

| | |
|---|---|
| 1 pound boiled haddock, boned | 3 drops Tabasco Sauce or 6 |
| 1¼ cups fresh lime or lemon juice | drops Hot Pepper Vinegar, |
| (the "reconstituted" juices do | page 163 |
| not work well in this recipe) | small dash Angostura or |
| 1 tablespoon white wine vinegar | Peychaud bitters |
| 6 to 8 whole cloves | 3 bay leaves powdered fine |
| 1 teaspoon dry mustard | ¼ teaspoon salt |
| ⅛ teaspoon powdered ginger | |

Flake the fish fine in a deep bowl or crock. Mix lemon or lime juice with vinegar and all seasonings and simmer 15 minutes—do not allow it to boil. Strain the hot liquid through a cloth over the flaked fish. Stir well, cover the top of the bowl or crock with a cloth, and let stand in a cool place 3 to 4 hours—or longer, if you wish. To use as a spread, strain the flaked fish and mash into a smooth paste. For a "dip," thin the paste with a little of the marinade liquid until it is the proper consistency. The mixture will keep several days in a covered container in the refrigerator, but should be brought to room temperature before serving.


## Halibut

A king-sized member of the flounder family, halibut is usually cut across its grain into steak. Because of this, halibut steak should be cooked in a basket grill to keep it from falling apart when it is done. A large chunk of halibut cut as a roast can be cooked by any of the recipes given here for baked or roast fish; the one on page 181 is especially recommended.


### GRILLED HALIBUT STEAKS

| | |
|---|---|
| 2 halibut steaks, about 6 inches | ½ cup white wine |
| in diameter and 1 to 1½ | 2 or 3 cracked peppercorns |
| inches thick | ½ teaspoon salt |

Marinate the steaks in the wine, peppercorns, and salt 30 to 45 minutes before cooking. (Do not refrigerate while marinating.) Using a basket grill, cook over medium-dark coals 6 to 8 minutes on each side, basting with the marinade liquid. If cooked in the kitchen stove's broiler, a somewhat shorter timing should be used. When done, the surface of the meat will show each layer of flesh in a white outlined pattern.

Serves 4.

### HALIBUT STEW

| | | |
|---|---|---|
| 2 | pounds halibut cut in 1-inch chunks | 1½ quarts cold water |
| 1½ | cups onions, chopped coarsely | 1 tablespoon cider vinegar |
| 1 | cup carrots diced ½ inch | 1½ teaspoons salt |
| 1 | cup green peas or green beans, fresh, canned, or frozen | 2 whole cloves |
| 1 | clove garlic | large dash of pepper |
| | | 6 biscuits, fresh or left over |
| | | butter |

In a deep pot, put the onions, carrots, green peas or beans, and garlic, cover with water, simmer until they are tender. The carrots will cook last, and by the time they are ready the garlic clove will be soft and mushy. Fish out the garlic and crush it to a fine smooth paste, and stir this back into the pot; or if you don't like garlic, discard the clove. Put in the pieces of fish and immediately add the vinegar, salt, cloves, and pepper. Cook very gently, 12 to 15 minutes. Split, butter, and toast the biscuits. Put them in soup plates and ladle the stew over them, or float the biscuits on top of the stew in each bowl just before serving. Potato may be substituted for the biscuit, in which case add ½ teaspoon of salt.

Serves 6 very handily.

## Octopus

In these days of scuba diving, octopus is no longer a rather frightening novelty. Scuba divers often encounter small to medium-sized octopus, and if the tentacled creature has a spread of three feet or less, it's eating-size. Several of our scuba-diving friends have surfaced with octopus attached, but it was Bill Briody of Daly City, California, who first cooked one for us to share. Share is the proper word. After chopping the tip ends off the tentacles and cutting them off the body sac, we shared the job of pounding the rubbery flesh (after flushing all the grit out of the suction cups) until it was limp and pliable. The flattened tentacles were then scalded, plunged into very cold water, and the skin peeled off—and after that, they were pounded some more. The flesh of the octopus is very like an unpounded abalone must be, or a huge and mightily muscled scallop. Octopus is the exception to the rule that fish should be cooked only a short time; simmer octopus long and gently.

### OCTOPUS STEW

| | |
|---|---|
| 2 pounds of octopus tentacles cut in 1-inch chunks | 2 cloves garlic |
| | 2 cups rice |
| 2 tablespoons finest light olive oil, or peanut oil | 3 ripe tomatoes or 303 can solid-pack tomatoes, drained |
| 1 large sweet onion | ½ lemon |
| *bouquet garni* containing a bay leaf, basil, celery tops, and a couple of allspice berries | ½ teaspoon salt |

Over gentle heat, bring the oil to the point where it will brown a 1-inch cube of bread in 1½ minutes. Chop the onions and sauté them until they begin to become transparent, then add the pieces of octopus; cook 5 to 8 minutes. Add enough water to cover the ingredients in the pot. Put the herbs of the *bouquet garni* in a small cloth bag; if you enjoy a strong garlic flavor, add the garlic separately and when it is tender crush it and stir it into the liquid. Cover the pan and simmer gently 1 to 1½ hours, until the meat is tender when prodded with the tines of a fork. Add more water if needed. Add the rice, quartered tomatoes, lemon, and salt. Cover, cook until the rice is tender; open to stir occasionally.

Serves 6.

## Salmon

Many people who have tasted no salmon except that from a can claim—justifiably—that they do not like this fine food fish. The salmon is very rich in oil, and when canned the oil is preserved with the flesh. A fresh salmon, cooked by a process that allows the oil to drain away, has little resemblance to the canned fish.

Frozen salmon steaks, commonly available in supermarkets, and fresh salmon seasonally available in fish markets usually are cut from the Humpback Salmon, which ranks about fourth in desirability among the salmon species, but is by far the most numerous. Graded by quality, the top salmon is the Silver (Coho), followed in order by the King Chinook, and Sockeye. These are all Pacific salmon, but all are distributed nationally by refrigerated airfreight. The Atlantic salmon is of a different species, and is a superior food fish. Landlocked, or freshwater salmon, include the Kokanee in the east, the Coho in the north central region. All are good, and the fresh-water Coho is even better than the salt-water.

A salmon should never be fried or cooked in a skillet, but should be grilled or broiled so that the fat escaping from its flesh will drain away. If baked, it should be on a rack. Small salmon can be roasted whole, or poached whole; these fish will be either Silverside or Atlantic salmon, not as oily as other varieties. If you are on good terms with your fish dealer, he will probably be able to supply you with a roasting-sized center cut from a large salmon. Recipes for salmon are equally suited to the preparation of large trout.

### GRILLED SALMON STEAKS

| | |
|---|---|
| salmon steaks cut 1 to 1½ inches thick | 3 drops Tabasco Sauce or ⅛ teaspoon Hot Pepper Vinegar, |
| ½ cup dry white wine | page 163 |

Grill the steaks 4 to 5 minutes per side over medium-bright coals, basting frequently with the white wine into which the Tabasco or

## Salt-Water Fish

Hot Pepper Vinegar has been stirred. The easiest way of telling when the steaks are done is to touch the skin occasionally with the butt of a knife or fork; when it slips easily from the flesh, remove steaks and serve at once. The basting liquid should provide all the seasoning necessary to point up the salmon's own flavor, but some people will feel lost without adding salt.

There is a wide variation in the size of salmon steaks, depending on the weight of the fish from which they were cut. It's a good idea to allow about ½ pound per serving.

### PLANKED SALMON, CAMP-STYLE

whole salmon of 12 to 15 pounds; this is about as big a fish as plank-style cooking will handle. Fish of 20 pounds or more are too thick in the body to cook in this fashion

salt, pepper

lemon juice

When opened for planking, a whole salmon of 12 to 15 pounds will measure 16 to 18 inches across at the widest part, and the board it is cooked on should be several inches wider. Either nail two boards together with cleats across the back, or split your fish in two and use a pair of planks. Plywood is not suitable—it will blister and bulge. Soak the boards in water for an hour or two before using. Clean the salmon by opening along the backbone, if it is to be cooked whole, leaving the belly skin and flesh intact.

Flatten the fish skin side to the board, and nail it on with black or blued roofing nails; do not use galvanized nails. Prop the board on stakes or rocks 18 to 24 inches from a thick bed of coals. Cooking time for a 12- to 15-pound fish will be about 45 minutes, and at midpoint in cooking the board should be turned end for end to assure even cooking. It is better to use dark to medium-dark coals and a longer cooking time than to try to hurry the job by using bright coals. When you can slip a blunt knife easily between skin and flesh, the fish is done. Serve with lemon wedges and season only after the fish has been cooked.

**200**

Incidentally, don't discard the head of the salmon. Wrap it in several thicknesses of dampened paper and bury it in the coals. Dig it out after about an hour and pop the cheeks out with a knife tip. Like the "oyster" on a roast turkey's back, these cheeks are prize morsels; they have a flavor that sums up the entire fish in a few bites.

## Snapper

Often called a red snapper, this fish belongs to the big family of bottom-dwelling sea bass. Most snapper are in the 5- to 8-pound class, which make them ideal for cooking whole. They respond well to grilling, but their cavities should be well buttered for this style of cooking, as the snapper falls into the "lean" category of fish.

### SNAPPER IN BLANKETS

whole snapper of 5 to 6 pounds, cleaned and scaled, head, tail, and fins removed
½ to ¾ cup fresh lemon juice
salt
3 cups unsalted nuts; almonds, peanuts, pecans, etc.
1 small onion
1 clove garlic
2 bay leaves
1½ cups fine dry bread crumbs
1 cup ricotta or farmer's cheese or cottage cheese
¾ cup milk thinned with ¼ cup water
butter

Brush the entire fish, inside and out, with lemon juice, and let it rest in a cool place for 30 minutes; brush again with lemon juice and let rest 30 minutes more; brush a third time with lemon juice and sprinkle the cavity with salt. When it has rested for 30 minutes after this final treatment, the fish is ready to be cooked.

Chop the nuts coarsely, grate the onion, mash the garlic with a knife blade on a board, powder the bay leaves after removing stems and veins. Mix nuts, onions, garlic, and bay leaf with the bread crumbs. Dice the cheese if it is dry enough, or crumble it coarsely if it is very wet. If you use cottage cheese, get the large curd type and drain it over a bowl, squeezing in a cloth to remove as much liquid as possible, then crumble the cheese curds. Combine the cheese with the bread-crumb mixture, then add the milk, stirring to moisten well. Your objective is a very thick paste about the consistency of cold honey. Butter the Dutch oven lavishly and put half the bread-crumb mixture in a layer on its bottom. Lay the fish on it and cover with the remaining bread-crumb mixture. Cover the Dutch oven and bury in coals 1 to 1½ hours. In the sheepherder stove, use a large, heavy casserole dish with a tightly fitting cover and cook 40 to 45 minutes; use the same utensil in the kitchen oven and cook 50 to 55 minutes at 350 degrees.

Serves 4 very generously.

## Squid

Don't confuse squid with octopus. The squid you want is a dainty little chap about the size of a baby's fist, with a translucent pearly body and spaghetti-thin tentacles. Fish markets usually sell squid intact, as many customers use the ink sac in cooking. To clean squid, chop off the tentacles where they join the body; reserve them. Slit the bottom of the body envelope, take out the small transparent "bone" and the stomach; with the stomach will come the intestines and ink sac. Reserve the ink sac, rinse the squid's body inside and out in lightly salted water and drain.

### BAKED STUFFED SQUID

Sometime in the middle 1940s, Russ Lazio, whose family operates commercial fisheries at several points along the Pacific Coast, introduced me to the delights of squid by demonstrating how to cook them.

12 squid, cleaned, washed and drained; ink sacs reserved
1 medium-sized sweet onion
1 clove garlic
2 tablespoons fine light olive oil or peanut oil
3 slices firm bread: sourdough, French, or Italian
2 sprigs parsley
¼ teaspoon salt
large pinch pepper
1 egg yolk
2 small tomatoes, fresh or canned; if canned, well drained
¾ cup dry white wine

Chop tentacles fine along with the onion and garlic and sauté this mixture in 1 tablespoon oil over gentle heat, for 3 to 4 minutes. Remove from pan with a slotted spoon, allowing juices to drain back into pan. Break the bread into small pieces, moisten with a few spoonfuls of the wine, and combine with the onion-tentacle mixture, adding chopped parsley, salt, and pepper. Pierce and drain the ink sacs, beat ink and egg yolk together, and work this liquid into the bread mixture. Stuff the squid with this, about 1¼ tablespoons to each squid. Reserve the remaining bread mixture.

Add remaining oil to the juices in the pan, then chop the tomatoes and sauté them until they can be pulped with a spoon or fork. Blend the reserved stuffing and the remaining wine with the tomato pulp. Put a layer of this on the bottom of a well-greased Dutch oven and lay the squid on it, distributing any remaining stuffing around and between the squid so they do not touch each other or the pan's sides. Cover the oven and bury in coals 35 to 40 minutes. In the sheepherder oven, use a casserole-type dish and cook 20 to 25 minutes; use the same dish in the kitchen oven and cook 25 minutes at 300 degrees.

Serves 4.

## Striped Bass

Formerly classed as an anadromous fish, living in salt water and entering the brackish waters of bays and river estuaries only to spawn, stripers have been very successfully propagated in big lakes, especially those of the TVA complex. The fresh-water striped bass is a less fat fish than his seagoing brothers, with a somewhat finer-textured flesh. But whether from salt or fresh water, the striped bass runs to fat, and the warmer the water from which it is taken, the fatter the fish. Stripers should not be pan-fried, but grilled; when baked, a rack is essential. Striped bass under 10 pounds are best when baked whole or filleted; the bigger fish can be baked in sections, or steaks cut from his thick body for grilling.

### GRILLED STRIPED BASS FILLETS, ITALIAN STYLE

| | |
|---|---|
| 8 medium-sized fillets, about 3 by 8 inches, ½ inch thick | 1 sweet red (Bell) pepper |
| 2 tablespoons fine light olive oil or peanut oil | 1 cup dry white wine |
| | salt, pepper |
| 2 small sweet onions | 12 to 14 stuffed green olives |
| 3 ripe tomatoes | large sprig of fresh parsley |

Grill the fillets over medium-bright coals 3 to 4 minutes per side. In the skillet, heat oil gently. Cut the onions and tomatoes into chunks, seed the pepper and cut it into strips. Sauté until the pepper begins to soften. Pour in the wine, slip in the bass fillets. Simmer very gently 8 to 10 minutes. Taste and adjust seasoning with salt and pepper during the final 2 or 3 minutes of cooking. Just before serving, drop in the well-drained olives and sprinkle the surface of the dish with chopped parsley. Serve a portion of the sauce with each.
Serves 4.

### GRILLED STUFFED STRIPED BASS

| | |
|---|---|
| 8- to 10-pound whole bass, or tail section of larger fish | 1 lemon, quartered |
| | salt, pepper |
| 1 large onion, quartered | paprika |
| 2 firm tomatoes, quartered | |

Wipe the fish thoroughly inside and out. With the tip of a sharp knife, make shallow cuts inside the cavity between the ribs. Dust the onion, tomato and lemon chunks with salt and pepper, put them in the cavity, and close by sewing or with small skewers. Rub the out-side of the fish with paprika; this will retard cooking of the outer layer of flesh just beneath the skin. Grill over medium-bright coals 20 to 25 minutes per side; cooking time may need to be extended when a section of a fish larger than 10 pounds is being cooked. When the skin begins to bubble away from the flesh, the fish is done. Or test by inserting a knife tip along the dorsal fin; if there is no flow of liquid when the knife is twisted gently, cooking is complete. Lift off the skin, run a knife along the backbone and lift off the top fillet; the ribs and backbone can then be lifted off the bottom fillet and this piece lifted from the skin. Discard the stuffing. A fish stuffed this way can be broiled in the kitchen oven, using a rack in a reflector-type pan; timing will depend on the thickness of the fish.

An 8-pound fish serves 6 to 8.

## Swordfish

Most of the outsized deep-sea fish are sought for trophies rather than food, but all make good eating. Their meat is commonly en-countered in commercial markets, usually in the form of steaks or big fillets, and though the swordfish is classified as fat, its flesh is leaner than fresh-water fish in this category. Pan-cooking should be avoided if possible, however. The meat is better grilled or broiled; when it is being cooked it should be coated with a mixture containing a small amount of oil or butter, or basted with an oil-based liquid. Roasts should be cooked on a rack with a film of water on the bottom of a closed roasting pan.

### ANCHOVIED SWORDFISH STEAKS

2 steaks about 4 by 8 inches, cut 1 inch thick
½ tablespoon butter
1 anchovy fillet, well drained
   or
1½ teaspoons anchovy paste

½ teaspoon peanut oil or other cooking oil
pinch of Nepal pepper or cayenne

Wipe the steaks well. Combine butter and the anchovy fillet, crushing the fillet as it is blended, and adding a scanty pinch of pepper. If anchovy plaste is used it should be thinned with the oil to make a paste that will brush on the meat easily. Coat the steaks with the anchovied butter or paste; grill over bright coals 3 minutes on one side, 5 minutes on the other. Cooked in the broiler of the kitchen range, the steaks should be on a rack in a reflector pan, cooked 6 to 8 minutes without turning, then turned only long enough to brown the bottom side.

Serves 2.

## Whiting

A close relation to the cod, the whiting lends its name commercially to a number of other fish. It is commonly filleted for cooking, and has a firm, fine-textured flesh that is without a really pronounced flavor of its own. When grilled or broiled as fillets or steaks, it should be cooked with a flavor-giving coating such as that in the preceding recipe; when poached, the recipes for flounder fillets beginning on page 193 and the one for Italian-style striped bass fillets on page 204 are recommended.

| | |
|---|---|
| 3 cups flaked cooked whiting | fat for deep frying, ⅓ lard or |
| 3 eggs, separated | solid shortening and ⅔ |
| 3 tablespoons flour | bacon drippings |
| ¼ cup minced onion | 2 to 3 tablespoons minced |
| ¼ teaspoon garlic salt | fresh parsley |

Mash the fish flakes fine. Beat the egg yolks until they froth, then beat in the flour. Combine the fish, onion, and garlic salt with the beaten yolks to make a batter. Beat the egg whites stiff and fold the batter into them. Have 3 to 4 inches of fat in a deep kettle, hot enough to brown a 1-inch cube of bread in 40 seconds. Drop the batter by tablespoons into the fat—turn when one side is browned, drain well, roll in chopped parsley. Any of the sauces given beginning on page 161 go well with these light, fluffy fritters.

Serves 4.

## Whitebait, Grunnion

On both Atlantic and Pacific coasts are are seasonal runs of tiny fish, finger-sized or even smaller, variously called whitebait, grunnion, smelt, candlefish, or one of several other names. The schools will sometimes appear in the shallows off ocean beaches, sometimes in bays or up the mouths of streams; usually, the fish are scooped up in nets or with buckets. Some insist on cleaning the pinhead-sized cavities of these small fry, others cook them just as they come out of the water, in a kettle of fat steaming over a driftwood fire on the beach.

### FRIED WHITEBAIT

| | |
|---|---|
| 1 quart whitebait | fat for deep frying, ⅓ lard or |
| 1 cup flour | solid shortening, ⅔ bacon |
| 1 teaspoon salt | drippings |
| | lemon wedges, or sauce |

Wash but do not dry the fish. Mix flour and salt together, roll the fish in the seasoned flour, drop into hot fat a small handful at a time. There should be 3 to 4 inches of fat in the cooking kettle, hot enough to brown a 1-inch cube of bread in 30 seconds. Cook the fish 2 minutes, which brings them to a crackling crispness. Drain well on papers before serving with lemon wedges or any of the sauces beginning on page 161. The fish are eaten bones and all.

Serves 4.

# IX

---

# Shellfish

AMONG THE SHELLFISH, crustaceans, and amphibians in this chapter, family resemblances abound. Abalone, scallops, clams, oysters, mussels; crab, lobster, crawfish, shrimp; frog, turtle; all share family characteristics as grouped, and in cooking can generally be interchanged, though each may present separate problems in preparation for grill, skillet, or kettle.

Molluscs and crustaceans all benefit by a light touch in cooking and saucing. Heat tends to toughen both, when applied for lengthy periods. Sauces should as a rule be on the bland side, with perhaps a pinpoint touch of piquancy. And all the amphibians require prolonged cooking and sturdy sauces.

Inland dwellers are no longer restricted to frozen or canned shellfish and crustaceans; air freight delivers fresh clams, oysters, crabs, mussels, shrimp, lobsters, to even the most landbound areas. Most of the recipes in this chapter begin with fresh molluscs or crustaceans, but the canned or frozen varieties can be used in most with satisfactory results. When substitution is inadvisable, warning will be given in the individual recipes.

# MOLLUSCS

## Abalone, Conch

While the abalone is a bivalve and the conch a univalve, which places them in separate genera, family differences do not extend to their preparation and cooking. Until a few years ago, both were regional specialties, the abalone on the Pacific coast, the conch in Florida waters. Now, frozen abalone from Mexico and Japan, and conch from the Carribean islands are both in supermarkets.

Flesh of both these molluscs is a single big muscle. Both should be sliced across their grain in half-inch-thick pieces and pounded with a hammer or tenderizing mallet until they are cardboard thin. Both should be cooked briefly and gently, for too much heat will toughen them.

### ABALONE STEAKS

| | |
|---|---|
| 4 well-pounded abalone (or conch) steaks | 1½ tablespoons flour butter |
| 2 egg yolks, or ¾ cup milk | salt |
| 1 cup fine-crushed unsalted cracker crumbs | lemon wedges |

Dip the steaks into beaten egg yolks or milk, mix cracker crumbs with flour, and press the steaks firmly into this mixture. Over very gentle heat, sauté in butter until both sides are a golden tan; turn only once during cooking. Do not cook until the outsides are brown; this will make the meat tough. Salt lightly after cooking, serve with lemon wedges.

Serves 4.

## CONCH STEW

6 to 8 small conches; 2 abalone can be substituted, or a dozen scallops
1 quart boiling water
1 teaspoon salt
4 slices bacon or salt pork
2 small onions
4 large ripe tomatoes, or a #2 can of solid-pack tomatoes

1 tablespoon fresh lime juice
2 bay leaves
3 drops Tabasco Sauce or ⅛ teaspoon Hot Pepper Vinegar, page 163
¼ teaspoon salt
⅛ pound (4 tablespoons) butter —no substitutes
½ cup medium-dry sherry

After pounding the meat, cut it into 1-inch squares and parboil 2 to 3 minutes in the water, to which the salt has been added. Sauté the bacon or salt pork in a deep skillet or heavy pot; if salt pork is used its rinds should be trimmed off and the meat blanched 1 minute in boiling water. When the bacon or salt pork begins to become transparent, slice and add the onions, and when the onions begin to soften cut the tomatoes in coarse chunks and add them to the pan, with the lime juice; stir this mixture well for 2 or 3 minutes. Put in the pieces of conch, and add 1½ cups of the water in which they were parboiled. Add bay leaves, Tabasco, and salt. Close the pan, simmer 5 to 7 minutes. Remove from heat, stir in the butter and sherry, and serve.

Serves 4 to 6.

## Clams

For such a meek, mild-mannered mollusc, the clam has generated more gastronomic controversy than anything its size. There will never be an end to the arguments over the relative virtues of cherrystones, littlenecks, quahogs, butters, razors, and goeducks, any more than the controversy over New England versus New York (or Manhattan) chowder will ever be settled. No drums will be beaten here for either side of either argument; advice will be offered in the best neutral traditions.

Let the manner in which you plan to cook them, modified by your personal preferences, guide you in choosing clams. Batter-fry or shell-bake the smaller types; use the more rugged specimens in chowders or chop them and mix with other ingredients, then stuff them back into their shells for baking.

If you dig your own clams, defer your feast until the day after digging. Scrub the shells thoroughly, using a stiff brush. Put the clams in a tub of sea water, or add ⅓ cup salt to each gallon of fresh water. For each quart of clams in the tub, sprinkle 2 tablespoons of corn meal on the water. Within 8 to 12 hours the clams will purge themselves of any sand they have ingested before being taken. Some people shorten the waiting period to 4 hours, and eat grit as a result.

An oyster knife is a vital tool if you are shucking clams to be used in chowder or soup. Open them over a bowl, to save their salty juice. The bigger varieties must be trimmed, the necks and hard muscle cut off; the muscle is discarded, the necks chopped for soup or chowder. If you want to be very delicate, skin the necks. Of course, the big clams such as the goeduck will require this treatment.

When buying clams, your nose is the best tester for freshness, but if you have doubts or a cold in the head, keep in mind that a bad clam will float in water, a good one will sink. And in self-preservation, remember that clams, oysters, and mussels are all susceptible to water pollution which only laboratory tests can reveal. Be sure of the area in which you dig clams and observe local warnings about polluted beaches and closed seasons.

## CLAM CHOWDER, NEW ENGLAND STYLE

| | |
|---|---|
| 1 quart shelled clams, their broth reserved | ¼ teaspoon salt |
| 4 cups diced potatoes | ⅛ teaspoon freshly ground black pepper |
| 2 cups salt pork in ½-inch cubes | 1 quart milk |
| 1 cup coarsely chopped onion | 3 tablespoons butter |

Parboil the potatoes 5 minutes; reserve the water. Rinds should be trimmed from the salt pork before it is cubed, and blanch the cubes 2 or 3 minutes in boiling water; drain, then crisp the cubed pork in a skillet, add the onions, and cook until the onions are transparent. Drain the potatoes and add enough potato water to the clam broth to make 1 quart. Pour this back over the potatoes, then drain the salt pork and onions from the skillet with a slotted spoon, allowing the fat to run back into the pan. Add the pork and onions to the potatoes, then put in the clams, whole or coarsely minced; edible portions of the necks should also go into the pot. Stir in the salt and pepper, simmer 10 minutes.

Pour in the milk, and from this point do not allow the chowder to boil. Let it simmer very gently while you taste and adjust the seasoning. Stir in the butter, and when it has melted, serve the chowder. Some very good chowder cooks add a big handful of oyster crackers an instant before dishing up; others equally good prefer to let each individual add his own crackers. The option is yours.

Serves 4 to 6.

### CLAM CHOWDER, NEW YORK (OR MANHATTAN) STYLE

1 quart shelled clams, their broth reserved
3 cups diced potatoes
1 cup salt pork cubed ¼ inch
¾ cup minced onion
4 large ripe tomatoes or a #2 can solid-pack tomatoes, well drained (those addicted to "instant" cooking now use tomato juice—follow them if you like, it's your chowder and your reputation that are at stake)
½ teaspoon salt
large dash black pepper
2 tablespoons chopped parsley

Parboil the potatoes 5 minutes, reserve the water. The pork should be trimmed of its rinds and blanched before being cut into dice. Crisp the pork in a skillet, then add the onions and cook until they are tender, but not brown. Drain the potatoes, add enough of their water to the clam broth to make 1½ quarts. Pour this liquid over the potatoes, strain the pork and onions from the skillet with a slotted spoon, letting most of the fat flow off them, and add the pork-onion mixture to the potatoes. Chop the tomatoes coarsely and put them in, with salt and pepper. Simmer until the tomatoes soften. Add the clams, minced fine, and edible portions of their necks. Simmer 8 to 10 minutes, stir in the chopped parsley, and serve.

If you belong to the tomato juice school, parboil the potatoes and prepare the salt pork and onions as directed. Combine the clam broth with 3 cups tomato juice and add potato water to make 1 quart; pour this over the potatoes, pork, and onions, add the clams, and simmer 10 minutes. Taste to adjust seasoning, and serve.

(There is another option. Some cooks try to carry water on both shoulders by adding milk to New York Chowder. It is a compromise, and like most compromises, satisfies very few.)

Serves 4 to 6.

## SHORE-BAKED CLAMS

Like its Western cousin, the barbecue, and its Southern kin, the fish fry, a Down East or Eastern Shore Clambake is a style of cooking combined with an event. It's possible—barely—to approximate the real thing in a backyard or patio, but it really requires quantities of lobsters, clams, corn, and potatoes all cooking in company with seaweed in a sealed pit to produce that mouth-tickling flavor found at a shore clambake. Here is the traditional menu and procedure; later, we'll look at the substitutes.

For each person, allow a quart of scrubbed but unshucked clams, one lobster, two ears of corn, and one or two potatoes. Sometimes onions find their way onto the list of ingredients and if they are on yours, allow one per person. The only other essentials are butter in incredible quantities, a few filled salt shakers, and the energy to dig a pit in the soft beach sand, line it with stones, and collect a huge pile of seaweed.

How long and wide your pit must be is determined by the number to be served. In soft beach sand, the pit should be long rather than deep. For a dozen, the pit would be about 6 feet long, 18 to 20 inches deep, and perhaps 3 feet wide. You need enough stones to cover the pit's bottom, enough firewood to create a healthy blaze for several hours, and enough seaweed to build the several layers on which the food will be cooked.

Line the pit's bottom with stones, build your fire on them, and keep it burning three to four hours. Shovel out the coals in a neat pile, to be used later, and lay wet seaweed on the smoking stones. On the seaweed go the clams, which are covered with a second seaweed layer to hold the lobsters, which are covered with a third seaweed layer to take the potatoes and corn. The corn should be peeled down to its last 3 or 4 layers of husk, the silk removed, and the husks smoothed back in place. A layer of seaweed is spread over the vegetables, the coals from the pit on this, and a final layer of seaweed spread over the still-glowing coals. Stretch a tarpaulin over the final layer of seaweed and shovel sand on top, especially along its edges to seal the pit.

About three hours later, open the pit, fish out the goodies, and distribute them, having plenty of melted butter and salt on hand.

You can approximate this result on a small scale by sinking a washtub or a galvanized garbage pail, or one of the big metal cans in which restaurants and bakeries buy shortening, into the sand or into the earth in your own backyard. Rocks are heated on a surface fire and lowered into the can; if you live inland where there's no seaweed, lettuce leaves soaked in salt water can substitute. The cooking time will be longer, since your heat source will be both smaller and cooler. You can also cook clams in a steamer, if you're willing to forgo the tangy flavor the salty seaweed adds.

Like a pitless barbecue, a ginless martini, or a ham that hasn't been smoked, a clambake's not a clambake unless you follow the traditions.

## BAKED STUFFED CLAMS

2 to 3 dozen unshelled clams
rock salt
3 slices crisp cooked bacon
3 or 4 fresh or canned mushrooms; ¾ cup when
chopped fine
2 tablespoons minced fresh
parsley

½ teaspoon salt
1 cup fine dry bread crumbs
Tabasco Sauce or Hot Pepper
Vinegar, page 163
butter

Scrub and purge clams as described. Spread a thick layer of rock salt on the bottom of a pan and press the clams into the salt to hold them upright; set the pan on coals until the clams open. Lift the clams out, pull from their shells, draining the juice into a bowl. Chop the clams fine, discarding the muscle and skinning the necks before chopping. Mince the bacon, mushrooms, and parsley and combine with the clams, bread crumbs, and salt; moisten with the clam broth to create a mixture that will hold its shape when pressed into half a clamshell. Stuff the shells, mounding generously. On top of each, put a drop of Tabasco or Hot Pepper Vinegar and a dab of butter. Return the stuffed shells to the pan of salt, cover the pan, and put it on coals 15 minutes. In a sheepherder oven, cook 8 to 10 minutes in an open pan; in the kitchen oven, in an open pan, 5 to 8 minutes under the broiler.
Serves 4.

## CLAMS FRIED IN BATTER

2 to 3 dozen shucked clams
2 eggs, separated
½ cup milk
1 cup all-purpose flour
¾ teaspoon baking powder

¾ teaspoon salt
fat for deep frying: ⅓ lard or
solid shortening and ⅔
bacon drippings

Beat the egg yolks until frothy, then beat in the milk. Sift together the flour, baking powder, and salt; stir the dry ingredients into the yolk mixture to form a thin batter. Beat the egg whites until stiff and fold the batter into them. Have fat to a depth of 4 to 6 inches in a deep kettle, hot enough to brown a 1-inch cube of bread in 40 to 45 seconds. Dip each clam into the batter separately, stir it around until thoroughly coated, then drop into the hot fat. It will sink, then rise to the surface, puffed up; turn the puff so it will brown evenly, and remove when richly tanned. Lift onto papers to drain, then serve at once. These fritters must be eaten as soon as possible without burning your mouth.

Serves 4 to 6.

## Mussels

Mussels have a bad reputation in some parts because when flooded with polluted waters they quickly become tainted. If you spent your life under similar circumstances, you would no doubt become tainted, too. Mussels are the easiest shellfish to gather; they favor shallow waters and cling to rocks and piers that are uncovered when low tides ebb. There are also mussels in fresh water, in most of the rivers that feed directly into the ocean, and these are as good as the salt-water or tidewater mussels. Inlanders can buy mussels, either shipped by refrigerated air freight or canned. Do not expect the canned ones to be as good as the fresh. Let Molly Malone and her cry of "Cockles and mussels, alive, alive o!" be your hint—live mussels are best. They should be scrubbed under running water with a stiff brush and their beards trimmed with scissors just before cooking.

### BUTTERED MUSSELS

| | | |
|---|---|---|
| 24 to 36 mussels in the shell | | young green onions |
| ¼ pound butter | ¼ | teaspoon salt |
| ½ cup minced fresh parsley | | rock salt |
| ⅓ cup minced chives or tender | | |

**216**

Scrub and beard the mussels. Knead together the butter, parsley, chives or onions, and salt. Have ready a long-handled spoon, such as an iced-tea spoon, warmed. Spread a thick layer of rock salt in the bottom of a heavy pan and press the mussels into the salt so they will stay upright. Put the pan on the coals. When the mussels open their shells, drop a scanty spoonful of the herbed butter into each one. Cook until the butter sizzles.

Serves 4 to 6.

## STEAMED MUSSELS, SAILOR STYLE

This is the famed *Moules à la Marinière* of France, a dish of such classic simplicity that it has not been improved in a couple of centuries.

| | |
|---|---|
| 24 to 36 mussels in the shell, scrubbed and beards trimmed | 6 to 8 shallots, chopped fine |
| | 1 clove garlic, chopped fine |
| 3 tablespoons butter (no substitutes) | ½ cup dry white wine |
| | pinch of fine-powdered bay leaf |

Melt butter and sauté the chopped shallots and garlic; when they begin to get tender, pour in the wine and sprinkle in the bay leaf. Simmer 2 minutes. Put the mussels in the pan, close the lid tightly, and cook 5 to 7 minutes over very bright coals. Open the pan after 5 minutes; if the mussels have not opened, cook 2 minutes more. When all the shells have opened, empty the pan into a heated bowl— mussels, shells, and sauce all together. Serve with crusty French bread, and certainly more white wine.

Serves 4 to 6.

## PICKLED MUSSELS

| | |
|---|---|
| 24 steamed or canned mussels, broth reserved | 1 teaspoon salt |
| | 2 or 3 whole cloves |
| 1 sweet onion | dash cayenne or Nepal pepper |
| 1 small carrot | ¼ cup fine light olive oil or peanut oil |
| 1 clove garlic | |
| 6 cracked peppercorns | 1 cup white wine vinegar |

**Shellfish**

Grate the onion, carrot, and garlic; combine with all the seasonings and the oil and vinegar. Add enough cool water to the mussel broth to make 1 cup. Stir well, then put in the mussels, making sure they are well covered. Let stand 6 to 8 hours in a cool but not refrigerated place, stirring occasionally. Remove the mussels and put them into their half-shells or in a shallow bowl. Strain the marinade, discard the solids; use the broth to pour over the mussels. Serve on crackers as an hors d'oeuvre, either whole or minced with some of the broth to moisten them.

Serves 4 to 6.

## Oysters

You probably like oysters or you don't. There seems to be no middle ground. If you're among the oyster afficionados, chances are that you'll have your own special favorites: Chincoteagues or bluepoints or Gardner's Cove or Barnegats; Mobile or New Orleans or Galveston; Pacific or Olympia.

There are no more public oyster beds, where an individual with energy enough to wield an oyster rake can gather his own, and some of the perennial favorites are diminishing in numbers. But there are enough to go around, and thanks to jet planes and refrigeration, oysters go around further than ever these days. It's relatively easy to enjoy fresh oysters on the half-shell, no matter how far inland you may be. And there are jar-packed and canned oysters on the shelves of most grocery stores.

### SPIT-BROILED OYSTERS (ANGELS ON HORSEBACK)

| | |
|---|---|
| 2 dozen oysters, fresh or canned | chopped parsley |
| thin slices of bacon | very fine dry bread crumbs |
| butter | |

Roll each oyster in a half-slice of bacon, and skewer; the oyster should be covered but not encased. Broil over bright coals 2 to 3 minutes; remove, take off the bacon, roll the oysters in butter, then parsley, and finally in bread crumbs. Return to the spit, broil until the crumbs brown.

Serves 4.

## CREAMED OYSTERS

2 dozen oysters, fresh or canned
½ cup butter (no substitutes)
½ teaspoon dry mustard
½ anchovy fillet, drained, or a pea-sized piece of anchovy paste
dash of Nepal pepper

1 cup celery, minced fine
1 pint cream (diluted evaporated milk can be used; dilute ⅔ pint milk from the can with ⅓ pint water)
½ cup medium-dry sherry

Melt butter in a deep skillet over low heat and stir in the mustard. Mash the anchovy fillet and add it, then the pepper, and stir until smooth. Put in the celery and cook over very gentle heat until tender. Pour in the cream and when it comes to a simmer—not a boil—add the oysters. Let simmer 4 to 5 minutes, remove from heat, stir in the sherry, and serve at once, over toast points or boiled rice.

Serves 4 to 6.

## OYSTER LOAF

2 dozen oysters, fresh or canned
1 loaf firm, crusty bread, unsliced
3 eggs
½ cup cream (undiluted evaporated milk can be used)

1 teaspoon salt
dash cayenne
butter

Use bread a day or two old. If all you can find is mass-produced squoosh bread, give up the idea of making an oyster loaf—there's no point in wasting good oysters. The best kind of bread is the firm-crusted French or Italian. Cut the top off your loaf of good bread an inch below its peak, and pull the insides out carefully, leaving a crust ¾ to 1 inch thick on sides, end, and bottom. Reserve the inside portion, and if it is at all soft, dry it in the oven, then make fine crumbs of it.

Beat the eggs lightly with the cream and seasonings. Sauté the bread crumbs in a dry skillet until they are light brown, or brown them on a cookie sheet in the oven. Combine bread crumbs with the egg-cream mixture to make a fairly dry stuffing. Fill the bread case with the bread-crumb mixture, dotting it generously with oysters as you fill. Put on the top of the loaf and secure it with toothpicks. Brush the outside of the loaf with butter. Put it on a rack in a Dutch oven and bury it in coals for 35 to 40 minutes. In a sheepherder oven, cook 20 minutes in an uncovered pan; in the kitchen oven, in an uncovered pan, 25 minutes at 250 degrees. To serve, slice thickly as you would slice bread. You can cook this in individual hard roll cases, but at the cost of some flavor.

Serves 6 to 8.

## Scallops

Two kinds of scallops are brought in by commercial fishermen, big ocean scallops and a smaller, sweeter bay scallop. Usually the scallops are sold without the shells, as the fishermen have a separate market for these. Frozen scallops are available both plain and "breaded," and the latter should be avoided for reasons already explained on page 158. Fresh or frozen scallops can be cooked by almost any recipe used for clams, mussels, or oysters, with the cooking time extended about 10 per cent.

If you come by scallops in their shells, clean them by the same method used for mussels—scrub well with a brush, and trim off the beard. When the scallop is taken from its shell either to be eaten or cooked, the tough hinge muscle should be cut off and discarded.

Don't look for a recipe for "Coquilles St. Jacques," because there is no such thing. The Pilgrim Scallop of European waters is called

"Coquille St. Jacques" in France; it is cooked in many ways, and customarily listed on menus as "Coquilles St. Jacques au Gratin," or "Coquilles St. Jacques Mornay," to identify not only the type of scallop cooked, but the manner of its cooking. So the mere listing of "Coquilles St. Jacques" on a restaurant menu makes as much sense as listing "Potatoes" without telling whether they are raw, boiled, fried, or mashed.

## GRILLED CREAMED SCALLOPS

| | |
|---|---|
| 2 dozen scallops, fresh or frozen | 3 tablespoons butter |
| rock salt, if cooking in scallop shells | ¼ teaspoon paprika |
| | 2 tablespoons fine-chopped chives |
| 1 pint cream (dilute ⅔ pint evaporated milk with ⅓ pint water, if desired) | ½ teaspoon salt |

You can cook this dish in scallop shells, available at many grocery stores and specialty houses, for dramatic effect, or you can cook it in a heavy skillet for utility. If cooking in shells, spread a layer of rock salt on the bottom of a pan and bed the shells into the salt by pressing them firmly in place. Put a scallop into each shell. Warm the cream in a saucepan, stir in the remaining ingredients. Do not allow to boil or even to simmer, just warm until the butter melts. Pour into the shells, filling each one about half full, then set on coals and cook until the cream begins to bubble lightly, 6 to 8 minutes. If you do not have a set of shells, prepare the sauce in a heavy shallow pan, such as a skillet, and add the scallops when the butter is melted, then place on coals and cook until the sauce bubbles up.

Serves 4 to 6.

## SEVICHE OR ESCABECHE OR SOUSE

There are dozens of regional names given this uncooked dish; the three given above are those by which it is known, respectively, in South America, Spain, and the Caribbean. It can be made from scallops, and in most places is, but in the Caribbean it is often made with conch. It is also made from mussels, clams, and raw fish of various kinds. All versions strongly resemble that which follows.

| | |
|---|---|
| 1 dozen raw scallops, chopped | ½ green (Bell) pepper |
| 1 cup fresh lime or lemon juice | ½ sweet onion |
| ¼ teaspoon salt | 1 tablespoon tarragon vinegar |
| 2 pimientos or sweet red (Bell) peppers | ¼ cup cool water |
| | ¼ teaspoon Nepal pepper |

Marinate the chopped scallops for at least 4 hours in the lime or lemon juice to which the salt has been added, stirring occasionally. Chop the pimientos, green pepper, and onion, and marinate in a second bowl in the vinegar mixed with the water and pepper. Marinate the same length of time as the scallops. Just before serving, drain the pepper-onion mixture and combine with the scallops and their marinade. The Seviche can be served as it is, in a bowl, or piled in scallop shells, or spread on toast rounds or crackers as an hors d'oeuvre.

## CRUSTACEANS

## Crab

Large and varied as the crab tribe is, you are apt to meet only two or three of its members in your cooking activities. These are the rock crab, often called the blue crab, which during its seasonal cycles of growth sheds its shell to become the soft-shell crab; the big Dungeness crab of deep Pacific waters; and the king crab of Alaska. Any recipe calling for use of rock crabs will serve for other small members of the clan unless the softshell is specified; any recipe for Dungeness crabs will also serve for the king. Parboiled and frozen rock and Dungeness crabs in the shell are now commonly available even in inland stores. If you live away from the coastal areas, ask your dealer to order for you if he does not stock them regularly, or use canned crabmeat. In dishes where this substitution is not advisable, warning will be given.

Crabs must be kept overnight after being taken, in a tub of seawater, or a brine made by adding ⅓ cup of salt to each gallon of fresh water. They will purge themselves during this holding period, and can then be cooked, in fresh water, in a tub or big kettle with an old bedsheet or towel folded to cover the vessel's bottom. Start the cooking in cold water, bring to a boil, then simmer 5 to 10 minutes. When they are cool, the crabs are ready to be cleaned.

Hard-shell crabs are all alike in construction, so whether you are cleaning a small rock crab or a big Dungeness the procedure is the same. A sturdy, sharp knife is run around the body between the top and bottom of the shell, and the bottom plate lifted off. Lungs (or gills) and sand sacs and the big intestinal vein are all recognizable on sight; these are lifted out and discarded. Then the meat is lifted out of the shell, the thin flat tendons interlacing it are removed, and the claws cracked and their meat extracted.

Soft-shell crabs are handled in a slightly different fashion. The flexible outer covering called the shell is actually part of their flesh, and is edible. Clean soft-shells by cutting away the face, the knife moving in an arc just back of the eyes. The ends of the arc you have cut house gills and sand sac, which can be scooped out with the knife tip. Then a similar but shallower cut at the center of the back apron removes the vent; since the crabs have purged themselves overnight, removal of the intestine is unnecessary.

All crabs must undergo parboiling and cleaning before they can be used in further cooking. If you live in an area where live crabs are sold, the market man usually will offer you a choice of live or boiled and cleaned crustaceans.

## BAKED DEVILED CRABS

At Sil Oliva's restaurant on San Francisco's Fisherman's Wharf, big Dungeness crabs are prepared this way.

4 Dungeness crabs and their shells, cleaned and parboiled, or 6 cups canned crabmeat

4 tablespoons butter (no substitutes)

4 tablespoons flour

1 cup heavy cream (evaporated milk diluted ¾ milk to ¼ water can be used)

4 or 5 drops Tabasco Sauce

1 teaspoon cayenne

¾ teaspoon salt

½ cup medium-dry sherry paprika

1 to 1½ cups fine dry bread crumbs

thin slices of lemon

Flake the crabmeat, including that from legs and claws, being sure to remove and discard all tendons. Melt the butter over gentle heat, stir in the flour to make a smooth white roux, and cook 3 to 4 minutes, but do not brown. Add the cream, stir until smooth. Put in the seasonings and the crabmeat, simmer very gently 5 minutes. Stir in the sherry and remove from heat. Fill the 4 crabshells with this mixture; if you have used canned crab, divide it among shallow gratin dishes or ramekins. Sprinkle the tops with paprika and a coating of bread crumbs, and put a slice of lemon in the center of each. If crabshells are being used, put them in a shallow pan with a layer of rock salt on its bottom, pressing the shells into the salt so they will stay upright. Cook 25 to 30 minutes in the sheepherder oven, 35 to 40 minutes in the kitchen oven at 300 degrees. Just before serving, brush the top of each shell or dish lightly with butter and sprinkle with more paprika.

Serves 4 very generously.

### FRIED CRAB CLAWS

One of the centers of the Dungeness crab fishery on the Pacific Coast is four hundred miles north of San Francisco, where the icy Humboldt Current swings to within a few miles of land. On shore, the tiny village of Trinidad is one of the points where crab boats put in to refuel. Dave Zebo of Trinidad gets his crabs fresh from the boats, and serves their big claws cooked in this fashion.

16 to 20 Dungeness crab claws, parboiled; there is no substitute
2 cups milk
2 eggs

3 cups fine unsalted cracker crumbs
½ cup butter
salt, pepper
lemon wedges or lemon juice

Crack the claws and remove the meat in one piece. Beat milk and eggs together, let the meat from the claws rest in this 5 minutes. Drain lightly, roll in cracker crumbs, and sauté gently over low heat, cooking only long enough to brown both sides to a crusty gold. Season after cooking with a minimum of salt and pepper and sprinkle with the lemon juice, or serve with lemon wedges.

Serves 4 to 6.

### GRILLED SOFT-SHELL CRABS

This is more a matter of procedure than a recipe. You should allow 4 crabs per serving, and quantities of ingredients required should be adjusted to the number of crabs you will cook. You will need about 1 teaspoon of butter—no substitutes—for each crab; for every 4 teaspoons of butter, ¼ teaspoon of fresh lemon juice; a pinch of powdered thyme or basil, and a modicum of salt and pepper. Combine the butter with the lemon juice and seasonings and brush a light coating on each cleaned, parboiled crab, putting a dab of the butter into the shell tips where the gills have been removed. Grill over medium-bright coals 5 to 7 minutes per side, brushing them with the seasoned butter as they cook. You can use the broiler of your kitchen range; timing will be about 8 minutes per side.

### DEEP-FRIED SOFT-SHELL CRABS

16 cleaned, parboiled soft-shell crabs
½ cup cooking oil
1 teaspoon salt
¼ teaspoon pepper
1 cup flour
2 beaten eggs

3 to 4 cups fine dry bread crumbs or unsalted cracker crumbs
fat for deep frying: ⅓ lard or solid shortening and ⅔ bacon drippings

**Shellfish**

Mix the oil, salt, and pepper. Let the crabs rest in the seasoned oil 5 minutes, then drain them well and roll in flour, dip in the beaten egg, and roll in the bread crumbs. You will need 3 to 4 inches of fat in a deep skillet or kettle, hot enough to brown a 1 inch cube of bread in 1 minute. Put in the crabs a few at a time so the temperature of the fat will not be lowered too suddenly. Cook 3 to 5 minutes, just long enough to brown evenly. Drain well on papers. One of the sauces given beginning on page 161, used very sparingly, or one of the herbed butters from page 164 used rather lavishly, make suitable accompaniments.

Serves 4.

## CRAB CHOWDER

1½  cups flaked crabmeat, fresh
    or canned
3  cups milk
2  hard-boiled eggs
2  tablespoons butter
1  tablespoon flour
peel of 1 lemon, grated fine

½  cup thick cream (or un-
    diluted evaporated milk)
dash of Angostura or Peychaud
    bitters
½  cup medium-dry sherry
¼  teaspoon salt
large dash pepper

Heat the milk but do not let it boil. Mash the egg yolks with the butter, flour, and lemon peel. (The easy way to grate lemon peel is to rub the whole lemon lightly on the grater, turning it when the first trace of the pith under the skin appears.) Blend the paste of egg yolks into the milk, adding it in small pieces and stirring until smooth. Chop the egg whites coarsely, and add them and the crab-meat to the milk. Simmer 5 minutes without boiling, stir in the cream and bitters, and simmer 2 or 3 minutes. Remove from heat and add the sherry and other seasonings.

Serves 4 to 6.

## Crawfish

To keep things straight, it's what is called in most sections of America the crawfish or crawdad, not the European crayfish, that we're taking up now. The crawfish is to be found in almost all North American waters, but is such a shy and retiring fellow that you'll seldom realize he's there. He is smaller than the European crayfish, seldom reaching more than 4 to 5 inches in length. The crawfish has a more delicate flavor than his seagoing cousins, the shrimp and prawn, though all belong to the same big family.

About half the fish that "get away" from bait fishermen are crawfish. Their quick, nervous, very light nips at baited hooks are like the first explorations of a taking fish. No hooks are needed to take crawfish, though. Tie a chunk of old raw meat or a thick slice of bacon to a line and drop it to the bottom of a lake or stream. Let it come to rest, then tighten gently. When the line quivers slightly, that's a crawfish at work. Wait a minute or so until he gets engrossed in the serious business of eating, then pull in the line very slowly and smoothly. The crawfish will hang on to his meal, and you can bring him up close enough to allow you to slip a fine-meshed dipnet under him, just before he gets to the surface.

Crawfish are cooked like shrimp, but should be cleaned before parboiling. Grasp the center tail segment, twist and pull. This removes the intestinal vein, and the crawfish can then be simmered 5 minutes in lightly salted water—1 teaspoon of salt per quart—and its thin shell peeled off. The head is cut off at the first segmented joint. Commercial crawfish farming has in recent years become a major farm industry, and frozen crawfish can be found in most supermarkets. They can also be bought live from bait houses in areas where warm-water fishing is done.

Recipes given for crawfish are also suitable for use with shrimp and prawns.

### CRAWFISH WITH BRANDY

2 to 3 dozen crawfish, cleaned but not parboiled
3 cups cold water
1 large onion sliced very thin
2 carrots peeled and cut in thin strips
1 clove garlic halved lengthwise or crushed
1 teaspoon salt
⅛ teaspoon powdered thyme
bay leaf
¾ cup brandy

**Shellfish**

Put the onion, carrots, garlic, salt, thyme, and bay leaf in the water and bring to a boil, then simmer 10 minutes. Strain the liquid through cloth into a clean saucepan, add the brandy, and bring to a slow simmer. Put in the crawfish a few at a time, cook 5 to 8 minutes. Remove and shell the crawfish into a warmed bowl, strain the pot liquid over them through a cloth, and serve. Or leave the crawfish in their shells and pile them on a warm platter. Strain ½ cup of the pot liquid into 1½ cups mayonnaise, mix well, and let each diner shell and sauce his own.

Serves 4.

## CRAWFISH IN WHITE WINE

2 to 3 dozen crawfish, cleaned but not parboiled
2 cups dry white wine
1½ cups fish stock or chicken stock
*bouquet garni* made up of 2 sprigs parsley, 3 or 4 shallots, bay leaf, a sprig of fresh thyme or pinch of powdered thyme
½ teaspoon salt
dash of cayenne

Heat the mixed wine and broth to a gentle simmer, with the *bouquet garni* in a cloth bag in the pot. Add salt and cayenne. Drop in the crawfish a few at a time to keep the temperature even. As they are done, after simmering 5 to 8 minutes, take them out and shell them into a warm bowl. When all the crawfish are cooked, re-move the *bouquet garni* from the pot, bring the liquid to a brisk boil over bright coals, and cook long enough to reduce ⅓ in volume. Pour over the crawfish and serve.

Serves 4 to 6.

## Lobster

Unless you're one of the few remaining New Englanders insisting on your right to drop a pot or two into the sea and rugged enough to do so, the king of crustaceans is only available across the fish-market counter. True lobsters come only from the American Atlantic coast;

the Pacific and Mediterranean lobsters are both types of *langouste,* a clawless crustacean. There are several firms listed in the Appendix on page 300 that guarantee live delivery anywhere of lobsters, so you can enjoy His Highness at his best wherever you happen to live. The best second choice is frozen rock lobster tails, found in most supermarkets, with canned lobster a third choice.

Regardless of your plans for him later on, a lobster must first be boiled. A live lobster put on the grill just shouldn't happen, though it has been done by a few novice outdoor chefs of my acquaintance. Drop your lobster live into a pot of cold water and bring it slowly to a boil, then let it simmer; time required will depend on the size of the lobster. As it cooks, the shell will change color from green to red, but this is no indication of the degree to which the lobster is cooked inside. However, an 8-pound lobster will be ready in about 12 minutes from the time the water first begins to simmer.

When cool enough to handle easily, turn the lobster on its back and slit its corrugated belly from head to tail with a sharp, sturdy knife. At its head you will find the queen, or lady, which must be removed; the dark intestinal vein running from the queen (which is the stomach) to the tail must also come out. Under the meat in the center of the body is lung tissue, called coral or tomalley; this should be spooned out to use in any sauce you prepare. Do not leave it in if the lobster is to be grilled. Now you can either pick out the meat, crack the claws, and serve the lobster or you can pick out the meat to go into a sauced dish, or you can put the whole lobster on the grill.

Frozen rock lobster tails have been cleaned before freezing, and are also parboiled. Grilling should be started without thawing and cooking time extended. When these tails are used in other dishes calling only for the meat, they should be thawed rapidly under running water and the meat cooked at once.

### GRILLED LOBSTER

| | |
|---|---|
| whole lobster or frozen rock lobster tails | melted butter<br>lemon wedges or lemon juice |

**Shellfish**

Before going to the grill a fresh lobster should have its tail broken; bend the tail back until it snaps or it will curl up tightly while cooking. Grill the lobster belly down over medium-dark coals for 3 to 4 minutes, then turn on its back to cook 8 to 10 minutes. After turning, dribble a generous quantity of melted butter, or one of the herbed butters given beginning on page 164, into the slit opened for cleaning. About midway during cooking, crack the big claws to allow steam to escape.

Frozen lobster tails will require about ⅓ more cooking time than fresh lobsters. Before putting unthawed on the grill, take off the bottom carapace if this has not been done before freezing. Spread a thick layer of butter or herbed butter over the flesh and cook shell side down without turning.

In kitchen cooking, put either fresh or frozen lobster shell side down on a rack in a reflecting broiler pan and cook without turning. Timing will be the same as grilling over coals.

Serve the grilled lobster with lemon wedges, additional melted butter, salt and pepper if you insist; and if you go that far, with one of the piquant sauces given beginning page 163. Allow one small lobster for each serving, split bigger ones to serve two.


**LOBSTER POLENTA**

This is probably the thriftiest way you can find to serve lobster to a large group and still retain its subtle, elusive flavor.

| | |
|---|---|
| 2½ cups flaked lobster meat, fresh, frozen, or canned | ¾ tablespoon salt |
| 1½ cups yellow corn meal | ⅛ teaspoon garlic salt or a pinch of garlic powder |
| 1 quart boiling water | 2 tablespoons butter |

Add the corn meal to the boiling water a little at a time, stirring often to prevent sticking. Stir in the salt while cooking. Cook 20 minutes, remove from heat, and set aside to cool. When firmly set, loosen the edges of the corn meal with a spatula or knife from the sides of the pot and turn it out on a plate. Slice across to get three rounds of corn meal. Choose a skillet or deep heavy pan roughly the size of the corn-meal rounds. Butter it, bottom and sides, and put one of the corn-meal slices on the bottom. Spread it with half the lobster meat and sprinkle very sparingly with garlic salt or even more sparingly with garlic powder. Put on the second corn-meal round and the remaining lobster, season, and top with the third corn-meal round. Dot its top generously with butter. Cover the pan and put over very low heat 10 to 15 minutes, until it is warmed through. The pan can be placed in an oven for warming, if you wish. To serve, slice in wedges like a cake.

There are several variations. One calls for the addition of thin slices of ricotta between the rounds of corn meal; another uses a sprinkling of grated Parmesan and chopped hard-boiled egg; another adds thin slices of barely ripe tomatoes between the rounds. Use your own judgment how far you want to go in diluting the lobster's flavor with these additions. The variation using ricotta, for which a domestic cream cheese could be substituted, is probably the best.

Serves 8 to 10.

## Shrimp

There are differences in body configuration and numbers of legs between shrimp and prawns, but these are important only to ichthyologists. To those interested primarily in cooking and eating, the differences are negligible, so let's just say that prawns are big shrimp and let it go at that. Cooking methods and recipes for one fit the other as stretch pants fit a female skier. So in this section read prawns as well as shrimp, and substitute freely. Crayfish can also be used in any recipe, and in the section devoted to crayfish beginning on page 227 are recipes suitable for use in cooking shrimp and prawns.

Both shrimp and prawns are available in three forms—fresh, frozen, and canned, in that order of preference for cooking. Fresh shrimp should be dumped into cold water, brought to a boil, and simmered 5 to 7 minutes, depending on their size. They are allowed to cool in the cooking water, then drained, their heads snapped off, the legs and shells removed, and a knife tip or deveining tool run up the back to scrape out the black intestinal line. If intended for further cooking, parboiling time can be reduced ⅓; this is long enough to firm their flesh, and separate flesh from shell.

Frozen shrimp come in four styles—uncooked; parboiled unshelled; parboiled, shelled, and cleaned; and breaded. For the reasons you should shun any breaded frozen fish product, see page 159. Frozen uncooked shrimp are treated like fresh ones, with cooking time extended by about ⅓; frozen unshelled shrimp should be thawed rapidly under cold running water and used at once; cleaned frozen shrimp should be added to the dish in which they will be cooked while still frozen, and the cooking time extended to compensate. However, do not overcook any shrimp or prawn, fresh or frozen; like all crustaceans, shrimp toughen when overcooked.

### SHRIMP IN BEER (BREWER'S SHRIMP)

| | |
|---|---|
| 2 to 3 dozen fresh or frozen shrimp, parboiled but unshelled | 1 tablespoon flour |
| | 1 tablespoon butter |
| | ½ cup cream (evaporated milk diluted ⅓ with water can be used) |
| 1 bottle beer or ale, at room temperature | |
| pinch powdered rosemary | paprika or cayenne |
| pinch powdered bay leaf | |

Whether frozen or fresh, do not shell the shrimp. Put them in a deep, heavy pan and pour the beer over them. Bring to a boil, then let simmer gently 6 to 8 minutes (10 to 12 minutes, if frozen). Add the rosemary and bay leaf as soon as the beer begins to simmer; before it boils. Strain the beer, return to the pan, and over brisk heat let it boil until it is reduced ½ in volume. Shell and devein the shrimp and put them in a deep warmed bowl. Knead flour and butter into a smooth paste, and when the beer is reduced, let it simmer without boiling further while the paste is flaked into it and the mixture stirred until smooth. Pour in the cream, return the shrimp to the sauce, and simmer gently 3 to 4 minutes. Sprinkle with cayenne or paprika just before serving.

Serves 4 to 6.

## SHRIMP CREOLE

| | |
|---|---|
| 2 to 3 dozen shrimp, fresh, frozen, or canned; if fresh or frozen they should be shelled and deveined | 2 stalks celery, chopped fine |
| | 1 teaspoon salt |
| | ½ teaspoon powdered thyme |
| | 4 small ripe tomatoes or 1 cup |
| 2 tablespoons butter or bacon drippings | solid-pack canned tomatoes, well drained |
| 1 medium-sized onion, chopped fine | 3 or 4 drops Tabasco Sauce |
| | 1 cup cooked rice |

Heat the butter or bacon drippings and brown the onion and celery very lightly over gentle heat. Stir in salt and pepper. Scald and peel fresh tomatoes and cut them in chunks over the cooking pan so their juices will go into the pan; if canned tomatoes are used, the juice they hold after draining will be just about the right amount. Let the mixture simmer until the tomatoes can be pulped with pressure from a fork or spoon. Add the Tabasco and rice, and cut the shrimp in thirds and add them. Close the pan tightly and leave on gentle heat 5 to 8 minutes.

Serves 4 to 6.

## SHRIMP FISHERMAN'S STYLE

A photographic assignment in the middle 1940s kept me for a week with the salmon fleet that once plied the Sacramento-San Joaquin River delta where it forms Suisun Bay. Those fishing boats were small, cramped for even their usual two-man crew, and the salmon they brought up in their long drift nets were collected daily by a fishery boat, which also brought the fishermen fresh bread and other supplies. On most trips, the fishery boat would drop off a bucket of fresh shrimp at the smaller craft, and the fishermen cooked them this way on their galley hot-plates.

| | |
|---|---|
| 2 to 3 dozen fresh shrimp, parboiled, shelled, and deveined; frozen shrimp, cleaned and thawed; or canned shrimp | 2 to 3 tablespoons brandy<br>1 tablespoon fine light olive oil<br>1 teaspoon Parmesan cheese, grated<br>¼ clove garlic, chopped very fine |

Put the shrimp in a heavy warmed pan. Heat the brandy, pour it over the shrimp, and light it. When the flames have burned out, pour in the olive oil, sprinkle with the cheese and garlic. Cook over high heat for 5 minutes, stirring and turning the shrimp and scraping the pan well. When lightly browned all around, the shrimp are done; eat them piping hot.

Serves 4.

## Frogs' Legs

Gigging frogs transfixed by a spotlight beam, or taking them on a big hook baited with a piece of red flannel, is a pastime small boys of today are missing. The pastime still exists where marshy ponds and brush-lined streams attract big frogs. One of the most glamorous movie-television stars, Dina Merrill, confessed to being a confirmed frog-gigger during a guest appearance on national television, but did not offer any recipes for cooking the legs of the gigged frogs. Here the omission is rectified.

First, it should be noted that frogs are grown commercially and shipped in the millions every year. Usually, the commercial legs are delivered trimmed and skinned, but not prepared. Legs from frogs you take yourself should be cut off close to the amphibian's body and the feet cut off. Make a slit along the leg and strip the skin free. (From this point, commercially prepared legs will need the same treatment given home-caught legs.) Push a skewer lengthwise through the legs two or three times in different spots. Drop the legs into a bowl of ice water, with some pieces of ice in the bowl, and let them soak four hours, completely covered. This whitens and swells the flesh, making it juicier and tender. Wipe the legs dry before cooking.

### CHICKEN-FRIED FROGS' LEGS

16 to 24 legs, prepared according    ¼ cup milk
    to directions above      2 to 3 cups fine dry bread
½ teaspoon salt            crumbs
⅛ teaspoon pepper       butter, or cooking oil
 2 eggs, lightly beaten

Sprinkle the legs with salt and pepper. Beat the milk and eggs together and dip the seasoned legs in it, and roll them in bread crumbs. Put in a warm place to dry 10 to 15 minutes, then dip into the egg-milk mixture a second time and roll again in bread crumbs. Have ½ to ¾ inch of hot fat in the skillet; a 1-inch cube of bread should brown in 40 seconds in the fat at proper temperature. Cook the legs no more than 3 to 4 minutes, rolling them so they will brown evenly. Once their coating is crusty brown, remove them to drain on papers, as overcooking will toughen them.

Serves 4 to 6.

### GRILLED FROGS' LEGS IN TOMATO SAUCE

16 to 24 legs, prepared according    1 clove garlic
    to directions on page 234     1 large sweet onion
 1 cup flour               2 very large ripe tomatoes, or
 1 teaspoon salt             equivalent in solid-pack
 ¾ cup cream or undiluted       canned tomatoes
    evaporated milk          1 tablespoon lemon juice
 ¾ cup fine light olive oil or     ½ teaspoon freshly ground
    peanut oil                white pepper

Mix flour and salt together, dip the legs in the cream, and coat them well with the seasoned flour. Cook on a small-meshed grill over bright coals for 10 minutes, turning to brown them evenly. In a deep skillet, heat the oil and sauté the garlic until it is very dark, then discard the garlic. Chop the onion and sauté in the flavored oil until it turns transparent, then add the tomatoes, chopping them coarsely over the skillet so their juices will be caught in the pan. Cook the tomatoes until they are very soft, mashing them with a fork or spoon as they cook, about 10 to 12 minutes. Add lemon juice and pepper, then the grilled legs, cooking only long enough to warm the legs and let them absorb some of the juices from the sauce; about 3 to 4 minutes.

Serves 4 to 6.

# Turtle

Fishermen and hikers still have an occasional chance to capture one of these slow-moving amphibians whose soft, fatty flesh is so toothsome in soups and stews. And turtle meat is available at some fish markets. The big 200 and 300 pound turtles that were such a prominent feature of pioneer diets have gone, though. A 12 to 15 pounder is a big turtle today, and is large enough to provide a few steaks and a generous pot of stew. The turtle most admired is the dome-shelled sea turtle, now protected in Florida where it is most commonly found, and should you meet one along the seashore of a neighboring state you should make sure of the local game laws before claiming it. The flat-shelled fresh-water turtle is almost as good, from the culinary standpoint, with the fierce snapper next in line. The land tortoise is not considered edible.

If you have a live turtle destined for the pot, pen it for four or five days without food. When cooking day arrives, chop off the head and hang the turtle by its tail to bleed for at least a half-hour. Then put it in a big pot of water, bring to a boil, and simmer 2 to 3 hours, depending on its size. Cook the head with the body, but discard it later.

Drain the turtle, discard the first cooking water, skin the neck and legs, and discard the skin. Start the turtle cooking in a fresh pot of cold water with 1 tablespoon of salt per quart added; cook the head this time, too. After 1½ to 2 hours cooking, remove the carcass and let it cool, and discard the head.

With the turtle on its back, cut around the joint where top shell meets bottom carapace. Lift off the lower shell. Remove and discard all intestines, including the round liver which contains the gall sac. If the turtle is female and has eggs in her, keep them for the stewpot. Cut and scrape the meat and fat from the shell; if your turtle is big enough to provide steaks, a flexible-bladed knife will help you get the meat out in large pieces. The steaks are sliced and grill-cooked without basting or flouring; remember, you are actually heating precooked meat that only needs to be browned and warmed through. The remainder of the meat goes to the stewpot.

### TURTLE STEW

| | |
|---|---|
| 2 to 3 cups turtle meat, chopped in bite-sized pieces | 2 to 2½ cups cold water |
| 1 cup green peas | 1 teaspoon salt |
| ½ cup tiny pearl onions or equivalent in sliced or chopped sweet onion | ¼ teaspoon freshly ground black pepper |
| 2 tablespoons flour | 1 cup medium-dry sherry or Madeira or 1½ cups dry red wine |

Sauté the turtle meat in the stewing pot; no fat will be needed. Cook over gentle heat and turn to brown on all sides. By the time the pieces of meat are browned they will have given up a quantity of fat; skim off all but a film of this. Add the green peas, parboiled briefly if they are fresh or frozen, well drained if canned. Put in the onions and stir until the peas and onions begin to tan, about 4 to 5 minutes. Sprinkle the flour over the ingredients in the pan and stir and turn to blend it with the pan juices. Add cold water and stir briskly as it comes to a simmer to blend it with the floured fat. Close pan and cook gently for 15 to 20 minutes. Add salt, pepper, and the sherry, Madeira, or red wine. When simmering resumes, remove the stew from heat, taste and adjust seasonings, and serve in deep warmed bowls.

Serves 6 nicely.

## A Pair of Unclassifiables

Since Cioppino contains representatives of fish, molluscs, and crustaceans; since spaghetti can be sauced with and combined with any kind of seafood, these two unclassifiables come in at the end of the line. Don't let the delayed treatment keep you from trying both.

### CIOPPINO

The origin of this dish is unknown, but since it strongly resembles the *bouillabaisse* of Marseilles, Cioppino is more likely than not the attempt of an Italian immigrant fisherman to duplicate this specialty soup stew of France's Mediterranean coast. Most of the Italian fishermen who emigrated to the San Francisco area beginning in the late 1890s were from the west coast of Italy, and the offshore islands along the front of the boot; not far by water from Marseilles. At any rate, Cioppino is a San Francisco specialty, and here is its traditional composition.

1 pint shrimp, fresh or frozen, unshelled
1 quart unshelled clams or mussels, or 1 pint of each
1½ pounds of halibut, sea bass, or other large fish
1 medium-sized lobster or langouste, parboiled and cleaned
1 Dungeness crab, parboiled and cleaned; or 4 Dungeness crab claws

1 large red onion—the "torpedo" onion is traditional
1 large green pepper (Bell)
4 ripe tomatoes or 4 cups solid-pack canned tomatoes
2 cloves garlic
2 tablespoons light olive oil
3 cups red wine
2 tablespoons tomato paste
1 teaspoon salt

Scrub the mussels and clams, trim beards from the mussels. Cut the fish in fairly uniform pieces, ¾ - to 1-inch cubes. Cut the lobster, shell and all, into 2-inch sections, crack the claws. Break the shell of the crab into pieces 1½ to 2 inches in diameter, letting the flesh cling to the shell. Crack the claws and legs.

Dice the onion coarsely, remove seeds and pith from the pepper and chop it coarsely, and chop the tomatoes coarsely, catching their juice in the bowl into which the chopped ingredients are going; mince the garlic very fine. Heat the oil in a Dutch oven or a similar big pot that can be tightly closed. Sauté the onion, peppers, garlic, and tomatoes in the oil at low heat. They should be allowed to get soft but not mushy or brown. Combine the wine, tomato paste, and salt. Scrape the pot in which the vegetables are cooking, then pour into it the wine mixture and all the seafoods, shells included. Close the pot tightly and put on dark coals. Cook very gently for 30 minutes. Taste and adjust the seasoning before serving.

Cioppino is served in big soup bowls, each portion containing some of each of the kinds of seafood in the pot and a generous ladleful of the liquid. Traditionally, each diner gets a big towel or dishtowel to tie around his neck like a bib, since dunking of the crusty Italian or French bread that should go with the dish is encouraged. This is the only seafood dish with which red wine *must* be served. And, finally, don't try to cook a small quantity of Cioppino. The recipe given serves 10, and is about as small a quantity as should be cooked.

## SPAGHETTI WITH SEAFOODS

On religious fast days before the ban on meats was removed, spaghetti was customarily served sauced only with butter and cheese, or perhaps with a few flakes of fish or crabmeat or some chopped bits of mussels and clams. The combination is a delicate one, with endless variations possible, but avoid the big, coarse pastas and choose tiny *spaghettini* or thin *farfarelle* or *stelle*.

**Shellfish**

1 to 2 cups flaked cooked fish or
  chopped shellfish
2 quarts boiling salted water—
  1 teaspoon per quart
2 tablespoons butter

tiny pinch of powdered basil
dash of garlic salt
⅓ pound small pasta, as above
salt

Stir the fish or shellfish into butter melted over gentle heat, add basil and garlic salt, mix well, cover the pan to keep warm.

Put the pasta in the boiling water a little at a time, stirring to avoid sticking. After 5 minutes, test the pasta by biting; it should have no white core of uncooked starch. As quickly as possible after the starch line vanishes, pour 1 quart cold water into the pasta pot, drain, and combine with the butter and seafood. Sprinkle with grated Parmesan if you like. (When boiled rice is substituted for pasta, you have a fish *rissoto*.)

Serves 4 adequately.

# X

---

# Soups, Stews, & Vegetables

THE VIRTUES OF vegetable dishes and meal-in-a-pot creations like rib-sticking soups and stews are not readily apparent to some. I'll tell you three—economy, novelty, and ease. One: outstanding vegetable courses can make meat courses simpler and less expensive, taking you off the hook of costly cuts of meat. Two: most of the "made" dishes from the outdoor cooking fire are a novelty, less commonplace than steaks or roasts, since the latter make up the entire repertoire of many who are still learning to cook over coals. Three: many of them do not demand constant attention while cooking, which allows you to relax more and take a greater part in the premeal activities.

Most of the "made" dishes you'll meet in this chapter originated when the cook was just a part-time cook, and had other things to do than to watch a hot grill. Many can be prepared well in advance, some can even be cooked overnight. Others are designed to disguise and use up leftovers in appetizing style.

Generally speaking, the ingredients of the recipes you will encounter in this chapter are commonplace, even homely. They are such things as turnips and cabbages and onions and beans. Beans are treated as they should be in the world's finest bean pot, the Dutch oven, a utensil too few cooks think of in connection with the succulent legumes. There are other ways to serve potatoes outdoors than fried or baked—you'll find a few of them here.

## Soups

The finest of all soups is the camp-style vegetable soup that simmers day after day in a permanent spot just within range of the cooking coals and is added to regularly with more ingredients and a fresh supply of liquid. This is a long-term soup, the kind worth starting only if you're going to camp at the same spot for a week or so. Quick soups are featured here. All of them are easy to prepare, all of them are sturdy enough to form a meal when served with hot biscuits and perhaps a sliver of cheese, and all of them fulfill the basic requirements of a good camp soup: filling, rib-sticking, yet not so highly seasoned as to make you thirsty a few hours after eating, while you're hiking to the deer-stand or kicking up pheasant across the fields. They all make fine breakfasts, too, and soup for breakfast in camp is a fine way to start a busy day. And they're equally good for beginning a meal in your patio or backyard.

### FIRST-DAY CAMP SOUP

| | |
|---|---|
| 2 thick slices bacon, diced | 2 carrots, sliced very thin |
| 1 slice ham, diced (optional; it does not replace the bacon) | 1 onion, chopped coarsely |
| | ½ head cabbage cut in 1-inch slices |
| 2 potatoes or 2 turnips, diced ½ inch | 1½ quarts water |
| 1 cup string beans or green peas | salt, pepper |

Sauté the bacon until it begins to yield some grease, then add the ham and vegetables; sauté the lot until they begin to become tender and lightly brown, about 4 to 5 minutes. Pour in the water, cold, and let the pot simmer. Add seasonings to taste. The soup will be cooked in about 20 minutes.

Serves 6.

## BUTTERMILK SOUP

| | |
|---|---|
| 1 cup milk | ½ cup raisins |
| 2 tablespoons flour | ½ cup cooked rice or ¼ cup |
| 3 cups buttermilk | fine unsalted cracker crumbs |
| ¼ teaspoon cinnamon | dash of salt |
| 1 thick slice lemon | pinch of sugar |

Warm the milk and stir in the flour over low heat; blend until smooth and free from lumps. Add the buttermilk, cinnamon, lemon, and raisins. Simmer—do not allow to boil—until the raisins are plump, about 4 to 5 minutes. Add rice or cracker crumbs, salt, and sugar, and stir vigorously. Simmer 5 minutes, taste and adjust seasonings; the soup should not be too sweet, but rather on the tangy side.

Serves 6.

## MARROW BALL SOUP

This can be prepared with marrow from big beef bones or from that taken from the legbones of any large game animal. Saw the bones into 4-inch sections and lay on dark coals until the marrow softens, about 5 minutes, then push the marrow out into a bowl while holding the bones in tongs or between folds of cloth or paper.

| | |
|---|---|
| ¾ cup marrow | 1½ to 2 quarts beef broth, or |
| 1 tablespoon milk or cream | extra-strength bouillon made |
| 2 eggs, separated | by dissolving cubes, granules, |
| ¼ teaspoon salt | or meat essence in ⅓ less |
| large dash cayenne or Nepal | water than package directions |
| pepper | specify |
| ½ cup very fine dry bread | |
| crumbs or unsalted cracker | |
| crumbs | |

Combine warm marrow with milk to form a smooth paste. Beat the egg yolks lightly and work into the paste, together with the salt,

**243**

pepper, and bread crumbs. Beat egg whites stiff and cut the marrow mixture into them to form a very light dough. Handling gingerly, form into small balls, ½ to ¾ inch in diameter. Drop the marrow balls into gently simmering broth and cook 10 to 12 minutes. Or half-teaspoonfuls of the marrow mixture can be dropped into the broth without handling to form into balls. The marrow mixture can be made up in advance of using, but will lose its lightness after 1 hour.

Serves 4 to 6.

### QUICK BROWN ONION SOUP

| | |
|---|---|
| 6 slices bacon | 1½ cups boiling water, or |
| 3 large onions | equivalent solution made with |
| 2 tablespoons butter | granules or meat essence |
| ⅛ teaspoon nutmeg | (BV, Bovril, etc.) |
| 1½ quarts beef broth, or 3 beef | salt, pepper |
| bouillon cubes dissolved in | grated Parmesan cheese |

Chop bacon coarsely and sauté lightly in the soup pot until a light brown; dice two of the onions and sauté with the bacon until they begin to become transparent. Add butter and nutmeg, stir well. Put the onion slices on the ingredients in the pot and pour over them 1½ cups of boiling beef broth, or the dissolved concentrate. Close the pan and let simmer 3 to 5 minutes. Add the remaining broth, or 1½ quarts boiling water if the concentrate is used. Simmer 5 minutes, add salt and pepper after tasting. Serve in soup bowls with a sprinkling of cheese floated on top of the soup.

Serves 6.

### QUICK POTATO SOUP

A little planning is needed to make this a "quick" soup, but if you soak the potatoes in advance, total cooking time is about 10 minutes. It is, by the way, a fine breakfast soup.

| | |
|---|---|
| 3 medium-sized potatoes | large dash black pepper |
| 1½ quarts cold water | 2 teaspoons cream cheese or |
| butter | ricotta |
| ½ to ¾ teaspoon salt | 1 cup milk or light cream |

One to 2 hours before the soup is to be cooked, peel the potatoes and slice them paper thin; put them to soak in a large bowl of cold water. If the soup is to be cooked for breakfast, this can be done the night before. When ready to cook, lift the potato slices out of the bowl, letting the starch that has soaked out stay in the bowl. Put the potatoes in the pot with fresh cold water and bring to a boil; by the time the pot boils, the potatoes will be cooked. Add butter, salt, pepper, and cream cheese or ricotta; stir until the cheese dissolves. Remove from heat, stir in the milk, taste and adjust seasoning, and serve.

Serves 6.

## Beans

Because they are easy to store, carry, and cook, dried beans are perhaps the most-used vegetables of the outdoor chef; they are also the most abused. Too many cooks toss a handful of dried beans into a pot of water, put it on the fire, and forget it. Even beans cannot survive such treatment; there is nothing less appealing than beans floating unadorned in a vapid, tasteless liquid.

A course in regional preferences should be required of anyone writing about beans in cooking. It's ludicrous to see a recipe for chili, for instance, that stipulates the use of kidney beans, which are native to the eastern U.S. and poorly thought of in chili country, where the favored bean is the speckled pinto. Midwesterners choose the lima, when there are no fresh green beans to be had. In the South, the black-eyed pea—which is a bean—is king. On the West Coast, sentiment splits between the big red bean and the tiny navy. The big navy bean is a New England bean, though far up in Maine John Gould swears by a purple-streaked white bean that's been handed down in his family for several generations and seems to prosper only on his own acres.

All beans of the dried variety require slow cooking. They're stubborn, and refuse to be hurried. As for canned beans, they are cooked quickly under steam pressure and then sealed into cans at such high temperature that they come out flabby and characterless. There's little excuse to accept this mass-produced mediocrity since beans cooked in a Dutch oven or over the slow, gentle heat of a bed of coals require no attention. And Dutch oven beans will show you what beans can taste like. No method of cooking beans compares to the Dutch oven; it was the original bean pot. One word of caution about bean cookery, though. The higher the altitude at which you operate, the longer it takes beans to cook. If you're in a mountain fishing or hunting camp, make allowance for this in planning your cooking schedule.

### DUTCH OVEN BEANS, EASTERN OR BOSTON STYLE

| | |
|---|---|
| 1 pound large white (navy) beans, washed and soaked at least 2 hours in cold water; they can soak overnight if you wish, and be better for it | ¾ cup molasses |
| | ½ cup tomato ketchup |
| | ¼ teaspoon ginger |
| | 1 teaspoon dry mustard |
| | 1 tablespoon salt |
| 3 or 4 large thick slices of salt pork or fat bacon | ½ cup hot water |

Drain the beans and put them in the Dutch oven. Trim rinds off salt pork or bacon; if salt pork is used, blanch it. Cut the slices in halves and bury them at random among the beans; reserve one slice to place on top of the pot. Stir the molasses, ketchup, and all seasonings together in the water and pour over the beans. Bury the Dutch oven in coals at least 6 hours; the oven can stay buried overnight with no danger of burning the beans.

Serves 8 to 10.

## DUTCH OVEN BEANS, SOUTHWESTERN STYLE

1½ pounds pinto beans, washed and soaked in cold water 2 to 4 hours
6-inch square of ham skin with a layer of fat left on it
2 ham shanks or a section of ham bone with some shreds of meat clinging to it
4 large ripe tomatoes or a #2 can of solid-pack tomatoes
2 hot chili pepper pods
1½ tablespoons salt

Drain the beans. Put the ham skin on the bottom of the Dutch oven, with about ⅓ of the beans on top of it. Chop the tomatoes coarsely and bury them in the remaining beans as they are added to the pot, along with the ham shanks and chili pods. Sprinkle the salt over the top of the beans and pour in cold water level with the beans in the pot. Bury the oven in coals at least 6 hours.

There are several variations. The most common is to add a heaping handful of minced-up pieces of beef, mixing the meat well with the beans. Chunks of onion are sometimes added. This method of cooking beans is distantly related to chili con carne—in fact it is called "chili beans"—but beans cooked this style are almost never served with chili. The bean going with chili is the plain boiled pinto bean, or refried beans. A recipe for genuine chili con carne is on page 55; for refried beans on page 248.

Serves 8 to 10.

## DUTCH OVEN BEANS, WESTERN STYLE

1 pound small navy beans or large red beans, washed and soaked in cold water 2 to 4 hours or overnight
¾ pound slab bacon on the rind
4 or 5 medium-sized onions
bay leaf
1½ tablespoons salt
2½ cups cold water

Drain the beans. Slice the bacon in ½-inch cuts down to but not through the rind; it remains in one chunk. Lay the bacon skin side down on the bottom of the Dutch oven and put in the beans, burying the peeled whole onions in them at random. Add the bay leaf, sprinkle the salt over the top of the beans, and pour the cold water over the beans. Close the Dutch oven and bury in coals at least 6 hours. Potatoes in large pieces are often added to the pot.

Serves 8 to 10.

### REFRIED BEANS

Almost any bean can be refried, but pintos, large white beans, and big red beans seem to respond to the treatment with the most gusto.

| | |
|---|---|
| 2 cups cooked beans with about 2 tablespoons of their pot juices | bacon drippings ½ cup grated cheddar cheese (optional) |

Mash the beans into a smooth paste, with the juice. Heat the fat to mild heat and spread the beans evenly over the bottom of the skillet. Stir often—no crust should be allowed to form. The beans will cook dry very quickly, and it may be necessary to add a bit of liquid. Cook only long enough to warm. Just before serving, stir in the grated cheese and let it soften but not melt completely. Some cooks like to add a spattering of minced onion or a dash of chili molido.

Serves 6.

## Cabbage

Outdoor cooking and cabbage are complementary; what is at best a mildly objectionable odor in the confinement of a kitchen becomes a fragrant aroma outdoors. There are few outdoor stews that will not benefit by the addition of some shredded cabbage leaves, and cabbage can also appear as a bonus in most soups. Cabbage is one of the few green vegetables that travels well and requires no refrigeration. It is essential to many traditional game dishes and to those using smoked meats.

## BRAISED CABBAGE AND SAUSAGE

½ head large cabbage or hearts of 2 small heads

10 to 12 small smoked sausage links, or equivalent in chorizo, linguesa, kolbasse, or other smoked sausage

bacon drippings

salt, pepper

If sausage other than small links is used, it should be cut into sections 2 to 3 inches long. Separate the leaves of the cabbage and wash; do not wipe dry, but shake the leaves lightly, leaving some drops of water clinging to them. Rub the bottom of a heavy skillet with bacon drippings. Put in layers of cabbage leaves, the sausages or sausage pieces buried among them. Close the skillet tightly and cook 20 to 30 minutes over medium coals. Test the cabbage at the thickest portion for tenderness. Season with salt and pepper by taste, using only enough to supplement the flavor the cabbage has drawn from the sausage.

Serves 6.

## BUBBLE AND SQUEAK

½ head cabbage

2 large slices cured ham

bacon drippings

salt, and a big dash of pepper

Parboil the cabbage 5 minutes in water to cover. Drain, cut in wide ribbonlike slices. Cut ham in 1-inch squares. Grease the bottom of a deep skillet with bacon drippings, put in cabbage and ham, stir together. Close skillet and cook over medium-dark coals 15 to 20 minutes. Season to taste, using only enough salt to supplement that from the ham, but use a heavy hand in peppering.

Serves 4 to 6.

### STUFFED CABBAGE

The Hot Pepper Vinegar on page 163 goes well with this.

1 large head cabbage
2 to 3 cups cooked meat, preferably from a roast: game, beef, pork, veal, chicken, ham
1 small onion
1½ cups fine bread crumbs or

unsalted cracker crumbs
2 tablespoons meat stock or thinned milk
½ teaspoon salt
large dash pepper
½ teaspoon caraway seed

Drop the whole cabbage into boiling water for 10 minutes; drain. With a sharp knife, cut out the stem and heart and pull out the inner leaves to form a cavity. Reserve the leaves removed. Chop the meat and onion, and combine with bread crumbs and all seasonings, using the meat stock or milk to moisten. Stuff the cavity with this mixture and use the reserved leaves to cover the opening, tying with string to hold in place. Cut a thin slice off the top of the cabbage so it will remain upright and set it on the bottom of the Dutch oven. Add water to cover the bottom of the oven ¼ inch. Close oven, bury in coals for 45 minutes to 1 hour. To serve, cut into quarters or sixths.
Serves 4 to 6.

## Corn

Count yourself lucky if you live or set up camp close to a place where really fresh corn is available, for corn is best when pulled off the stalk and carried at a dead run to the fire where it will be cooked. Good fresh corn really needs no accompaniment except butter and a few grains of salt. Aged corn, whether it has grown old by traveling to market or by freezing, needs the help of friendly accessory ingredients to enhance its flavor.

## CORN ROASTED IN THE SHUCK

There are two methods of cooking corn in its own covers, and both give similar results—grilling the whole ears over coals, or burying it in coals. Choose the one you find most convenient and satisfactory.

To grill: select the freshest corn you can find. Strip off all but the 3 or 4 inner layers of husks, pull these back, and remove the silk. Press the shucks back in place and secure the top with a twist of wire. Grill over medium coals, turning frequently, 15 to 20 minutes.

To bury: again, use the freshest corn you can get your hands on. Pull back the tops of the husks and remove the silk, press the husks back into place and secure with a twist of wire. Bury in coals 35 to 40 minutes.

All that's needed in addition to the corn is a slathering of sweet butter and a few grains of salt. Allow at least 2 ears per person.

## CORN SLUB

Except for a fisherman's accident, Corn Slub might never have come to my attention. Ralph Lyman, perennial mayor of Arcata, California, had his new rod and reel yanked from his hands by an especially active salmon, and before the fishing tackle had reached the bottom of the Pacific Ocean, Ralph swore off fishing forevermore. Refusing all offers to lend him equipment, Ralph spent the remainder of the trip recalling his boyhood days in Nebraska, and some of the camp-cooked goodies he'd enjoyed. Among them was Corn Slub.

| | |
|---|---|
| 2 cups absolutely fresh young corn | 2 eggs, lightly beaten |
| 1 cup fine bread crumbs | 1 tablespoon salt |
| 2 tablespoons melted butter | bacon drippings |

Cut the corn off the cob, holding it over a bowl to catch the milk that drips as the knife shaves the kernels. (If you can't find corn this young and fresh, add a tablespoon or two of thin milk.) Mix the kernels and their milk with the bread crumbs, butter, eggs, and salt. Beat well with a fork. Heat a griddle or big heavy skillet and grease with bacon drippings. Test by dropping a sprinkle of water on the pan; when the water dances wildly and disappears in 15 seconds, the pan is hot enough. Drop the batter by tablespoonfuls on the hot griddle, turn when the bottom browns—1½ to 2 minutes—and cook until the other side is brown. Serve smoking hot.

Serves 4 to 6.

## SUCCOTASH

Originally a simple stew of corn and beans, given to the Pilgrims by the Indians, succotash has fallen on evil days in its later years. Recipes of today include peppers, onions, and other ingredients foreign to the straightforward nature of pristine succotash.

| | |
|---|---|
| 2 cups fresh lima beans | ⅛ teaspoon freshly ground |
| 2 cups fresh green corn right | pepper |
| off the cob | 3 tablespoons butter |
| 1 teaspoon salt | |

Heat water to boiling, put in the corn, beans, salt, and pepper, and cook 10 to 12 minutes at a low boil until the beans are tender. Drain well, stir in the butter, and serve at once.

You can use canned or frozen ingredients. Heat canned beans and corn in their own liquids from the cans, combine, butter, season. In using frozen ingredients, drop a package each of beans and corn, unthawed, into boiling water; cook until the beans are tender, drain, butter, season. But succotash from very fresh ingredients wins hands down.

Serves 4 to 6.

## Eggplant

The eggplant has a long background in outdoor cooking. It is a native of the Middle East, where desert nomads still cook all their meals outdoors. The eggplant is virtually ignored in outdoor cookery, but it can provide a few surprises. Use it in place of one of the root vegetables in a stew, adding it late to the pot, to give it time to soften and impart flavor, but not enough time to get mushy. In selecting eggplant, choose firm, unwrinkled fruit with bright green stems. If it is to be cubed and cooked kabob-style on skewers, peel it deeply, for the flesh just beneath the skin is bitter. Before being cooked as kabobs—or before it is sautéed, for that matter—the cubes or slices should be put in a bowl of cold water to which a pinch of salt or a few drops of vinegar or lemon juice has been added, and soaked 20 to 30 minutes; this firms the flesh and keeps it from discoloring and also improves its flavor.

### GRILLED EGGPLANT MIX

This old Armenian method is an outdoor cook's showpiece, and unlike too many showpiece dishes, it is as delicious as it is dramatic. No utensils are used except a bowl.

| | |
|---|---|
| medium-sized eggplant, very fresh and very firm | 4 or 5 pitted ripe olives |
| 2 small green onions | 1 teaspoon fine light olive oil or peanut oil |
| 1 sweet green (Bell) pepper | 1½ teaspoons salt |
| 2 small firm-ripe tomatoes | |

There are two methods you can use. In the first, cook the eggplant on the grill, over medium coals; in about 5 minutes put the pepper beside it, then the onion a moment or two later, and the tomatoes five minutes after that. (Total cooking time for the eggplant will be 20 to 30 minutes, depending on its size, so you can time the addition of the pepper, onion, and tomatoes to have all ingredients finish cooking at the same time.) In the second method, put the eggplant directly on dark coals, the pepper, onion, and tomatoes on a flat rock beside the bed of coals. In either method, all the ingredients must be turned often so they will cook evenly. Handle them with cooking mitts, folded cloths, or several thicknesses of paper.
When cooking is complete, slip the skins from the tomatoes by

making a few short slashes at the stem and peeling back. Drop the tomatoes into a mixing bowl. The skin of the pepper will slip quickly after it has been dipped into a bowl of cold water when removed from heat. Open the pepper and remove seeds and pith, put in the bowl with the tomatoes. Peel the onions and put them in the bowl. Slash the eggplant into halves and spoon its soft flesh into the bowl. Add the olives, oil, and salt. Using two knives, chop the tomatoes, pepper, and onions in the bowl; this mixes the dish thoroughly, and it is ready to serve. It makes an unusual spread for toast or crisp crackers as an hors d'oeuvre. (Zucchini can be substituted for eggplant.)

## Mushrooms

Almost any outdoor activity—hunting, fishing, camping, hiking, picnicking, bird-watching—that takes you across uncultivated ground at the proper time will sooner or later bring you into contact with field mushrooms. They grow almost everywhere when the right combination of soil temperature, humidity, and sunshine brings them popping up. Depending on where you are, the season might be spring, summer, or autumn, but when mushroom spores are present in fallow soil, they will appear.

Now, there's no middle ground with most people where mushrooms are concerned. Either they have a total fear of eating any mushroom not store bought or canned, or they grab every specimen they encounter on their rambles. For the timid, there are quick rules of thumb in picking field mushrooms. One, feel them. If they feel startlingly like human flesh, they're edible. Two, examine them. If the gills range from a beautiful dusky pink to dark brown, they're edible. Avoid any mushroom that feels slick or slimy or clammy, or that has white, yellow, green, or orange gills. Puffballs, white all around and without gills, are generally safe, though many avoid them on general principles. Tree fungi are also usually safe, but

**254**

neither puffballs nor tree fungi have features that afford such positive identification as do mushrooms. When in doubt, of course, leave a mushroom alone. Anything you're afraid to eat will give you nervous indigestion, anyhow.

Fresh mushrooms, whether picked yourself or bought at the store, should be washed in several changes of cold water and the caps and stems scrubbed with a soft brush. They need not be skinned. Any mushroom old enough to require skinning is too old to eat.

### GRILLED MUSHROOMS

| | |
|---|---|
| medium to large-sized fresh mushrooms | salt |
| | freshly ground white pepper |
| butter | |

After washing, parboil the mushrooms by dropping into boiling water 2 to 3 minutes. Drain well. Snap off the stems and reserve them to use in dishes calling for chopped-up mushroom. Brush the caps with buttter and put gill side down on the grill over medium coals for 1 minute. Turn, and put a generous amount of butter in the gills while the mushrooms cook 2 to 3 minutes more. Dust scantily with seasonings after taking off grill.

## Onions

Without onions the outdoor chef would almost be forced to turn in his apron. There is a type of onion compatible with almost every type of dish; their pungency ranges from the delicacy of the thin scallion or green onion in an ascending scale through the sweet small pearl onions and white Bermudas to the purple-veined torpedoes and reds up to the hot, sharp yellow ones. By choosing the suitable variety you can control the onion flavor in your dishes from a fragrant undertone to an overpowering blast. And even by themselves, onions make a pretty good outdoor dish.

## BAKED ONIONS

10 to 12 whole sweet white
    onions 2 to 3 inches in
    diameter
nutmeg

salt
bacon drippings
thin slices of bacon or salt pork

Peel the onions and score a shallow cross on the root end to keep them from popping their cores as they cook. Mix nutmeg and salt in a ratio of about ¼ teaspoon nutmeg to 1 tablespoon salt. Rub the onions with bacon drippings and roll them in the seasonings. Line the bottom of the Dutch oven with thin slices of bacon or salt pork; if pork is used, blanch it; set the onions in it; they should not touch each other or the pan's sides. Bury the oven in coals 35 to 40 minutes. In the sheepherder oven, cook in a tightly closed pan 15 to 20 minutes; in the kitchen oven, 25 minutes at 325 degrees. Some like to use very fine dry bread crumbs with the salt-nutmeg mixture.

Serves 6 to 8.

## ONION SHORTCAKE

6 large sweet onions
2 tablespoons butter
salt, paprika
½ batch Light Biscuit Dough,
    page 273, baked as a single

pan-sized biscuit
2 cups beef broth or bouillion
    made from cubes, granules,
    or meat extract such as BV,
    Bovril, etc.

Peel and slice the onions about ¼ inch thick. Using 1 tablespoon butter, sauté the onions over gentle heat until they just begin to become transparent. Sprinkle lightly with salt and paprika as they cook. Split the biscuit, butter it with half the remaining butter, and put the bottom half in a shallow bowl; put the onions on the biscuit, top with the other half biscuit and pour the hot broth over all. Butter the top before cutting like a cake to serve in wedges.

Serves 6 to 8.

## Potatoes, Turnips, Carrots

Baked and fried potatoes are probably the most overworked items on outdoor menus. They require little skill, and only enough imagination on the part of the cook to refrain from wrapping the baked kind in foil and to drain the fried version on papers to remove excess grease. No recipes for either of these old stand-bys will be found here; for baked potatoes and foil, see page 20. As for powdered, or "instant" potatoes, it is kinder not to mention them. There is some excuse for their use in back-pack trips where lightness of load is a factor, but they generally have all the flavor of a first-grade library paste.

Turnips, with their two-fisted flavor, can be baked whole in coals like potatoes; peeled, boiled, and buttered as a side dish; and used with or as a substitute for potatoes in pot roasts, soups, and stews.

Carrots bring important flavor to pot roasts and stews, or can be served by themselves when boiled and buttered or served with one of the herbed butters on page 164. Carrots boiled, drained, and heated with a tablespoon of honey and a teaspoon of lemon juice make an unusual side dish.

### POTATO POT PIE

| | |
|---|---|
| 4 large potatoes | large pinch of pepper |
| 6 large carrots | 3 slices uncooked ham |
| 1½ tablespoons flour | 1½ cups milk |

Peel potatoes and carrots, cut in ¼-inch slices. Grease the bottom and sides of the Dutch oven and put a layer of potato slices on the bottom, then a layer of carrot slices. Sprinkle lightly with flour and pepper, and put on a slice of ham. Build up the pot with alternate layers of potato, carrot, and ham, dusting with flour and pepper as above. Top off with a layer of potatoes. Pour the milk over the dish, close the Dutch oven, and bury in coals 1 to 1½ hours—longer, if it

**257**

suits your convenience. The dish will not overcook, but if extended cooking is planned, add extra milk. In the sheepherder stove, cook in a tightly covered pan 45 minutes. In the kitchen range, cook 1 hour at 300 degrees.

Serves 6 to 8.

## POTATO GHOSTS

In cooking, these puff into light, fluffy balls, a ghost of the solid vegetable.

| | |
|---|---|
| 1½  cups cooked mashed potatoes | 1  egg |
| ½  cup flour | fat for deep frying: ⅓ lard or |
| 1  teaspoon baking powder | solid shortening and ⅔ bacon |
| ½  teaspoon salt | drippings |

Sift together the flour, baking powder, and salt and blend with the mashed potatoes. Beat the egg lightly, then continue to beat while adding the potato mixture a little at a time to produce a smooth thick batter. Have the cooking fat 3 to 4 inches deep in the kettle and hot enough to brown a 1-inch cube of bread in 40 seconds. Drop in the batter by tablespoonfuls, a few at a time, and turn so the balls will brown evenly. Remove to drain as soon as the outside is crisply browned. A sprinkle of salt should be added just before serving.

Serves 4 to 6.

## CREAMED PEPPERED TURNIPS

| | |
|---|---|
| 6  medium-sized turnips | 1½  teaspoons freshly ground |
| 1  teaspoon salt | black pepper |
| 2  cups milk or light cream | |

Peel the turnips and cut in ½-inch slices. Cover with cold water in a deep pot, add salt, and cook briskly for 30 minutes, or until tender. Drain the cooking water, pour in the milk or cream, add the pepper, and return to heat for 3 to 4 minutes, but do not allow to

**258**

boil. Be sure to spoon a portion of the milk over each serving. A dollop of butter on each individual serving, or on the bowl in which the turnips are served, is a nice touch.

Serves 6 to 8.

## CLAPSHOT

| | |
|---|---|
| 2  medium-sized potatoes | 1  teaspoon salt |
| 2  large turnips | large pinch of pepper |
| 1  cup milk | 1  teaspoon butter |

Peel and quarter potatoes and turnips, cook in lightly salted water. Drain, mash together, and beat in the milk, seasonings, and butter. When shredded boiled cabbage is added to this old Scottish dish, it is called Colcannon.

Serves 6.

# Rice

Outside the Deep South's rice belt, rice is often neglected in outdoor cooking, yet it is the basis for many dishes that originated in the South during plantation days and have since migrated elsewhere. Use rice in place of starchier potatoes, if you are a waistline-watcher; it combines with almost any meat, can be seasoned in a multitude of ways when served as a side dish, and is the base on which many rib-sticking outdoor dessert dishes are based. In cooking rice the heavy Dutch oven again proves its versatility, for it produces light, fluffy grains that would be the envy of any Oriental or Creole cook. When buying rice, choose the long-grain, or Patna variety; brown rice is a toothier version that goes well with outdoor-style foods and can substitute for the very expensive wild rice (which is really a variety of oats). The "converted" or "quick" rice products on the market today are useful only if they are not used in dishes to be reheated; avoid them in any dish calling for precooked rice that will undergo a second heating. One and half cups of dry rice produces 3 cups of cooked rice; to increase the quantity, use only 1 additional table-spoon water to each ½ cup of rice.

### DUTCH OVEN RICE

| | |
|---|---|
| 1½ cups rice | 1 teaspoon salt |
| 1 cup water | |

Bring the water to a brisk boil in the Dutch oven. Add rice and salt, close at once, bury in coals for 30 minutes. The rice will neither burn nor stick, but will be light and fluffy.

Rice cooked this way can be served plain with melted butter or butter and brown sugar; or with Green Sauce, page 32, or Barbe-cue Sauce, page 31. It can be served with any of the herbed butters on page 164, or with an herbed butter of your own devising. The plain rice can be used to stir into sautéed chopped vegetables, such as onions, green peppers, mushrooms; it can also be converted into a cheese dish. And plain rice is the base for a number of desserts.

### SPANISH or CREOLE RICE

| | |
|---|---|
| 1½ cups uncooked rice | pack canned tomatoes |
| 1 slice bacon, chopped coarsely | 2 tablespoons cold water (only |
| 1 small onion | with fresh tomatoes) |
| 1 teaspoon mild chili molido | ½ teaspoon salt |
| 2 ripe tomatoes or 1 cup solid- | |

In a deep skillet sauté the bacon until it begins to crisp. Chop the onion fairly fine, add it and the chili molido, and sauté until the onion starts to become transparent, then chop fresh tomatoes over the pan to preserve their juices and add them; handle solid-pack canned tomatoes by chopping them in the pan itself. If fresh tomatoes are used add 2 tablespoons cold water. Add rice and salt, stir thoroughly, close the skillet tightly, and cook over gentle heat 20 to 25 minutes. Stir occasionally.

Serves 6.

### RICE-STUFFED PEPPERS

| | |
|---|---|
| 2½  cups cooked rice | game, fowl, beef, etc. |
| 6  large Bell peppers | 1  tablespoon chili molido |
| 3  cups minced precooked meat: | ½  teaspoon salt |

Circle the stems of the peppers with a knife-cut, remove seeds and pith. Drop into boiling water for 1 minute, then plunge into cold water so their skins will slip off easily. Skin. Combine rice, meat, and seasonings and fill the peppers with this mixture. (Don't be inhibited about adding to the stuffing almost any ingredients you fancy—chopped onion, celery, grated cheese, whole-kernel corn, etc. This dish is more versatile than hash in making use of small quantities of leftovers.) Put the filled peppers into a deep skillet that can be tightly closed, with ¼ inch cold water on the bottom of the pan. Cover and cook over very low heat 20 to 25 minutes, or until the pepper cases are tender. The dish can be oven-cooked—in the sheepherder stove, cook 12 to 15 minutes; in the kitchen oven, 20 minutes at 350 degrees. Use a tightly covered pan when oven-cooking, and remove the cover for the final few minutes to brown the tops of the peppers.

Serves 6.


## Squash

Squash is a real veteran of outdoor cooking. It was a principal vegetable of the Indians and their small cooking-fires. It is also a versatile vegetable for the outdoor cook to keep in mind, for some of the big hard-skinned squashes can serve as cooking utensils as well as food.

### GRILLED SQUASH

Soft-skinned squash such as zucchini and pattipan should be washed and rubbed well with cooking fat or oil, then placed whole on the grill over medium-bright coals. Cooking times will vary according to size and the type of squash; from 6 to 8 minutes for zucchini, pattipan, and small yellow gooseneck to 12 or 15 minutes for cherimoya, acorn, and turban. While cooking, the squash should be turned once or twice. After putting them on warmed serving plates, slash them deeply in a crisscross pattern and brush with melted butter. The herbed butters on page 164 are all good for seasoning soft-skinned squash cooked this way.

Hard-skinned squash can be cooked directly on the coals, if you prefer. Brush their flesh with butter as they cook; again, the herbed butters from page 164 are good. For squash with naturally sweet or semi-sweet flesh, try blending the butter with powdered allspice, mace, cinnamon, nutmeg, or even a tiny pinch of ginger.

### BAKED STUFFED SQUASH

| | |
|---|---|
| whole or half thick-skinned squash such as Hubbard | salt, pepper, nutmeg |
| 1 cup cooked rice | 3 tablespoons butter |
| 1½ cups chopped cooked meat, or sausage sautéed in crumbles | ¼ to ½ cup grated Parmesan |

Bake the squash in halves on the grill or on coals until the flesh is tender, basting occasionally with a little butter. When done, remove from heat and scrape out most of the flesh with a spoon, leaving about ¼ inch on the shell. Combine the squash flesh with the rice and meat; the squash can be minced or mashed, as you choose. While mixing, season with salt, pepper, and a dash of nutmeg to taste. Blend the remaining butter and cheese. Fill the shell of the squash, coat the top of the mounded stuffing generously with the butter-cheese mixture, and return to grill or coals for 10 minutes.

Serves 6 to 8 as a side dish; 4 to 6 as a main dish.

# XI

---

# Bread, Cakes, & Eggs

CAMP COOKS OF OLD were judged by their breads even more than by the meat dishes they turned out. The cook who offered leaden biscuits and soggy pancakes soon moved on—by request. If you have shied away from outdoor baking under the impression that it's difficult, perhaps this chapter will release your inhibitions. If the frontier bakers could do it, you can bake bread, too.

Bread was baked in the fireplaces of settlers' cabins, in the coals of cooking fires kindled by immigrants crossing the Cumberland Gap or heading for California on the Santa Fe Trail. In the shanties of the forty-niners, sourdough bread was a mainstay, just as it was in the icy cabins of those who struggled over Chillikoot Pass to join the Alaska Gold Rush forty years later. Shanty-cooks in lumber camps and chuck-wagon cooks on the cattle ranges baked breads regularly.

"Pinch-offs" was the common chuck-wagon name for biscuits, the term deriving from the cook's contempt for rolling pin and biscuit cutter. A good chuck-wagon cook blended his dough in the top of an open flour sack and from the mass pinched off biscuit-sized blobs directly into the Dutch oven or metal pan that went to the sheep-herder stove.

## Bread, Cakes, and Eggs

Even before their day, bread was baked by the Pueblo Indians of the Southwest in beehive ovens; by the eastern tribes in the coals of their cooking-fires, out of a flour made by pounding corn; and by the northwestern tribes in watertight baskets, of a dough compounded from chestnuts or acorns and wrapped in corn husks to boil. From the days of the Indians onward, bakers had less to work with than you do. And most of their breads put to shame the squishy loaf that is the product of today's bread factories, worked up by chemists in laboratories instead of bakers.

For oudoor baking, the sheepherder stove is the best investment you can make. If you plan to embrace the art, complete details of its construction will be found on page 303. The double skillet is best for baking biscuits buried in coals, but does not do as well with loaves as the Dutch oven. At the bottom of the list for outdoor baking is the reflector oven; it is as variable as the winds that affect its performance, temperamental and uncertain in any but expert hands.

All breads, whether baked indoors or out, fall into two categories. There are "risen" breads that rise once or twice before baking, and "quick" breads that rise only in the pan. Most of the loaf breads are in the first group, while biscuits and pancakes fall into the second. Corn breads are quick breads; whether leavened with baking powder or salt, they are not put to rise before baking. You will meet them all in this chapter.

In the recipes that follow, you will encounter yeast among the ingredients of pioneer breads baked before yeast was widely distributed or easily shipped. In these recipes, yeast has been substituted as a convenience and a method of securing more certain results than the leaven used a century or more ago, which was freshly grated ginger and sugar. The combination was explosively effective, but using it successfully took learning.

As for the yeast used, it matters little whether you stick to the moist compressed cakes or use the more modern dry yeast. As a matter of convenience in storing, dry yeast is recommended. When mixing yeast to use in any baking recipe, mix it with lukewarm water or liquid, never boiling water. Heat kills yeast spores, which is why bread stops rising after it has been in the oven a short time.

Finally, the flour. Avoid any of the "soft" flours, the extramilled, presifted, modified flours. These are sometimes suitable in modern recipes for cakes, but none of them works well in breads, whether quick or double-raised. A good durum wheat flour was the bedrock of pioneer breads (though perhaps bedrock is a bad choice of words). The hard-wheat flour so difficult to find today did and does produce a firm-textured loaf, though all the recipes in this chapter have been tested with modern all-purpose flours, which are milled from the soft hybrid wheats. If you can find a good hard-wheat flour, use it. You'll get a superior bread.

## Loaf Breads

### ANADAMA BREAD

Variously called "Anadama" and "Amadama" in old cookbooks, this pioneer bread is said to have been named for a pioneer wife named Anna, who served her husband a soft corn-meal spoonbread with molasses every day at every meal. Finally tiring of the mixture, the husband in a hot rage tossed flour and yeast into the spoonbread mixture served him one evening, poured the result into a Dutch oven, and baked it, muttering while he waited for it to cook, "Anna, damn her!" It's as good as any of the stories purporting to tell how a dish got its name.

| | |
|---|---|
| ¾ cup white corn meal | 1 teaspoon salt |
| 2 cups boiling water | 1 yeast cake dissolved in ½ cup |
| ½ cup molasses | warm water |
| 2 tablespoons bacon drippings | 5 cups flour |

Sift the corn meal into the boiling water a little at a time, cook 5 minutes. Take off heat, stir in the molasses, bacon drippings, and salt. Let stand 15 minutes to cool.

Begin adding the flour to the dissolved yeast, stirring as you add, until 1 cup of flour has been used. Mix with the corn-meal-molasses batter, then continue to add the remaining 4 cups flour a little at a time until a stiff dough is formed. Turn this out onto a floured board and knead vigorously for 10 minutes. Put in a greased mixing bowl and let stand in a warm place until it doubles in bulk—1½ to 2 hours, depending on the temperature of your warm place. Knead again, but very lightly this time, on a floured board. Shape into 2 or 3 loaves of equal size. Put into a well-greased Dutch oven and let rise until the dough has increased in bulk ⅓. Close the Dutch oven and bury in coals 1 hour; during the last 15 minutes of cooking, scrape the coals off the top of the oven and replace with very bright fresh coals (without opening the oven). In the sheepherder stove, cook 35 to 40 minutes; in the kitchen oven, 40 minutes at 350 degrees.

Makes 2 standard or 3 small loaves.

### POTATO BREAD

One of the easiest of all outdoor breads to make, potato bread was favored by emigrants who had learned to shy away from sourdough (see page 268).

| | |
|---|---|
| 1 small raw potato | lukewarm water |
| 2½ cups water | 1 tablespoon sugar |
| 1½ teaspoons salt | 1 tablespoon solid shortening, |
| 1 yeast cake, or 1 package | lard or vegetable |
| dry yeast, dissolved in 1 cup | 4 cups flour |

Peel and boil the potato; reserve the water after the potato cooks. Remove the potato and mash it. Dissolve the salt in 2 tablespoons of the potato water. Combine dissolved yeast with the mashed potato, then blend into this the salted potato water, sugar, and shortening. When well blended, begin adding the flour by tablespoons, with alternate dashes of the remaining potato water, until all 4 cups of flour and 2 cups of the water have been used. Cover the mixing bowl with a cloth and let it stand in a warm place until the dough doubles in bulk; 1 to 2 hours, depending on temperature.

Grease the Dutch oven well, grease your hands well. Turn the dough out onto a very lightly floured surface, and *without* kneading shape it into 2 or 3 loaves or balls. Space these evenly in the pan, brush the tops lightly with cooking oil, and let stand until the dough increases ⅓ in bulk—about 2 hours at 70 degrees, longer if the air is cooler, a shorter time if it is warmer. Cover the oven, bury in coals, and cook 35 to 40 minutes; overtime rather than undertime. In the sheepherder oven, in an open pan, cook 20 to 25 minutes; in the kitchen oven, 25 to 30 minutes at 350 degrees.

Makes 2 standard or 3 small loaves.

## SALT RISEN BREAD

Notice the correct name: Salt *Risen* Bread. Salt *Rising* Bread is a modern corruption; this is a risen bread, as opposed to quick breads, with salt rather than yeast triggering the fermentation by chemical action with corn meal.

| | |
|---|---|
| 1½ tablespoones white corn meal, or 1 tablespoon stone-ground meal | ½ teaspoon salt<br>3 cups lukewarm water<br>6 cups flour |

Stir corn meal and salt into water, add 2 cups flour. Set in a warm place until the mixture begins to bubble; this will take about 2 hours, depending on air temperature. When bubbling is well established, add the remaining 4 cups flour to the corn-meal mixture. Add the flour 2 to 3 tablespoonfuls at a time, alternating with teaspoonfuls of lukewarm water. Knead thoroughly between each addition. You want a very firm, resilient dough. Since the leavening action will vary slightly between brands of corn meal, you might find it necessary to use a bit more or less than the indicated quantity of flour.

When the dough is kneaded, shape into 2 or 3 balls of equal size and put into a well-greased Dutch oven. Let stand in a warm place until the dough increases in volume by ½. Cover the oven, bury in coals, cook 45 minutes. In the sheepherder stove, use an open pan and bake 25 to 30 minutes; in the kitchen oven, 35 minutes at 350 degrees.

Makes 2 standard or 3 small loaves.

## SOURDOUGH BREAD

This is the most famous and notorious of all pioneer breads. It earned its fame because good sourdough bread is perhaps the best and most satisfying loaf ever baked. It got its notoriety from two causes, one old, one modern. The leavening for sourdough bread is provided by a "starter," which is renewed at each baking by preserving a bit of the spongy dough produced midway in the mixing process. This starter is what causes the bread to rise and what gives sourdough bread its unique flavor. In theory, the starter lives indefinitely; in San Francisco there is a restaurant using a sourdough starter first mixed in 1850.

Sourdough got its notoriety in the early days when flour milling was a hit-or-miss affair, with local mills producing different types of flour from different varieties of wheat and wheat varieties were as little standardized as milling. Most of the wheat grown was hard durum, and a sourdough starter begun with hard wheat will not survive the addition of a low-gluten soft wheat. This is the explanation for the failure of much early sourdough bread. The sourdough process got an undeserved reputation for being tricky, troublesome, hard to handle.

The modern reason for sourdough's notoriety is the cussedness of mankind. Many bread factories today manufacture a long oval loaf out of the same sponge used to produce their oblong squoosh bread. They brush the top of the oval loaf with milk or water to give it a thick crust, and label the result "Sour French" bread. Buyers confuse it with sourdough, and are disappointed to find it the same loaf as that in the shiny plastic wrapper.

You can make a good sourdough bread with today's standard all-purpose flour. Your starter does not have to be used daily or weekly, as was once the case; it can be refrigerated or frozen and used when you get the craving for real sourdough bread. As long as you remember to reserve the portion of the dough sponge necessary to renew the starter each time you bake, a sourdough starter will go with you through life and can be handed down to your children and grandchildren. It's worth it, too.

In spite of what you may have heard, sourdough baking is neither tricky, troublesome, nor time consuming. There's a lot of waiting involved, but you can find other things to do while the bread rises; the total amount of time you will be personally involved in mixing or other operations is about 45 minutes, after you've made up your starter for the first time. That step requires an additional 30 minutes, but need not be repeated as long as you remember to reserve a portion for the next baking. If you'd like to skip making a starter, there are firms listed on page 304 that will sell you one. But making your own isn't all that difficult.

### SOURDOUGH STARTER

| | |
|---|---|
| 3  medium-sized potatoes | 3  tablespoons all-purpose flour; |
| 3½  cups water | do not use cake flour |

Peel and quarter two of the potatoes and boil until they are very soft. Pour off 2 cups of the cooking water into a sterilized crock or jar, let it stand until it is lukewarm. Peel the third potato and scrape off 2 level tablespoons of pulp. Add this pulp to the water in the jar or crock. Stir in the 3 tablespoons flour and cover the crock lightly; do not seal. Put it in a warm place.

Between 36 and 48 hours later, this mixture in the crock will begin to ferment. The solids will form a bubbly layer and separate from the liquid. Pour off the liquid, reserving 3 tablespoons, which is returned to the crock. This is the starter: the contents of the crock. You will know it is ready for use by several signs. It will be pure white, with no tinge of gray or yellow; it will give off a clean, sharp, yeasty odor; and the solid portion will be a mass of bubbles the size of rice grains. If your starter is gray or yellow or has no bubbles, you will know that you've used an unsuitable flour and must start again with one that is "hard" rather than "soft."

One starter is used for all sourdough baking: bread, rolls, biscuits, pancakes. Each time you bake, at the proper step in the mixing a portion of the sponge is removed and becomes the starter for the next baking. Nothing needs to be added to the portion you remove. It can be kept at room temperature for up to four days, in the refrigerator for up to three months, or in the freezer for six months. When refrigerated or frozen it must be brought to room temperature by setting its container into a pan of warm water.

### SOURDOUGH BREAD

| | |
|---|---|
| sourdough starter, prepared as above | ½ teaspoon baking soda |
| 3 cups lukewarm water | 3 tablespoons sugar |
| 7 to 8 cups flour—the same kind used with the starter | 4 tablespoons liquid fat; melted shortening or cooking oil |
| 3 eggs | 1 teaspoon salt |
| 1 cup milk | |

Put the entire starter into a mixing bowl and stir in 3 cups lukewarm water. Add 3 cups unsifted flour, mix well. Cover the bowl with a cloth and set aside for 4 hours. This is the working time at 70 degrees; if it is cooler, the time will be longer, if warmer, shorter. You can tell when the mixture, called the sponge, is ready for you to go to the next step: its surface will be covered with slowly forming, bursting bean-sized bubbles.

*At this point remove 1 cupful of the sponge and put it in the crock or jar in which it will be stored; the container must be sterilized. This is your next starter. It can be used at once, or stored as described. At this point in each baking you must remove and reserve this cup of sponge.*

After reserving the starter, beat the eggs, milk, salt, sugar, soda, and fat together and mix with the sponge remaining in the mixing bowl. Beat well, then add the remaining 4 cups of flour; combine it with the sponge by hand, adding a little at a time. Your objective is a very firm, very resilient dough, and it may be necessary to use a little

**270**

more or less than the 4 cups of flour indicated to get the right consistency. You will know the dough is ready when it resists further mixing.

Turn out the dough on a lightly floured board and knead it until it has a satiny sheen and will no longer stick to your hands or to the kneading surface. Lift the ball of dough; when properly kneaded, it will not sag or string. Put the dough into a greased bowl and let it stand until it doubles in bulk. This will take 2 to 4 hours, depending on temperature.

Turn the dough out onto the floured mixing board and work it just enough to press out all air bubbles created by its rising. Divide the ball of dough into 2 or 3 balls, put them in the well-greased Dutch oven and let stand until they double in bulk. Close the oven and bury it in coals for 50 minutes to 1 hour. In the sheepherder oven you can use open loaf pans or form the dough into ovals rather than balls and let it rise for the last time on baking sheets; baking time will be 25 to 30 minutes. In the kitchen oven in loaf pans or on baking sheets, time it for 35 minutes at 350 degrees.

Procedure for making sourdough biscuits will be found on page 275; for sourdough pancakes on page 282. Sourdough rolls are made from the dough used for bread; bake 40 minutes in the Dutch oven, 15 minutes in the kitchen oven at 350 degrees.

Now, one thing more. There are many, many recipes for sourdough bread. Some are "simplified" to the point that the bread they produce isn't sourdough bread at all. Some are even more complicated than this one. During a dozen years, I've tested at least a recipe a year for sourdough bread, and the old-timer above is still the easiest one I've found that results in a good sourdough loaf.

## Biscuits

If you think an oven is necessary for you to produce good biscuits, you're wrong. A couple of the following recipes turn out good biscuits in an open skillet. The others prove that all biscuits needn't be alike. You can even use biscuit dough to make Squaw Bread, by cutting the dough into squares, punching a hole in the middle (to avoid a soggy center) and cooking it like doughnuts in deep fat.

## BEATEN BISCUITS, CAMP STYLE

These biscuits should only be eaten hot. They do not hold over well or take kindly to reheating, so make only enough for one meal. If you want a biscuit that holds well and can be reheated without damage, use the Skillet Biscuits on page 274 or the Sourdough Biscuits on page 275.

| | |
|---|---|
| 2 cups all-purpose flour | margarine |
| ½ teaspoon salt | ½ cup water |
| 1 teaspoon lard, butter, or | |

Mix the flour and salt together, work the shortening in with your fingertips. When the fat is blended in, add water, a teaspoon at a time, mixing it into the solid dough between each addition. You want a very firm, stiff dough.

Now the fun begins. Turn the dough out on a floured board and sprinkle the dough with flour. Beat it gently with some kind of club: a peeled branch, hammer-handle, small baseball bat, rolling pin. Beat the dough into a sheet about ¼ inch thick. Fold the sheet double, double again, then double once more and begin beating until the dough is back to that sheet about ¼ inch thick. Repeat this 6 or 8 times—the more you beat, the better the biscuits will be. When you're tired of beating, fold the sheet into that familiar series of doubles, but this time pat it very gently into a sheet about ½ inch thick. Cut out the biscuits and put them into the Dutch oven or double skillet, well buttered, and brush their tops with melted butter. Cover the pan and bury in coals 30 minutes. In the sheepherder oven, use open pans or a baking sheet and cook 12 to 15 minutes; timing for the kitchen oven is 18 to 20 minutes at 350 degrees.

Makes 20 to 24 biscuits, 2 or 2½ inch diameter.

## LIGHT BISCUITS

These biscuits hold over reasonably well; when served as left-overs they are best when split and pressed into hot bacon drippings in a skillet. They also make excellent cobblers and shortcakes.

| | |
|---|---|
| 1¾ cups all-purpose flour | 2 tablespoons butter |
| 2½ teaspoons baking powder | ¾ cup milk (diluted evaporated |
| 1¼ teaspoons salt | milk or dry milk can be used) |
| 1 tablespoon sugar | |

Sift together the flour, baking powder, salt, and sugar; put them through the sifter twice. Cut the butter into the dry mix with a knife or wire pastry blender. Stir in the milk, but stir only long enough to get all the lumps out of the dough. Turn onto a floured board, sprinkle the dough with flour, and knead very gently, with a light touch, for 3 to 5 minutes. Pat—do not roll—the dough into a sheet ¼ inch thick. Cut out the biscuits and put them in a well-oiled Dutch oven or double skillet, and bury in coals for 25 minutes. In the sheepherder oven, in pans or on a baking sheet, bake 10 minutes; in the kitchen oven, 12 to 15 minutes at 350 degrees. You can also cook these biscuits like pancakes, in a heavy skillet, very lightly greased, over medium-bright coals. Put in a few at a time, cook 5 to 6 minutes per side.

Makes 20 to 24 biscuits, 2 or 2½ inches in diameter.

## POTATO BISCUITS

These are leavened biscuits, very firm, with a texture almost like that of bread. They keep well, can be reheated with no noticeable loss of quality, and are excellent toasted and floated on soups, or at the bottom of a bowl of stew, or with gravy.

| | |
|---|---|
| 4 large potatoes | dry yeast |
| 2 tablespoons lard or solid shortening | 4½ to 5 cups all-purpose flour |
| 1 yeast cake or package of | ½ teaspoon salt |

Peel, quarter and boil the potatoes; reserve 1 cup of the water in which they cook. Drain the potatoes and mash with the shortening. Dissolve yeast in the cup of lukewarm potato water and blend it with the mashed potatoes. Stir the flour into the potatoes a little at a time, adding the salt with the first 2 cups of flour. You may need a bit more or a bit less flour than indicated; your dough should not be excessively stiff.

Turn the dough out on a lightly floured board and with floured hands pat it into a sheet ½ inch thick. Cut the biscuits and put them into the lightly greased Dutch oven or double skillet. Allow space for them to rise. Put the pan aside and let the biscuits double in bulk; this will take 30 to 45 minutes, depending on temperature. Close the pan, bury it in coals, cook 30 minutes. In the sheepherder oven, use open tins or a baking sheet, cook 15 minutes; in the kitchen oven, cook 20 minutes at 350 degrees.

Makes 20 to 24 biscuits, 2 to 2½ inch diameter.

### SKILLET BISCUITS

These biscuits are surprisingly light and delicate in texture. They hold over well for a day or two and can be reheated successfully. When split and toasted they are almost like unsalted soda crackers.

| | |
|---|---|
| 1¾ cups all-purpose flour | ½ cup solid shortening or ¾ |
| 3½ teaspoons baking powder | cup bacon drippings |
| 1 teaspoon salt (if bacon drippings are used, only ½ teaspoon) | 1 cup milk |

Sift together the flour, baking powder, and salt. Work in the fat with your fingertips, then stir in the milk to make a fairly thin dough. Stir until smooth, turn out on a lightly floured board and knead very gently—just 3 or 4 quick passes. Pat—do not roll—the dough into a sheet about ¼ inch thick. Grease the skillet very lightly over medium heat; it must be hot when the biscuits go in. Cook a few at a time, turn when browned on the bottom; about 4 to 5 minutes per side is the right cooking time. As they cook, the biscuits will rise until they are ½ to ¾ inch high.

Makes 20 to 24 biscuits, 2 to 2½ inch diameter.

## SODA BISCUITS

This is the Western "sore finger bread," and it has a bad name, received when lazy cooks served soda biscuits cold or tried to reheat them. It can't be done. They get tougher than sin and sour as alkali water. Hot, they're delicious—cold, they're for the birds, so feed the birds any cold soda biscuits.

| | |
|---|---|
| 4 cups all-purpose flour | ½ teaspoon lard or solid |
| 1 teaspoon salt | shortening |
| 1 teaspoon cream of tartar | ¾ cup milk—if none is available, |
| 1 teaspon baking soda | use water |

Sift the dry ingredients together. Rub in the shortening with your fingertips. Mix the milk with ¾ cup water, or if you're not using milk, use 1½ cups water, and add slowly to the solids, mixing with your fingertips. (That's how they got their nickname.) By tradition, soda biscuits are not cut, but pinched off onto the bottom of the Dutch oven or double skillet or the baking sheet, if you're using an oven. If you don't trust your eye, pat the dough flat, about ½ inch thick, and use a cutter. In the Dutch oven or double skillet, bury in coals 18 to 20 minutes; on a baking sheet or in tins in the sheepherder stove, cook 6 to 8 minutes; in the kitchen oven, 10 minutes at 350 degrees. Don't overcook. Overcooked soda biscuits are just as tough as cold ones.

Makes 20 to 24 biscuits, 2 to 2½ inch diameter.

## SOURDOUGH BISCUITS

Sourdough biscuits have all the qualities of sourdough bread. They hold over well, can be warmed with no noticeable loss of quality. They are made by following the procedure for making sourdough bread, page 268. Consult this recipe and follow it to the point where the starter is removed. From that point:

Use ½ the quantities called for in the bread recipe, and proceed to the first kneading. Let the dough rise, then turn out onto a lightly floured surface and knead just enough to remove air bubbles. Roll or pat the dough into a sheet ¼ to ½ inch thick. Cut the biscuits and put them in the greased Dutch oven or double skillet, allowing room for them to rise; if an oven is to be used put them in pans or on a baking sheet. When the biscuits have doubled in bulk, close the Dutch oven or skillet and bury in coals 30 to 35 minutes. In open pans or on a baking sheet in the sheepherder stove, cook 12 to 15 minutes; in the kitchen oven, cook 20 minutes at 350 degrees.

Makes 20 to 24 biscuits, 2 to 2½ inch diameter.

## Panbreads

### BANNOCK

What the Johnnycake was to the traveler of the American frontier, bannock was to the French-Canadian *voyageurs* who opened the north central section of the continent with their trapping operations in the seventeenth century. Though one of the great regional outdoor breads, bannock is not widely known, and it deserves to be. There are two kinds, a bread and a cake; the latter will be found on page 287.

| | |
|---|---|
| 3 cups all-purpose flour | (use water if there is no milk) |
| 1 tablespoon baking powder | 2 tablespoons bacon drippings, |
| large pinch of salt | melted butter, or cooking oil |
| 3 tablespoons milk | 1¼ cups warm water |

Sift or stir the dry ingredients together, stir in the milk and fat. Add warm water and stir into a smooth dough, thicker than pancake batter but thinner than biscuit dough. Grease a deep heavy skillet and pour in the dough; let it stand and rise 20 to 25 minutes. Cover the skillet tightly and cook over bright coals until done, about 25 to 30 minutes. Test it as you would a cake, by pushing a straw into the center; when the straw comes out clean, the bannock is done.

Every northwoodsman has his own ideas about bannock. Some prefer to let the dough rise in the mixing bowl and bring a thick film of grease to high heat in the skillet before pouring in the dough; this method produces a flatter bannock with a crusty bottom. Some form the dough into pones, much like corn pones, and let them rise in the skillet before cooking. Bannock can be oven-baked, in an open pan, 10 to 12 minutes in the sheepherder stove; 20 minutes at 375 degrees in the kitchen oven.

Makes a loaf about 8 inches around and 2 inches thick.

## KNACKBRÖD

Knackbröd needs no refrigeration, travels well, and is more satisfactory than soda crackers as a base for spreads. It stays fresh indefinitely without having to be sealed in an airtight wrapping, and when used as a trail bread creates little thirst because of its low salt content. It is especially good when warmed and eaten buttered or with a cheese. Knackbröd is widely available commercially, but is very easy to make.

| | |
|---|---|
| 3 cups rye flour | 1 teaspoon baking soda |
| 1 cup white flour | 1 pint buttermilk (dry |
| ½ cup sugar | buttermilk can be used) |
| 1 teaspoon salt | ¾ cup oil or melted shortening |

Sift or shake the dry ingredients together. Stir in the buttermilk and shortening until smooth. You want a fairly stiff dough. Turn out on a lightly floured board and knead gently. Divide dough into 12 balls of equal size, roll them very thin, about ⅛ to ¼ inch thick. Slide the rounds onto a lightly greased baking sheet, and prick each one over its entire top surface with a fork. In the sheepherder oven, bake 8 to 10 minutes; in the kitchen oven, bake 15 minutes at 400 degrees. Let cool before using.

Makes 12 large rounds or wafers.

## Bread, Cakes, and Eggs

## Corn Meal Breads

Each culture has its traditional unleavened breads, and those of the North American Indian cultures were baked with corn meal. White settlers fell into the cultural pattern of the continent, but improved on the methods of producing meal. The oak-stump mortar and small hand *metate* was replaced by the grist mill where water power was harnessed to rotate huge stone discs between which the kernels were ground. Later, high-speed steel rollers replaced the stone discs, and the meal they ground was finer and more even in texture than the stone-ground type. Texture is the principal difference between "corn meal" and "stone-ground corn meal," both of which are available everywhere today. Either type can be used in any corn meal bread, though a smaller quantity of stone-ground meal will be needed in most recipes. The difference between white and yellow corn meal is largely a matter of regional preference, and the two are readily inter-changeable.

### JOHNNYCAKE

Grandpa of all unleavened corn breads is the Johnnycake, a name which historians generally agree was corrupted from "journeycake," the pones being favored by travelers because they keep almost indefinitely after baking. Several regional variations are given in this recipe.

| | |
|---|---|
| 1 cup corn meal or ¾ cup stone-ground corn meal | 2 cups boiling water |
| 1 teaspoon salt | fat for frying |

Sift the cornmeal and salt together and add the boiling water gradually while stirring into a thick batter. Drop spoonfuls in a hot skillet with a thick film of fat on its bottom. Turn when the bottom is browned; cooking time should be 3 to 4 minutes per side. Drain on papers before serving. Some cooks form the batter into oval pones instead of dropping spoon-scoops into the skillet.

A lighter textured version of Johnnycake results when an egg is beaten into the batter. Some cooks using the egg version substitute 1 cup of milk for one of the cups of boiling water; some add a pinch of baking soda; some put in a pinch of sugar. The result is still Johnnycake.

Ashcake is a thick Johnnycake batter formed by hand into pones and buried in hot ashes over coals, with more coals heaped over the ashes. It was usually cooked outdoors or at an open hearth indoors.

Hoecake is a Johnnycake made from a batter using only 1 cup of boiling water plus ½ cup hot bacon drippings or lard. This is a Southern variation; its name derives from the pones having been cooked on the blade of a hoe by field workers during their noon lunch period.

Crackling Bread is a Johnnycake, generally made with white corn meal, to which chopped crisp crackling—fried pork skin or pork fat —is added when mixing the batter.

Hush Puppies are a variation of Johnnycake; they can be cooked only in the hot fat in which fish have been fried. The recipe is on page 170.

Yield of this recipe in any of its variations is 8 to 10 pones.

## CORN MEAL CRISPS

| | |
|---|---|
| 1 cup corn meal | ¼ teaspoon baking soda |
| ½ cup flour | ⅓ cup bacon drippings |
| ½ teaspoon salt | ½ cup milk |

Though these crisps can be made with any corn meal, you will get best results in both taste and texture by using a fine-ground yellow meal.

Sift the dry ingredients together and add the fat, then the milk, stirring into a smooth batter. Turn out onto a corn-meal-covered board and knead thoroughly, at least 5 to 6 minutes. Roll into 1-inch balls, and roll these very flat, very thin—about ⅛ inch. Cook over high heat in a lightly greased skillet until brown on one side, turn. Cooking time will be 4 to 5 minutes per side. The cakes should be quite brown and very crisp, almost brittle. Brush with butter, sprinkle with salt, and eat them very hot. The crisps can be oven-baked. On a baking sheet in the sheepherder stove, cook 10 minutes; in the kitchen oven, 15 minutes at 375 degrees. Do not turn when oven-cooking them.

Makes 18 to 20 crisps.

## Pancakes

Pancakes are often the refuge of a camp cook unsure of his skill with other breads, and who serves hotcakes with every meal. Other camp breads may be as easy to cook, but this poor fellow has the crutch of a prepared "mix" to lean on, which makes him feel secure. In cold fact, these "mixes" don't help you much. By the time you add an egg and milk or water, you might as well have taken another 30 seconds, which is all the time needed to shake together the flour, salt, baking powder and sugar; these are what "mixes" contain, plus a few assorted chemicals to keep them from smelling rancid after several months of sitting around waiting to be used. If you insist on a "mix," the home-mixed one on page 309 will stay fresh for a couple of weeks and serves for both pancakes and biscuits; stir up a batch and avoid the preservatives in the packaged mixes. Here's a trio that will give you a little variety.

### CRUMB PANCAKES

| | |
|---|---|
| 1 cup very fine dry bread crumbs | 1½ teaspoons baking powder |
| 3 tablespoons flour | 2 eggs, separated |
| 1 tablespoon sugar | 1 cup milk |
| 1½ teaspoons salt | 2 tablespoons melted butter or cooking oil |

Stir or sift the dry ingredients together. Beat the egg yolks lightly with the milk, add to the dry ingredients and stir in the oil. Beat the egg whites stiff and fold them into the batter.

At this point you have two options. Number one: Drop spoonfuls of the batter onto a lightly greased griddle or skillet, wait for bubbles to show on top, then flip the cakes and wait until they're browned. Do this and you'll have a light, fluffy pancake with a unique texture. Number two: stir into the batter ¾ cup chopped fresh strawberries, minced or grated apple, chopped soaked raisins, crushed fresh huckleberries, blackberries, boysenberries, blueberries, or almost any other minced fruit or berry that strikes your fancy. Then cook the pancakes in the usual way, serving them with butter and perhaps a dusting of sugar laced with a touch of nutmeg or cinnamon.

Makes 12 to 14 pancakes, 3 to 4 inches in diameter.

## JOE O'DONNELL'S PANCAKES

Of my many pancake-making friends, none turns out hotcakes equal to those made by Joe O'Donnell on the woodstove in his kitchen. Joe lives near Orleans, on California's upper Klamath River, and is as adept with griddle and turner as he is with a flyrod. That's saying a lot, for Joe fishes every day of the 6-month steelhead season on the Klamath, and has for almost 50 of his 80 years. Joe O'Donnell's cabin is the unofficial headquarters for a dozen or so fly fishermen, but when you're fishing from Joe's you don't get pancakes for breakfast. In the presunrise dark, you eat a handful of graham crackers with your coffee, then head for the river and fish "until the sun hits the water," usually about 10 A.M. Then everyone heads back to the cabin and Joe cooks the hotcakes.

| | | | |
|---|---|---|---|
| 4 | cups all-purpose flour | 3 | teaspoons sugar |
| 3½ | teaspoons baking powder | 3½ | cups lukewarm milk or water |
| ½ | teaspoon salt | 2 | eggs |

Stir the dry ingredients together in a bowl, beginning with the flour and stirring continuously while the others are added. Pour in the milk, adding it slowly, while beating it into the dry ingredients. Add the eggs and beat vigorously for 5 minutes, to produce a batter just a little thicker than a rich cream. Have the griddle hot, but below the smoking stage; drops of water sprinkled on its surface should not dance, but just sizzle and vanish in about 90 seconds. Pour on the batter, or ladle it onto the griddle, and never try to spread or smooth the top of the cakes once the batter's on the griddle. When the very first bubbles rise to the tops of the cooking pancakes, turn and cook until browned.

Makes 20 to 24 pancakes, 3 to 4 inches in diameter.


### SOURDOUGH PANCAKES

Sourdough pancakes are chewier than most others, and stay edible longer; they do not seem to get old and soggy. These are the pancakes you fold over a spoonful of jam and wrap in waxed paper to tuck into your fishing creel or hunting coat pocket for a midmorning munch.

A word of caution: sourdough pancake batter must be started 12 hours before cooking.

| | |
|---|---|
| 1 cup sourdough starter, page 269 | 2 eggs |
| 2 cups lukewarm water | 1½ tablespoons sugar |
| 3 cups all-purpose flour, preferably the same flour that was used in making the starter | 2 tablespoons liquid fat; oil or melted shortening |
| | ⅓ cup milk or water |
| | 1 teaspoon baking soda |

At least 12 hours before the pancakes are to be cooked, mix the starter with the lukewarm water and 2 cups flour; let stand in a covered bowl. Before beginning to mix the pancake batter at the end of 12 hours, return 1 cup of this mixture to the starter crock.

Beat eggs lightly and continue to beat while adding the sugar, fat, milk or water, baking soda, and remaining flour. When the mixture is smooth, blend it with the starter, let stand 15 to 20 minutes. It can stand longer, up to 1 hour. Grease the skillet or griddle very lightly, heat until a few drops of water spattered on its surface dance wildly and vanish in 1 minute. Pour pancakes, when bubbles form on the uncooked tops, turn and cook until brown.

Makes 20 to 24 pancakes about 3 to 4 inches in diameter.

## Eggs

Eggs cooked outdoors have a distressing tendency to show up in only one style: fried hard in bacon drippings. It's certainly the easiest way, but monotonous. In another cookbook of mine you will find almost six hundred ways to cook eggs, many of them suited to open coals. To avoid repetition (and to encourage you to add another cookbook to your shelves) the subject of eggs is touched on very lightly here. Incidentally, if you are auto camping and traveling rough roads, or back-packing, eggs placed in a sack with oatmeal, corn meal, or breakfast cereal will survive the roughest journeys unbroken.

### SCRAMBLED EGGS, COUNTRY OR CAMP STYLE

6 eggs                                   salt, pepper
butter or other cooking fat

Be very sparing of both the amount of fat used and the amount of heat under the skillet. Break the eggs directly into the pan, scrambling with a fork as each egg goes in. Season as you stir. Serve the moment the tops film. Eat at once, as eggs cooked this style dry to a leathery toughness very quickly. To make a crude omelet, scatter minced onion or green pepper, bits of cooked crumbled ham or bacon, or other meat or flaked fish over the bottom of the pan before putting in the eggs.

Serves 4.

## KENTUCKY SCRAMBLE

| | |
|---|---|
| 6 eggs | kernel corn |
| 1½ cups fresh corn or | butter or bacon drippings |
| well-drained canned whole | salt, pepper |

Grease the skillet very lightly. If fresh corn is used, sauté it about 4 minutes over very low heat, stirring frequently. Break the eggs into the pan over the corn, season, scramble at once with a fork. This dish is never called "Kentucky Scrambled Eggs," but always is a "a Kentucky Scramble."

Serves 4 adequately, 6 sparingly.

## SHEEPHERDER EGGS

Sheepherders in the plateau country of Nevada and Utah and in California's big valleys prepare their eggs this way, mixing the dish in a small Dutch oven or a heavy skillet and letting it cook in coals or in the sheepherder stove while they go out for a prebreakfast checkup of their flocks. By the time they return, their eggs are cooked and waiting.

| | |
|---|---|
| 6 eggs | large pinch of thyme or |
| 2 or 3 boiled potatoes | marjoram, powdered |
| 2 sweet onions or their | 4 patties of precooked |
| equivalent in small | country-style sausage, or large |
| green-topped fresh young | link sausage, or an equivalent |
| onions | quantity of thin-sliced hard |
| bacon drippings | sausage such as salami |
| salt, pepper | |

Dice the potatoes and onions. Heat bacon drippings in the bottom of the Dutch oven or skillet and sauté them lightly, sprinkling with the thyme while stirring. Beat the eggs lightly with salt and pepper. Break the sausage into thumbtip-sized pieces, or chop coarsely. Stir the beaten eggs and sausage into the potatoes and onions. Cover the

Dutch oven and bury in coals 30 minutes or more. In the sheep-herder stove over low coals, cook in a tightly covered skillet 15 to 20 minutes; in the kitchen oven in a tightly closed casserole, cook 20 minutes at 250 degrees. The dish should have a brown bottom crust, but a rather soft center when it is served.

Serves 4 to 6.

## EGGS ROASTED ON THE SPIT

This is another of those showpieces for the outdoor chef, a good dish on which to win a bet or face down a dare. It happens to work, unlikely as you might think it, and also tastes good.

| | |
|---|---|
| 4 eggs | very fine, very dry bread crumbs |
| ½ pound butter (no substitutes), chilled | of 8 bread slices |

Beat the eggs until they froth. Form the chilled butter into a ball, roll it in bread crumbs, then in eggs, and repeat this until all of the bread crumbs and eggs have been absorbed. Put the ball on the spit and cook slowly over very dark coals until it is crisply browned, about 15 to 20 minutes.

Serves 4, lightly.

## A COWBOY BREAKFAST

When she was a tiny tot, my wife was taught this cowhand break-fast by her grandfather, James Grisba, who worked as a cowhand, then as a Texas Ranger, until the opening of the Oklahoma Strip in 1889, when he joined that land rush and acquired a ranch of his own.

| | |
|---|---|
| a boiled, unpeeled potato | a strip or two of bacon |

Fry the bacon crisp. Cut the potato in half lengthwise and gash its exposed surfaces deeply, press gently to open the slits. Pour the hot bacon drippings into the open cuts, and eat the now-hot potato with the bacon.

Serves 1 lonely cowhand riding fence or range-herding.

# XII

---

# "A Little Something Sweet"

EMILE BONDURANT, better known as Frenchy to several generations of fishermen seeking the monster rainbow trout that lurk in the deep holes of California's Lake Almanor, gave this chapter its title. After every meal we shared on Almanor's shores while he was teaching me to read the lake, Frenchy would sigh with contentment as he spooned jam on a biscuit, saying, "A meal's no good unless you finish with a little something sweet."

A camp cook really wins his spurs when he offers a dessert comparable in quality with the good meal he's just prepared, but there is seldom time for him to deal with a fancy dish to offer as a topper for the dinner. The most practical desserts to offer with outdoor meals are those that can be prepared in advance and put on to cook while the meal is being eaten, or served cold. And like all outdoor foods, desserts should be simple and hearty.

Most of the dessert dishes meeting those specifications have come down to us from pioneer days, when there were no handy corner bakeries or confectionery stores offering pies and cakes and cookies; no sections in supermarkets and drugstores devoted to displaying an infinite variety of candy bars; no drive-ins vending sweet soft drinks and ice-cream concoctions. The ingredients used for desserts were fresh fruits in season, dried or canned fruits in the wintertime, pre-

**286**

pared by methods that used a minimum of what was then a scarce and expensive commodity, granulated sugar.


## APPLE SLUMP

This old New England favorite can also be made using peaches, pears, apricots, or any other fruit, as well as berries. Though the recipe calls for fresh fruit, it can be made with canned fruits, well drained, and the indicated quantity of sugar cut in half.

| | | | |
|---|---|---|---|
| 8 | tart cooking apples | 1½ | cups all-purpose flour |
| 1 | cup sugar | ¼ | teaspoon salt |
| 1½ | teaspoons cinnamon | 1½ | teaspoons baking powder |
| 2 | cups water | ½ | cup milk |

Peel and core the apples, slice them into a lightly buttered pan that can be tightly closed—a Dutch oven or double skillet does very well. Sprinkle the sugar and half the cinnamon over the apples, pour water in the pan and bring to a gentle simmer. Sift together the flour, salt, and baking powder; add the milk, stirring until smooth. You want a stiff batter rather than a dough. Drop the batter in tablespoonfuls on the simmering apples and sprinkle with the remaining cinnamon. Close the pan tightly and cook over low heat 35 to 40 minutes.

Serves 6 to 8.


## BANNOCK DESSERT BREAD

Prepare the Bannock bread recipe, page 276. Before putting the dough aside to rise, stir in 1½ cups brown sugar, or 1 cup brown and 1 cup white sugar. Add raisins, pitted chopped prunes, diced apples, coarsely chopped apricots or peaches, or almost any other fruit or berry. Canned fruits can be used if they are drained well. Use 1 to 1½ cups fruit. Set the dough to rise, which will take 25 to 30 minutes, then cook in a tightly closed pan over bright coals 25 to 30 minutes, or until a straw thrust into the center of the bannock comes out clean. Oven time will be 12 to 15 minutes in the sheepherder stove; 25 minutes at 375 degrees in the kitchen oven; in either oven use an open pan.

Serves 8 to 10.

## BISCUIT COBBLER WITH DRIED FRUIT

3  cups dried fruit; apples, apricots, peaches, etc.—one kind of fruit or a mixture of several can be used

1  cup sugar

1  teaspoon lemon juice

½  teaspoon cinnamon

½  batch Light Biscuit Dough, page 273

2  tablespoons butter

Cover the fruit with warm water and soak 20 to 30 minutes; drain; reserve 1 cup of the water in which the fruit soaked. Mix this water with the sugar, lemon juice, and cinnamon, boil 3 minutes. Butter the Dutch oven very heavily and put the fruit in it. Pour the boiled seasoned water over the fruit. Prepare the Light Biscuit Dough, pat into a round the size of the pan, and lay on the fruits in the pan. Cover the Dutch oven, bury in coals, and cook 35 to 40 minutes. In the sheepherder oven, cook in an open pan, 15 to 20 minutes; in the kitchen oven in an open pan, 20 to 25 minutes at 350 degrees. Dot the top of the biscuit crust with butter just before serving; if the cobbler is to go to the table cold, butter it while still hot.

A second version of this cobbler uses a half batch of Light Biscuit Dough baked into a single pan-sized biscuit, which is then split, buttered, and filled with the stewed fruit. Juices from the pan are poured over the top before serving. In this version the dish is improved if 2 tablespoons of brandy are added to the syrup after it boils and just before taking it off the fire.

Serves 6 to 8.

## BREAD PUDDING, CAMP STYLE

12  slices dry bread
    any kind of jam or jelly, enough to cover each slice of bread

generously

1  tablespoon butter

1  cup milk

Spread the bread thinly with butter, thickly with jam or jelly. Butter the Dutch oven or a heavy skillet with a tightly fitting cover, arrange the coated bread slices in layers. Pour over the bread all the milk it will absorb; add the milk slowly to let it soak into the bread. Do not cover the bread with milk. Dot the top of the dish with butter, cover the pan, put over low coals 20 to 30 minutes—or long enough for everyone to eat dinner. The pudding will be ready when it's time for dessert, it will not spoil if it waits a while in the pan.

Serves 6 to 8.

## BREAKFAST PUDDING

| | |
|---|---|
| 12 slices very dry firm bread | 3 tablespoons sugar, white or |
| 1 teaspoon powdered ginger | brown |
| 1 teaspoon nutmeg or powdered | 1 cup raisins or currants |
| allspice | 2 tablespoons butter |
| ½ teaspoon salt | ½ to ¾ cup milk |

Soak the bread in warm water and gently squeeze it dry while still preserving its shape. Mix the spices, salt, and sugar, spread on a flat surface, and gently press both sides of each slice of bread into the mixture. Butter a Dutch oven or double skillet generously and arrange the slices of bread in alternate layers with the raisins or currants. Pour the milk over the top layer of bread, let it soak a minute or two, then with a flat pancake turner or big spoon press the bread down into the pan, packing it firmly. Dot the top with chunks of butter. Bury the oven or skillet in coals before going to bed. The next morning, turn the still-warm pudding out onto a big plate and slice into wedges like a cake, or cut in thick slices and sauté until the outsides are crisp. It can be eaten as it comes from the pan, or sprinkled with sugar, or doused with honey, syrup, or jam.

Serves 6 to 8.

## BROWN BETTY

Apple is the traditional filling for this Down East dessert of earlier days, but you will find peaches, pears, apricots, even cherries or berries work equally well. Canned fruits can be used; drain them well, reduce the recipe's indicated quantity of sugar by ½, and mix ¼ cup of the fruit's syrup with ¼ cup lemon juice rather than using pure lemon juice.

| | | | |
|---|---|---|---|
| 3 | cups peeled, sliced apples | 1½ | tablespoons cinnamon |
| 1½ | cups fine dry bread crumbs or graham cracker crumbs | 1 | teaspoon powdered nutmeg |
| | | ½ | teaspoon powdered cloves |
| ½ | cup melted butter | ½ | cup lemon juice (see above) |
| 1½ | cups brown sugar (see above) | | |

Mix crumbs and butter, grease the sides and bottom of the Dutch oven, and press the crumbs thickly on bottom and sides to form a crust. Mix the sugar and spices together. Peel and core the apples and slice about ¼ to ½ inch thick. Put a layer of apples on the bottom of the pan, sprinkle with the brown sugar mixture and a few drops of lemon juice. Add layers of apple slices until all apples are used, sprinkling between each layer with the spiced sugar and lemon juice. Spread a thick layer of the buttered crumbs on top of the last layer of apples, dot with butter. Close the Dutch oven, bury in coals, cook 30 to 40 minutes. In the sheepherder stove use an uncovered pan and cook 15 minutes; in the kitchen oven in an uncovered pan cook 20 minutes at 300 degrees. Traditionally, the Brown Betty is served in bowls with cream poured over each serving.
Serves 6 to 8.


## CALAS

Lost to modern ears is the calling of the street vendor. Even if city health laws would permit him to operate, the crying of his wares would be drowned by traffic noise. The last of the Calas traymen vanished from New Orleans streets years ago, but old residents of the Crescent City would still be able to translate his slurred crying, "Bellacala" into its meaning: "Belle calas." Since the Calas were cooked while you waited, it is an authentic outdoor dish.

3 eggs

¼ teaspoon almond or vanilla
   extract

¼ teaspoon powdered cloves

½ teaspoon powdered nutmeg

2 cups cooked rice

½ cup sugar

½ teaspoon salt

6 tablespoons flour

3 teaspoons baking powder

fat for deep frying, a neutral oil
   such as peanut oil

Beat the eggs until frothy, adding the extract, cloves, and nut-meg during the final moments of beating; combine with the rice. Stir or sift together the sugar, salt, flour, and baking powder and blend with the rice mixture. Have 3 to 4 inches of fat in a deep kettle hot enough to brown a 1-inch cube of bread in one minute. Drop in the dough by spoonfuls, a few at a time so the temperature of the fat will not be lowered. Turn to brown evenly, remove and drain well after about 4 minutes of cooking. Sprinkle with sugar and eat at once. Calas must be eaten piping hot or their charm is lost.

Makes 12 to 14 Calas.

## FRIED PIES

fruit for filling (apples,
   peaches, cherries, berries,
   etc.); 1½ canned, 2 cups
   fresh

1 cup all-purpose flour

2 tablespoons butter

1 egg yolk

3 tablespoons hot milk

⅛ teaspoon salt

fat for frying: ⅓ solid
   shortening and ⅔ light
   cooking oil

Stew fresh fruits until soft in 3 cups water to which 1 tablespoon sugar and a dash of lemon juice have been added. If canned fruits are used, drain well and mash into a thick purée.

Sift the flour into a mixing bowl and cut the butter into it. Beat egg yolk with milk and salt and stir into the flour. Turn out on a floured board and knead until smooth and elastic, then pat or roll into a sheet ⅛ to ¼ inch thick. Cut the dough into squares or circles. Put a dollop of fruit into the center of each and close the pie by folding its edges together; use a touch of cold water along the joint to make them stick, then crimp the edges with a fork.

## "A Little Something Sweet"

Have 4 to 5 inches of fat in a deep kettle hot enough to brown a 1-inch cube of bread in 30 to 40 seconds. Drop the pies into the fat two or three at a time, let cook until the outsides are browned. Remove, drain well, dust with sugar.

Makes 8 to 10 pies.

## FRUIT DUMPLINGS

fruit for filling—fresh apples, pears, firm peaches, seeded prunes, raisins, or apricots make the best fillings, in the order given. Canned fruits are not recommended. You will need 1¼ to 1½ cups of coarsely cut fruit.

4 cups all-purpose flour

2 teaspoons salt
1 teaspoon baking powder
1½ cups butter
⅔ cups water
2 cups sugar
½ cup butter
2 tablespoons lemon juice
1½ cups warm water

Sift or stir together the flour, salt, and baking powder and blend the butter into it with your fingertips. Add the warm water a tablespoon at a time, while continuing to blend. You want a smooth, elastic dough and may need a bit more or a bit less water than indicated. Turn the dough out onto a floured board and pat it into a thin sheet, about ⅛ to ¼ inch thick. Cut into 3-inch squares.

Put 1 tablespoon of chopped fruit in the center of each square of dough, sprinkle with sugar, and top with ½ teaspoon butter. Bring the corners of the square up to encase the fruit and press the edges of the dough together; moisten with water to get a firm seal.

Mix 1 cup of the remaining sugar with the lemon juice in 1½ cups warm water. In a small pan, bring this to a rolling boil. Arrange the dumplings in the bottom of a heavy pan with a tightly fitting cover and pour this syrup over them. Close the pan and cook over very bright coals for 20 minutes. The dumplings are best served hot, with a dab of butter melted in cream and several tablespoonfuls put over them.

Makes 16 to 18 dumplings; allow 2 or 3 to a serving.

## LAZY COOK'S DESSERT

Leftover biscuits are the foundation for this dessert. The best biscuits to use in constructing it are Light Biscuits or Potato Biscuits, page 273.

| | |
|---|---|
| 2 eggs | ¼ teaspoon nutmeg or allspice |
| 2 cups milk | 12 leftover biscuits |
| 1½ tablespoons sugar | 3 tablespoons butter |
| ¼ teaspoon cinnamon | |

Beat the eggs, adding the milk, sugar, cinnamon, and allspice or nutmeg while beating. Split the biscuits and soak them in this, letting them absorb all the liquid they can hold without getting soggy. Drain the soaked biscuits on papers. Heat butter in a skillet and sauté the biscuit halves until browned, cooking on both sides. For those with an extra sweet tooth, mix sugar and cinnamon with which to sprinkle the biscuits while they are still hot, or pass syrup or honey. This dish is sometimes called Lazy Cook's Pancakes.

Serves 4 to 6.

## PEACH POT PUDDING

Apricots, apples, pears, berries, cherries, or other fresh fruits can be substituted for peaches, but canned fruits are not advised.

| | |
|---|---|
| 2 cups fresh peaches, diced ½ inch | ½ cup milk |
| | ½ cup brown sugar |
| 1 cup sugar | 1 teaspoon nutmeg or cinnamon |
| 1 cup all-purpose flour | 1 tablespoon butter |
| 2 teaspoons baking powder | 1 cup hot water |
| ½ teaspoon salt | |

Sift or stir together ½ cup of the sugar and all the flour, baking powder, and salt. Stir in the milk to form a smooth batter, then add the diced peaches and mix well. Grease the bottom and sides of the Dutch oven quite heavily, and pour this batter into it. Combine the

remaining ½ cup sugar with the brown sugar and nutmeg or cinnamon, rub it into the butter, pour hot water over it. Stir until the
butter and sugar are dissolved and pour into the Dutch oven over
the batter. Close the oven and bury it in coals 45 minutes. As the
pudding cooks, the syrup and peaches will sink to the bottom and
the batter will rise to the top, forming a crust as it floats on the fruit
and syrup. The dish can be cooked in the sheepherder stove in a
deep open pan, 20 to 25 minutes; in the kitchen oven, cook 30 minutes at 325 degrees. Good hot or cold.

Serves 6.

### PIONEER'S COVERED WAGON CAKE

This recipe was given to my mother sometime in the early 1920s
by a family friend, then in her eighties, who had crossed the country
from Virginia to Texas in a covered wagon in the years after the
Civil War. You will get a better cake if you use butter or margarine
instead of lard. The cake is dark and very solid, much like a moist
fruitcake. To pretty it up, add a few chopped nutmeats to the ingredients and sprinkle the top lightly with chopped glacé fruit.

| | |
|---|---|
| 4 cups raisins | 3 cups sugar |
| 3 cups prunes | 2 tablespoons vinegar |
| 4 cups currants | 1 tablespoon molasses |
| 3 to 4 cups warm coffee—enough to cover the above fruits | 1½ teaspoons baking soda |
| | 3 cups all-purpose flour |
| | 2 cups chopped citron |
| 3 cups lard | |

Chop the raisins (the original recipe calls for seeding the raisins,
as there were no seedless raisins at the time it was originated) and
seed and chop the prunes, put in a bowl with the currants and soak
overnight in enough coffee to cover them. Drain before using. Cream
together the lard and sugar, then mix with the vinegar, molasses, and
baking soda, and combine with the flour. Work until well mixed,
then work the chopped raisins, prunes, currants, and citron into the
dough. Grease the bottom and sides of a Dutch oven and pour in the

dough. Close the oven and bury it in coals to cook 1½ hours. This cake can be oven-baked, in loaf pans or an angel-food pan. In the sheepherder oven, cook 40 to 45 minutes; in the kitchen oven, 35 to 40 minutes at 325 degrees. Test for doneness by inserting a straw in the thickest portion—when the straw comes out clean, the cake is done.

## PORK CAKE

| | |
|---|---|
| ½ pound raisins | ½ cup molasses |
| ½ pound currants | 1½ cups all-purpose flour |
| ½ pound fresh uncooked pork fat | 1 teaspoon baking powder |
| 1 cup boiling water | 1 teaspoon each nutmeg and cinnamon |
| ½ teaspoon baking soda | |

Shred or grind the pork fat; be sure there is no lean meat left on it. Pour boiling water over the fat in a mixing bowl, combine the baking soda and molasses and pour into the fat. Stir well. Sift together the flour and baking powder and blend with the fat and liquids to make a stiff batter. (A little more flour than indicated may be needed, as the batter should be very stiff.) Combine the raisins, currants, and spices with the batter. Grease the bottom and sides of a Dutch oven and pour in the batter. Close the oven, bury it in coals for 2½ hours. You can bake this cake in an oven; in the sheepherder oven use loaf pans or an angel-food cake pan and cook over dying coals for 1¼ to 1½ hours; in the kitchen oven cook 1½ hours at 300 degrees. Test with a straw stuck into the cake, when the straw comes out clean, baking is completed.

## RICE AND FRUIT PUDDING

| | |
|---|---|
| 2 cups cooked rice | ½ cup sugar |
| 2 cups fresh or canned fruit of your choice (see below) | ¼ teaspoon cinnamon |
| 1 cup raisins | ¼ teaspoon nutmeg or allspice |
| 1 cup milk | 3 tablespoons melted butter |

### "A Little Something Sweet"

Virtually any fruit or combination of fruits, fresh, canned, or dried, can be used. Fresh fruits should be parboiled 5 minutes in 1 quart water with 1 tablespoon sugar added; dried fruit soaked 2 hours in water to cover and a dash of lemon juice; canned fruits are used just as they come from the can. All fruits should be well drained before adding to the pudding.

Combine rice and fruit in a heavy, well greased pan with a tightly fitting cover. Mix the milk, sugar, and spices. Pour the melted butter over the rice-fruit mixture in the pan, then at once pour in the seasoned milk. Close the pan tightly and cook on low heat for 25 to 30 minutes. A sprinkling of chopped unsalted nut meats on the top of the pudding is an option that adds crispness to the dish.

Serves 6 to 8.

### SWEET POTATOES, CREOLE STYLE

| | |
|---|---|
| 4 boiled sweet potatoes | rinds of 1 orange and ½ lemon, |
| 3 tablespoons butter | grated fine |
| ¼ cup brown sugar | ¼ cup dark (Jamaica) rum |
| ½ teaspoon cinnamon or allspice | |

Butter a heavy skillet that has a tight-fitting cover. Peel the sweet potatoes and quarter them lengthwise, spread them thickly with butter and put them on the bottom of the skillet. Combine the sugar, cinnamon or allspice, and grated peel and sprinkle over the potatoes. Warm the skillet and the rum, pour the rum over the potatoes and set afire. Before the flames die away, smother them by closing the skillet. Cook 20 minutes over low heat, until the sugar melts.

Serves 6 to 8.

### TURNIP PUDDING

| | |
|---|---|
| 4 large yellow turnips (rutabagas) | ½ cup melted butter |
| 2 tablespoons vinegar or lemon juice | 2 tablespoons brown sugar |
| ½ cup milk | ½ teaspoon salt |
| 1 tablespoon molasses | ½ teaspoon allspice or powdered cloves |

Peel and cube or slice the turnips and boil in salted water until tender. Drain well. If vinegar is used, heat to the boiling point and pour over the turnips; if lemon juice is used, no boiling is necessary. Mash the turnips, combine with them while mashing all the remaining ingredients. (An egg lightly beaten and added after mashing will make the pudding fluffier.) Pour the mixture into a greased pie tin, put on a rack in the Dutch oven, pour water into the bottom of the oven to a depth of about ¼ inch. Close the oven and bury in coals 45 minutes. To oven-cook use open pie tin—in the sheepherder stove, cook 20 minutes; in the kitchen oven, 30 minutes at 325 degrees.

## CAMP FRUIT CANDY

Here's a cookproof recipe that can safely be trusted to youngsters who want to "help" around the cooking fire.

| | |
|---|---|
| ½ cup each of dried apricots, pears, and raisins; or of apples, peaches, and pitted prunes | 2 tablespoons sugar |
| | 2 tablespoons warm water |
| | 18 marshmallows |
| | butter |
| ½ teaspoon cinnamon or allspice | |
| ½ cup chopped unsalted nutmeats | |

Chop the dried fruit fine, dust with the spices, and add the nutmeats to them. Dissolve the sugar in warm water. Spread the chopped fruits and nutmeats in an even layer over the bottom of a buttered shallow skillet and sprinkle them with the spices, then with the sugared water. Cut or pull the marshmallows in half and cover the fruits with these pieces. Put the skillet over very low heat until the marshmallows melt and run down over the fruits. Chill the skillet at once by letting it sit on the ground 5 to 10 minutes, then put it into a larger pan filled with cold water until the candy sets. Cut into squares.

Makes about 36 pieces, 1½ to 2 inches square.

## Camp Coffee

Even the best outdoor meal fails to satisfy most people unless there's good coffee to top it off. Traditionally, camp coffee is boiled, and a lot of otherwise sensible outdoor cooks have gotten so hooked on instant coffee that they've not only forgotten how to boil up a pot of the real brew, they've forgotten what genuine coffee tastes like. If you're among them, shock treatment is your best hope. Brew a pot of camp coffee and drink a cup or two.

Making coffee over coals calls for an old-fashioned conical-shaped coffeepot made from enameled steel. They come in sizes from six cups up to a couple of gallons. Pick the size that fits your needs and then buy one having double that capacity. Determine how much water your pot holds by filling it until the water level is a half-inch below the bottom of the spout; use a standard eight-ounce coffee cup for this job, not the oversized mugs commonly used outdoors.

Always brew to the pot's full capacity. Put in the proper amount of cold water—you already know how many cups that translates into —and then put in one level tablespoonful of coffee for each cup and one for the pot. Set the pot on a bright, healthy bed of coals and forget about it until the spout begins to discharge dense white steam and the lid jumps nervously. Take the pot off the coals and pour in ½ cup of cold water, to settle the grounds. An eggshell tossed in the pot will do the same thing.

One easy way to handle coffee-making is to use a number of small cloth bags, each one holding the exact amount of coffee required to brew a potful. When the coffee is done, pull out the bag, dry it by the fire, empty the grounds on the coals, and save the bag to wash and use again.

Soap should never touch the inside of a coffeepot. When oils accumulate on its sides after it's been used a few times, fill the pot brimful of water and bring it to a bouncing boil. Let the water bubble 5 minutes or so, pour it off, and wipe the inside of your pot clean with paper towels or a cloth. An outdoor coffeepot gets a sooty bottom, and you can ease your clean-up job by rubbing the outside of the pot with soap before it goes to the coals. Even in cold water, the soot will wash off with the soap. And it's an easy job to renew the coating before the pot is used again.

Now that the coffee's finished, it's time to leave the cooking fire. Be sure your coals are dead, though. Whether in the backwoods or in your backyard, stray winds can whip almost-dead coals into fresh life and scatter them as embers onto combustible surfaces. You might save several thousand acres of growing trees, or you might save your own roof, by putting out your cooking fire before you leave it.

# APPENDIX

## COMMERCIAL SUPPLIERS OF GAME MEATS

SALE AND SHIPMENT of meat classified as wild game is illegal in some states, but the classification varies from state to state. In some the ban extends to animals and fowl bred and sold by game farms or imported from abroad; in others, it is applied only to game taken by hunters. Federal laws probit sale and shipment of wild waterfowl, but not those same species from commercial breeders. Depending on the way your state's laws are written and interpreted, your butcher can generally order most game meats for you. If he cannot find sources of supply, the following list might help.

The list is by no means all inclusive, but one or another of the firms named can supply you with all but three or four of the sixty-five kinds of game animals, birds, fish, and shellfish used in the recipes in this book. Most of the firms handle specialties besides those under which their names are found, so inquiries are in order. You should inquire before ordering, anyhow. Some items are available only seasonally, minimum purchases or quantities may be required on some, and you should pre-arrange with any supplier the details of shipping.

### Antelope, bear, wild boar, most kinds of venison

Czimer Foods Co., 953 West 63 Street, Chicago, Illinois 60621
Jurgensen's, 601 South Lake Street, Pasadena, California 91109
Les Eschalottes, Ramsey, New Jersey 07446

**300**

## Buffalo

B-Bar-B Ranch, Gillette, Wyoming 84716
Brittain Ranch, Conway, Texas 79020
J. A. Ranch, Clarendon, Texas 79226
Wichita Mountain Wildlife Reserve, Cache, Oklahoma 73527

## Elk

Wichita Mountain Wildlife Reserve, Cache, Oklahoma 73527

## Ducks and geese

Bird Island Resort, Route 2, Box 142, Afton, Oklahoma 74331
Czimer Foods Co., 953 West 53rd Street, Chicago, Illinois 60621
Mrs. Loren Holcomb, North Branch, Minnesota 55056
Iron Gate Products Co., 424 West 54th Street, New York, New York 10019
E. Joseph, 183 Van Brunt Street, Brooklyn, New York 11231
Jurgensen's, 601 South Lake Street, Pasadena, California 91109
Maryland Gourmet Mart, 414 Amsterdam Avenue, New York, New York 10024
Saunders Poultry Shop, 3rd & Fairfax, Los Angeles, California 90036
George H. Shaffer Market, 1097 3rd Avenue, New York, New York 10028

## Pheasant, quail, chukkar partridge, wild turkey

Archbold Associates, East Aurora, New York 14502
Bird Island Resort, Route 2, Box 142, Afton, Oklahoma 74331
Cavin Game Bird Farm, North Little Rock, Arkansas 72114
Czimer Foods Co., 953 West 53rd Street, Chicago, Illinois 60621
H & L Game Farms, Baldwin, Mississippi 38824, or Box 123, Ridge Farm, Illinois 61870
Mrs. Loren Holcomb, North Branch, Minnesota 55056
Iron Gate Products Co., 424 West 54th Street, New York, New York 10019

## Appendix

E. Joseph, 183 Van Brunt Street, Brooklyn, New York 11231
Jurgensen's, 601 South Lake Street, Pasadena, California 91109
Kraft's Game Farm, Princess Anne, Maryland 21853
L & M Quail Farm, 1730 Picher, Joplin, Missouri 64801
LeJune's Quail Farm, Box 112, Sulphur, Louisiana 70663
Lucky Star Ranch, Chaumont, New York 13622
Maryland Gourmet Mart, 414 Amsterdam Avenue, New York, New York 10024
Meadowbrook Game Farm, Richfield, Pennsylvania 17086
Saunders Poultry Shop, 3rd & Fairfax, Los Angeles, California 90036
George H. Shaffer Market, 1079 3rd Avenue, New York, New York 10028
Sun Sportsman's Supply, Box 856, Salina, Kansas 67401

### Abalone

Eureka Fisheries, Box 217, Field's Landing, California 95537

### Crabs in shell

Booth Fisheries, 600 Lombard Street, San Francisco, California 94106
Wakefield Food Sales, 32 South 5th Avenue, Mt. Vernon, New York 10550

### Clams and lobsters in shell

Capn's Corners, Camden, Maine 04843
Saltwater Farms, Damariscotta, Maine 04543

### Oysters in shell

J. & J. W. Ellworth Co., Greenpoint, Long Island, New York 11944
Geo. Thompson & Son, 236 Water Street, New York, New York 10020

### Frog legs, snapping turtles

J. R. Schettle Frog Farms, Stillwater, Minnesota 55082

**Beef jerky**

Round-Up Distributors, Box 7456, Denver, Colorado 80209
Western Brand Co., Savannah, Georgia 31402

**Sourdough starter**

Frank Drew, 729 Main Street, Klamath Falls, Oregon 79601

## SHEEPHERDER STOVE & SELF-POWERED SPIT

For a permanent or semi-permanent installation such as you would want in your backyard, patio, or summer cabin, a rigid sheepherder stove would be the most satisfactory. If you require portability, the snap-together version is what you're after.

Plans and construction details for the portable sheepherder stove are shown in the accompanying sketch and instructions. A rigid sheepherder stove can easily be built by any welding or sheet-metal shop on the basis of plans for the portable version. Dimensions can be altered to suit your individual space and needs, of course. Ideally, the rigid stove is built from a single piece of sheet iron, no lighter than 11-gauge. The metal is cut and bent to form an open box, corner seams welded, grill rods welded to the sides, and one end opened with a cutting torch for a flap door. The cutting torch is also used to remove the hole at the top back where the stovepipe is placed.

There are several different versions of the sheepherder stove. Some have legs that raise them to a convenient working height, and are completely enclosed, with the firebox an integral part of the oven compartment. All of them give the same results in use, providing a quick and very dry heat in their ovens and a convenient top surface that is as useful for keeping foods warm as it is for cooking.

Plans for the self-powered spit are also shown in a sketch. A cage is bent from #8 black iron wire to hold the roast or fowl being cooked. At the top of the cage a loop is formed by which the cage is suspended from a slanting pole or branch over a circular bed of coals, with a doubled rope of the required length used to hang the cage from the pole.

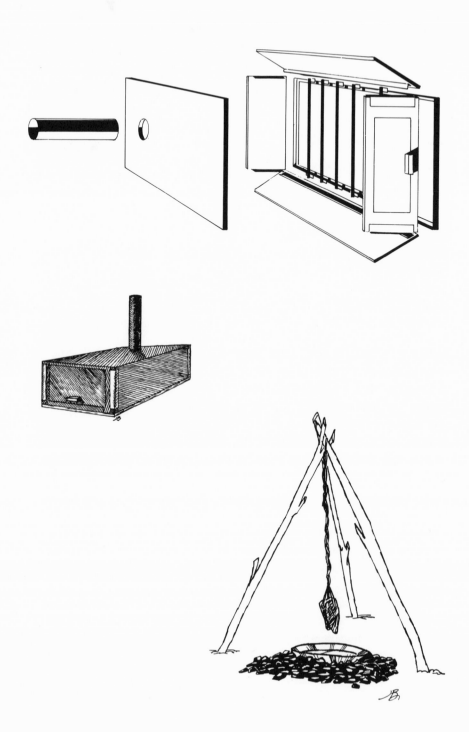

In use, the roast is placed in the cage and the rope twisted tightly, so that it unwinds itself just as a child unwinds in a playground swing. At the end of its twisting, the rope rewinds itself and continues to revolve the meat in its cage for a substantial period of time before rewinding by the cook is necessary.

Anyone who can hold a pair of pliers can make the cage in a half-hour or less. For permanent or semi-permanent installations, a length of concrete reinforcing rod can be driven into the ground and bent in an arc that will hold the twirling cage in the proper position in relation to the firepit. This type of spit should be used with the fire at ground level, or raised only slightly, in order to get the power provided by a long rope. When used with a raised brazier, the supporting pole or rod must either be very high, or the rope short. A long rope will twirl the roast for a longer period before needing to be retwisted by hand.

Here is an exploded sketch of the knock-down Sheepherder Stove built for me by Tony Villines of Borger, Texas. Top is 20 by 30 inches, and has a frame of ¾-inch angle iron welded to its underside. Ends are 20 by 14 inches, with angle iron brackets welded to their short dimensions. Sides are 14 by 29⅞ inches and have strips of angle iron welded along their insides, 1½ inches from the bottom edges. Grill bars are 19⅞ inches long, with 1-inch lengths of angle iron welded to each end. A frame of ¾-inch angle iron, 20 by 30 inches, supports the stove on the ground over a firepit 10 to 12 inches deep. One end has a flap door cut in it, hinged to swing up and out. A collared hole at top back holds a 20-inch length of standard 6-inch stovepipe. Top, sides, and ends are of 11-gauge sheet iron; grill rods are ⅜-inch bar iron. The bottom frame, end brackets, and top frame hold the stove rigid. It knocks down into a flat bundle about 4 inches thick, can be assembled in five minutes without tools, knocked down as soon as it is cool enough to handle after being used. For a permanent or semi-permanent installation the top, sides, and ends can be bent from one piece of sheet metal and grill rods welded into place.

Bottom sketch gives details of the self-powered spit. Over a ring of coals, meat being cooked is held in the cage at the end of a doubled rope supported by a slanting limb. When twisted, the rope unwinds and rewinds to allow the meat to cook evenly. A drip pan should be placed under the meat, in the center of the ring of coals.

## SMOKE-COOKING, DRYING, AND SALTING

Those who have grown up in a world addicted to shortcuts and married to refrigerators and freezers may find it hard to believe that when properly cured almost all meats and fish will stay edible for an indefinite time without being refrigerated, canned, or frozen. Those whose experience has been confined to the modern version of ham and bacon are sometimes shocked when they discover that these meats formerly did not spoil when kept unrefrigerated. And there are a few diehards who maintain that the terms "ham" and "bacon" should not be applied to today's wet-cured meats any more than a bottle of carbonated sauterne should be labeled champagne.

Only a small quantity of today's ham has ever been in a smokehouse. It is "aged" by shooting chemicals into its flesh with a hypodermic needle and by painting another chemical on the outside to impart a synthetic "smoky" flavor. In one process, the veins of a raw leg of pork are connected to tubes which carry chemicals through the veins into the meat, under pressure. The meat is then "aged" in a heat chamber for a few hours and labeled "ham."

Federal law now requires that certain types of wet-processed "ham" carry a label warning the buyer of what he's getting, but when the local butcher skins the leg, the label goes with it. These wet-processed pieces of pork are neither ham nor bacon, nor are they smoked meats. From one to two years is the shortest time in which a true ham can be produced by the traditional brining, drying, and smoking process; from six months to a year of this time is spent in aging the ham. A few specialty houses still produce real ham, both in the hard-cure and the softer sugar-cure. If you want ham and bacon of quality, seek them out. The meat is more expensive than that you will buy at the supermarket, but you will be paying for solid meat, not chemicals and water.

Ham, bacon, fish, fowl, almost any meat can be home-cured if you want to take the time; it is not a project for the impatient. The meat must be submerged in a brine of salt, sugar, saltpeter, and pepper for ten days to six weeks, then hung in an enclosed smokehouse where it dries for up to a year while bathed in smoke from a smouldering fire some distance away. The meat is never exposed to direct heat; fire from some pleasantly aromatic hardwood such as hickory, apple, pear, or others burns in its own compartment and the smoke travels to the smokehouse via a tunnel or large pipe. There is ample literature on this subject if you care to try it.

Air-drying fish is another matter. For this you need only a rack that will hold a few chicken-wire frames and a cover to shield them from the sun. Fish to be dried must be cleaned by opening them at the back. They are then soaked in brine 36 to 48 hours, rubbed well with salt, and laid on the frames 10 days to 2 weeks, depending on the weather. The drying fish must be turned several times each day and taken indoors at night to avoid being wet by dew. When a thumb will not dent their surface, the fish are cured. Stored in a cool place, they will keep up to six months without refrigeration. Before being used they must be soaked in several changes of water to remove the salt their flesh has absorbed. Such fish as salmon, big trout, and the fattty salt-water fish such as cod, herring, and mackerel are the best with which to work. Again, there is ample and detailed literature available on the subject.

Smoke-cooking should not be confused with curing. In smoke-cooking the food is cooked over coals artificially smothered, as in a barbecue pit or one of the modern versions of the ancient Chinese smoke ovens. The barbecue pit is ancient indeed. It is found in most aboriginal cultures, and whether the meat being cooked is beef in the Southwest, where the barbecue emigrated from the Caribbean via Mexico, pork in a Hawaiian luau, or geese and duck in Hong Kong, the process is the same.

Commercial versions of smoke cookers, patterned after the old Chinese models, are available from several manufacturers. The main thing to look for is one that will seal itself properly to hold in the smoke. A 50-gallon oil drum can be adapted for use as a smoke cooker by any competent welder. The drum can be laid on its side, grill-rods welded across its midsection, and a door cut to give access to both the rods and the fire compartment. Or the drum can be stood on end and doors cut at top and bottom to allow access to either firebox or cooking compartment separately. Again, the main thing to consider is proper sealing of the cooker.

**Appendix**

## OUTDOOR GRUB-BOXES

What follows is a brief, bare outline of suggestions based on a reasonable number of years of outdoor living in all sorts of climates and all conditions of terrain. It seems logical to begin with the back-packer, who can carry only necessities, then go to the auto camper, who isn't bothered by the weight of his supplies, and wind up with the backyard cook who's just a step from his own kitchen and for whom the sky is the limit.

### Back-Packing, Horseback-Packing

Planning is nine tenths of the job. If you're hiring a guide for a horse-back-packing trip, leave the planning to him; he's done it more often than you have and really doesn't need your suggestions. If you're doing it yourself:

List in detail every meal you'll eat and quantities of all ingredients needed for each, then add one full meal for extras or emergencies. This will save you from having to throw away or carry home what should have been left behind in the first place. Don't plan to live on the fish you catch or the game you kill; the fish and game may have other ideas.

Weight economies that should be obvious are often overlooked. Water is the heaviest thing you can carry, and most canned foods contain at least 50 per cent water, some much more than that. Most freeze-dried soups, meats, and vegetables are now reasonably edible; even dehydrated potatoes can taste good after you've lugged a pack uphill all day. Dry milk saves both weight and space. If you carry fresh meat for your first meal or two, take out bones to reduce weight.

Dry cereals are wasteful. They take up bulk far out of proportion to the food value you get from them and do not deliver the lasting protein energy you require. They are very largely starch, a carbohydrate that converts to sugar in your body, and gives a quick spurt of energy that soon passes. Meat protein gives a sustained release of energy. Solid-cured ham, sausages such as dry salami, and beef jerky give maximum food value and when eaten with a vegetable such as potatoes, don't make you unduly thirsty. Well-aged dry cheese is next in delivery of

**308**

food value; don't bother with "processed cheese foods," though, they're 40 per cent to 60 per cent water. Except for Knackbröd page 277, baked breads waste weight and space and salted crackers create thirst. Cook extra biscuits or pancakes at evening camp and carry them for a noon trail snack.

You can make for yourself an all-purpose mix to carry in plastic bags that provides both biscuits and pancakes. Sift together dry ingredients in this ratio: 1 cup flour to 1 teaspoon salt and ½ teaspoon sugar, work in 1 tablespoon solid shortening until you have a dry, crumblike mixture. Carry baking powder separately; for pancakes use 1½ teaspoons baking powder to each cup of the mix, adding water or reconstituted dry milk to make the batter. For biscuits, use 1 tablespoon baking powder per cup of mix with enough liquid to form a spongy dough. This mix will stay usable up to 3 or 4 weeks without refrigeration.

Buy slab bacon rather than sliced; not only is thin bacon miserable to cook and eat, but it suffers in a back-pack and slab bacon doesn't. Use the rind to render for fat for other cooking. Carry flour in a plastic bag and rub your bacon with it before cooking; pour a little hot water or reconstituted dry milk into the pan drippings and stir into a gravy. Forget eggs, on a pack trip they're a luxurious nuisance.

Don't stint on spices. Small plastic bags closed with twistums carry a lot of flavor in an ounce or two of weight and virtually no bulk. Take thyme, basil, oregano, paprika, cinnamon, nutmeg, powdered cloves, and any others that you favor. Back-packing is about the only time when instant coffee is justified, but dump it in a plastic bag and throw away that heavy glass jar. Transfer anything you take from glass or metal or cardboard containers into plastic bags, whenever possible.

Powdered fruit concentrate to mix with water is a good trail item; get a presweetened type. Chocolate bars are greatly overrated as a source of quick energy since their manufacturers began putting 20 per cent to 25 per cent air into them through hydrogenation. And chocolate is a thirst-maker. So are most excessively sweet or salty foods. The pemmican recipe page 268, gives you a compact snack food, easily carried, that does not produce thirst and needs no cooking. It also takes a lot of slow chewing, which alleviates both thirst and hunger. Until the question of the possible radiation effects on humans from irradiated foods have been settled, these are best avoided.

## Appendix

### Auto Camping and Cookouts

With pickup campers and vans, virtually no weight or bulk restrictions need apply. If you use a family car or station wagon for your camping trips and cookouts, you'll save work by making up two or three outdoor cooking boxes that can be kept packed and ready to go. These can be made of plywood of a size and shape to fit your car's luggage space. Make several small boxes instead of one big one. Put handles on them —rope handles are most satisfactory.

Until I got into a camping van that's kept loaded and ready to roll, my boxes and their contents were something like this:

Box 1—Short-handled camp axe, machete, bowsaw. Butane lantern with extra cylinders of fuel, extra mantles. Two nested galvanized buckets into which the kettle fitted. Folding canvas bucket that doubles as refrigerator when saturated with water and hung on a tree limb. Wood matches. Cloth bag of assorted size nails. Coil of stovewire. Folding shovel. Everything packed and kept from rubbing and rattling between layers of old newspapers (handy firestarters) and old cloths that could be torn into sizes needed for dishrags, towels, handcloths, then burned after use.

Box 2—Dishes, knives, cooking and eating utensils. Paper towels, toilet tissue. Spices and seasonings in plastic screw-top bottles. Iron rations for emergencies: pressed ham, freeze-dried soups, dried beans, rice, tea, coffee. The emergency items replenishd as used, the spices after each trip. By nesting all pots, pans, and dishes, filling the coffeepot with items in plastic bags or bottles, enough room was left to hold most of the food needed for a week. The Dutch oven traveled separately wrapped in a burlap bag. It, too, was filled with supplies: fresh meats, fresh vegetables, perishables and soft items. Staples such as flour, sugar, shortening, corn meal, etc., went into the kettle or into chinks in the boxes. Perishables such as potatoes, onions, carrots, cabbage, etc., went into heavy paper bags and were tucked into any odd corner available.

For years I carried no ice chest, but most of my camping was in mountain areas at altitudes where the air was cool and dry and springs plentiful. For arid areas, both icebox and water containers are needed. And somewhere in the dunnage room was always found for a few bottles of wine and a bottle of brandy, both important ingredients in any kind of cooking.

**310**

# Index

Abalone, preparation, 209
Aging, *see Hanging*
Albacore, baked with pepper, 190
Albondigas, Mountain Sheep, 63
Alsatian Style Goose, 119
Anadama Bread, 265
Anchovied Swordfish Steaks, 205
Angels on Horseback, 218
Antelope (*see also Deer*):
  cleaning, 28
  braised with dumplings, 35
  chops, Piedmontese, 33
  rack or saddle roast, 34
  meatballs (Sferia), 35
Aoudad Sheep, steaks, 64
Apple Slump, 287
Ashcake, 279

Bag-braised Jacksnipe, 126
Bannock, bread, 280
  dessert bread, 287
Barbecue, basic procedure, 39
  marinade/sauce, 31
  sauce, 39
Barbecued Fresh Boar Ham, 39
Barracuda, steaks or fillets, 191
Basic procedures for:
  baking, 264
  barbecuing, 39
  broiling, 13, 10, 160
  cleaning birds, *see individual species*
  cleaning fish, 158
  cleaning large game, 28
  cleaning small game, *see individual species*
  equipment, 9
  fires for outdoor cooking, 21–22
  foil cookery, 20
  salting and smoking meats, 307
  sheepherder stove, 15, 11, 303–305
  skewer cookery, 65
  spit-roasting, 10
  substituting, 27, 85, 107, 160
  testing temperatures, 24
  utensils, 13
Basque Sheepherder Eggs, 367
  Shepherd's Pie, 82
Bass, black (*see also Panfish, Trout*)
  cleaning, 165
  baked stuffed, 165
  pan-fried, 166
  poached in wine, 166
Bass, striped (*see also Halibut, Shad*)
  fillets, Italian Style, 204
  grilled, 204
Beans, in Cassoulet of Game, 81
  in Dutch oven, 246–247
  refried, 248
  sausage stew, 77
Bear, care of meat, 36
  paws, 38, 48
  tenderloin, 37

Beaver, cleaning, 86
  braised, 37
Beef, *see large game recipes*
  to give flavor of game, 30–31
Bigarade, duck, 113
Bigos, Polish Game Stew, 74
Biscuits, beaten, 256
  cobbler with dried fruits, 288
  light, 273
  potato, 273
  skillet, 274
  soda, 275
  sourdough, 275
Bluefish (*see also Barracuda, Snapper*)
  baked stuffed, 192
Boar (*see also Bear, Javelina*)
  cleaning, 39
  barbecued fresh ham, 39
  chops, smothered, 42
  scrapple, 43
  spareribs, 41
Breads:
  Anadama, 265
  Bannock, 280
  Bannock dessert, 287
  corn meal, 278
  Knackbröd, 277
  Potato, 266
  puddings, 288, 289
  Salt Risen, 267
  Sourdough, 268
Breakfast Pudding, 289
Brewer's Shrimp, 232
Brown Betty, 289
Brown Onion Soup, 244
Brunswick Stew, 103
Bubble and Squeak, 249
Buffalo (*see also Caribou, Elk*), 45
Burgoo, 104
Buttermilk Soup, 243

Cabbage, braised with sausage, 249
  bubble and squeak, 249
  with grouse, 132, 133
  stuffed, 250
Cake, 294–295
  Pork, 295
Calas, 290
Candy, 297
Caribou (*see also Buffalo, Deer, Elk*)
  ribs with vegetable sauce, 48
  spiced shanks, 49
Carp (*see also Shad, Suckers*), 167–168
Cassoulet of Game, 81
Cast-iron cookware, 14
Catfish (*see also Panfish, Cod*), 169–170
Chicken: *see Pheasant, Quail; also Rabbit, Squirrel*
Chili con carne, 55
Chops, antelope, 33
  boar or javelina, 42
  deer, 50

# Index

Chowder:
　clam, 211, 212
　codfish, 192
　crab, 226
Chukkar: *see Pheasant, Grouse*
Cioppino, 238
Clams (*see also Mussels, Scallops*), 210–215
Clapshot, 259
Cobbler, dried fruits, 288
Codfish (*see also Haddock, Halibut*), 192
Coffee, 298
Colcannon, 258
Conch (*see also Abalone, Scallops*), 209–210
Cook's Corrector, 84
Coots, 123
Corn, 251–252
Cornish Game Fowl: *see Quail, Grouse*
Cornmeal breads, 276
　ashcake, 279
　crackling, 279
　crisps, 279
　hoecake, 279
　Hush Puppies, 170
　Johnnycake, 278
Cowboy's Breakfast, 369
Crab (*see also Lobster*), 222–225
Crackling Bread, 279
Crawfish (*see also Shrimp*), 227–228
Crumb Pancakes, 280
Cullen Skink, 243

Deer (*see also Antelope, Caribou, Elk*), chili, 55
　chops, 50, 51
　cleaning, 28
　cooked like beans, 56
　hanging, 28
　liver, 50
　mincemeat, 56, 57
　rack or saddle roast, 52
　Son-of-a-Bitch Stew, 53
　steaks, 50, 51
Deviled Crab, 223, 224
Deviled Haddock, 194, 195
Doves (*see also Pigeons, Jacksnipe*)
　braised, 201
　fried in deep fat, 131
　spit-roast, 130
Duck (*see also Goose*), 109–116
Dumplings, with antelope, 35
　elk liver, 38
　fruit, 292
　potato, 47
Dutch oven (*see also cast-iron cookware*)
　beans, 246
　dumplings, 292
　meatloaves, 70, 71
　onions, 255, 256
　rice, 259

Eel, 171
Eggs, 283–285
Elk (*see also Caribou, Deer, Moose*)
　cleaning, 28
　hanging, 27, 28
　heart, stuffed, 58
　liver dumplings, 58
　shortribs, salt-baked, 59, 60
Escabeche, 221, 222

Fillets, barracuda, 191
　black bass in wine, 166
　flounder (sole) grilled, 193
　flounder (sole) in tomato sauce, 194
　muskellunge in cream, 174
　pike, sweet and sour, 176
　striped bass, Italian style, 203
First-Day Camp Soup, 242
Fish (*see also individual species*)
　classified as fat or lean, 160, 189
　cleaning, 158
　cooking time, 160
　judging freshness, 159
　salt-curing, smoking, 307
Flank, antelope, 35
　deer, 53, 54, 56
　moose, with apricots, 60
　rolled stuffed, 69
Flounder (sole), 193–194
Fricassee, goose, 120
　woodchuck, 102
Fried Pies, 291
Fries, 80
Fritters, whiting, 206
Frog legs, 234–235
Fruit Dumplings, 292

Game birds (*see also individual species*)
　cleaning, 128
　hanging, 109
　giblets, 154
　preserving, 154
　soup, 155
Game Pot Pudding, 76
German Style Rabbit, 93
Gingered Duck, 115
Goose (*see also Duck*), 109, 116–122
Greek Style Rabbit Stew, 96
Green Sauce, 32
Greyling (*see also Trout*), 184
Grill area, planning, 9
Grouse (*see also Quail, Woodcock*), 132–134
Guinea Fowl (*see Pheasant, Turkey*)
Gumbo, goose, 121

Haddock (*see also Cod, Halibut*), 195
Halibut (*see also Cod, Haddock*), 196–197
Hanging to age, large game, 28
　small game, 85
　upland birds, 128
Ham, barbecued fresh, 39
　with beans, 246
　in Brunswick Stew, 103
　in potato pot, 257
　smoking, 306
Hamburger, 73
Hash, Lake Trout, 172, 173
　patties, 83
Hassenpfeffer, 94
Heart, stuffed, 58
Herbed Butters, 164
Hoecake, 279
Hors d'oeuvres suggestions:
　corn meal crisps, 279
　grilled eggplant mix, 253
　grilled mushrooms, 255
　pickled mussels, 217
　potato ghosts, 258
　potted trout, 187
　seviche, 221
　stuffed goose necks, 122

Hot Onion Sauce, 32
Hot Pepper Vinegar, 163
Hot Pot or Hotchpotch, 84
Hot Turkey Pot, 149
Hush Puppies, 170

Jacksnipe (*see also Doves, Pigeon*), 126
Javelina (*see also Boar*)
  cleaning, 39
  scrapple, 43
Joe O'Donnell's Pancakes, 281
Johnnycake, 278

Kabobs, 65
Kidneys, 80
Knackbröd, 277
Knives, selection, care, 17

Lake Trout Hash, 173
Lamb (*see Antelope, Mountain Sheep*)
Larding, 52
Lazy Cook's Dessert, 293
Leftovers, dishes using, 74, 75, 78, 82, 83,
  84, 116, 120, 153, 154, 239, 260
Lime Sauce, 162
Liver, deer, 50
  elk, dumplings, 58
  moose, roast, 61
Lobster (*see also Crab*), 228–230
Louis Dressing, 223

Marinades, marinating, 29–31
Marrow, to prepare, 243
  ball soup, 243
  with steaks, 45
Marsh birds (*see also individual species*),
  125
Meatloaf, 71–72
Meatrolls, stuffed, 70
Mincemeat, venison, 56
Mix, pancake and biscuit, 309
Molé, turkey, 150
Moose (*see also Caribou, Elk, Buffalo*)
  cleaning, 28
  flank with apricots, 60
  liver, roast, 61
  meatballs, 62
Mountain Oysters, 80
Mountain Sheep Albondigas, 63
  shepherd's pie, 82
Mudhens, 123
Mulligan, 72
Mushrooms, 254, 255
Muskellunge Fillets In Cream, 174
Muskrat (*see also Beaver, Rabbit*)
  cleaning, 86
  fried, 89
Mussels (*see also Clams, Scallops*), 215–
  216

Octopus, 197, 198
Onions, baked, 256
  shortcake, 256
  soup, 244
Opossum (*see also Bear, Boar*), 89–90
Oysters (*see also Clams, Mussels*), 218–219

Pancakes, crumb, 280
  Joe O'Donnell's, 281
  mix for campers, 309
  sourdough, 382
Panfish (*see also Black Bass*), 175

Peach Pot Pudding, 293
Pemmican, 66–67
Pepper Vinegar, 163
Peppers, stuffed, 261
Pheasant (*see also Grouse, Quail*)
  hanging, 128
  judging age, 135
  grilled, 136
  Hunter's Style, 137
  Russian Style, 139
  in sour cream, 136
  with vegetables, 138
  sauced, spit-roast, 140
Pickled Mussels, 217
Pie, fried, 291
  pigeon, 141
  quail, 146
  shepherd's, 82
  squirrel, 100
Pigeon (*see also Doves, Jacksnipe*), 141
Pike, Sweet and Sour, 176
Pioneer's Covered Wagon Cake, 294
Planked Salmon, 200
  Shad, 179
Porcupine, fried, 91
Pork (*see Bear, Boar, Opossum*)
Pork Cake, 295
Possum (*see Opossum*)
Potato, biscuits, 273
  bread, 266
  ghosts, 258
  pot, 257
  soup, 244
Pot pudding, game, 76
  peach, 293
Potroasts, 69
Potted Trout, 187
Prairie Oysters, 80
Prawns (*see Crawfish, Shrimp*)
Preserved Game Birds, 156
Pudding, bread, 288
  breakfast, 289
  game, 76
  peach, 293
  rice and fruits, 295
  turnip, 296

Quail (*see also Grouse, Pheasant*), 143–145
Quick Bread Pudding, 288
Quick Brown Onion Soup, 244
  Potato Soup, 244

Rabbit (*see also Squirrel, Upland Birds*),
  92–96
Raccoon (*see also Porcupine, Woodchuck*),
  97–98
Reed birds (*see individual species*)
Refried Beans, 248
Ribs, boar spareribs, 39
  caribou, with vegetables, 48
  elk shortribs, salt-cooked, 60
Rice, Calas, 290
  in Dutch oven, 259
  fruit pudding, 295
  Spanish or Creole, 260
  in stuffed peppers, 261
Roasts:
  antelope, 34
  boar, 39
  deer, 52
  doves, 130

# Index

Roasts (*continued*)
 duck, 110, 111
 goose, 116
 grouse, 134
 moose liver, 61
 pheasant, 140
 potroasts, 69
 quail, 144
 raccoon, 98
 turkey, 148, 149
Rock Cornish Fowl (*see Pheasant, Quail*)
Roti, or vertical grill, 12

Salmon (*see also Trout*), 199–200
Salt-cooking in coals, 60
Salt-curing fish, meats, 306
Salt-Risen Bread, 267
Sashlik, 65
Sauces, barbecue, 31, 39
 green, 32
 herbed butters, 164
 hot onion, 32
 hot pepper vinegar, 163
 Louis Dressing, 309
 sour lime, 162
 white wine, 163
Sauerbraten, 77
Sausage, braised with cabbage, 249
Scallops (*see also Conch, Clams, Mussels*),
 220–221
Scrapple, 42
Sea Urchins, 239
Seviche, 221
Sferia, 35
Shad (*see also Black Bass, Suckers*), 178–
 179
Shanks, Caribou, spiced, 49
Sheep, Aoudad and Mountain, 64
Sheepherder Stove, 12, 303–305
Shepherd's Pie, 82
Shrimp (*see also Crawfish*), 231–233
Skewer cooking, 65
Skillet Biscuits, 274
Slumgullion, Skilligalli, 85
Smoking fish, meats, 306
Snapper Baked In Blankets, 201
Soda Biscuits, 275
Sole (*see Flounder*)
Son-of-a-Bitch Stew, 45, 53
Soup, buttermilk, 243
 chowders, 211, 212
 first-day camp, 242
 game bird, 155
 marrow ball, 243
 onion, 244
 potato, 244
 squirrel, 138
Sources supplying wild game, 300–304
Sourdough Bread, 268
 biscuits, 275
 pancakes, 282
Sour Lime Sauce, 162
Souse, 221
Spaghetti, with game, 78
 with seafood, 239
Spareribs with barbecue sauce, 39
Spiced Caribou Shanks, 49
Squash, grill-baked, 262
Squid, 202
Squirrel (*see also Rabbit, Upland Birds*),
 99–101

Steaks, abalone, 209
 Aoudad Sheep, 64
 barracuda, 191
 buffalo with marrow, 55
 deer, 50, 51
 halibut, 196
 salmon, 199
 swordfish, anchovied, 205
Steelhead (*see also Salmon, Trout*), 186
Stifado, Greek Rabbit Stew, 96
Striped bass (*see also Muskellunge, Pike*),
 204
Stew, Bigos, 74
 Brunswick, 103
 Burgoo, 104
 Cioppino, 238
 deer, 53
 duck, 116
 gumbo, 121
 halibut, 197
 Jambalaya, 105
 liver, 58
 Mulligan, 85
 with potato dumplings, 75
 rabbit, 95, 96
 Skilligalli, Slumgullion, 85
 Son-of-a-Bitch, 45, 53
 turtle, 237
Stuffed Goose Necks, 122
Sturgeon, baked with potato sauce, 181
Succotash, 252
Suckers, suckerburgers, 182
Sweetbreads, 80
Sweet and Sour Pike, 177
Sweet Potatoes Creole, 296
Swordfish Steaks, anchovied, 205

Tenderizers, use of, 28
Tenderloin, bear, 37
Tongue, buffalo, boiled, 46
Trout (*see also Salmon*)
 Amandine, 183
 au Bleu, 184
 baked in corn husks, 183
 cleaning, 158
 baked stuffed, 186
 grilled, 185
 pan-fried crisp, 184
 potted, 187
Turkey, preparation, 128
 judging age, 146
 Hot Pot, 149
 Molé, 150
 oven-roast, 148
 spit-roast, 149
 Terrapin, 153
Turnips, 258–259
Turtle, 236–237

Upland game birds, 128 (*see also individual
 species*)

Venison (*see individual species*)

Whitebait, 206
Whitefish, 181
White Wine Sauce, 163
Whiting Fritters, 206
Wild game, commercial sources of, 300–304
Woodchuck (*see also Raccoon*), 102
Woodcock (*see also Grouse, Quail*), 127